THE BOBBS-MERRILL SHAW SERIES

Under the General Editorship of

JOHN HENRY RALEIGH AND LOUIS CROMPTON

This photograph of the bust of Julius Caesar formerly in the Berlin Museum served as the frontispiece for Caesar and Cleopatra *in the first edition of* Three Plays for Puritans *in 1901.*

CAESAR

AND

CLEOPATRA

by
BERNARD SHAW

Edited, with an Introduction and Notes, by
GALE K. LARSON
California State University, Northridge

THE BOBBS-MERRILL COMPANY, INC.
Indianapolis · New York

BERNARD SHAW
1856–1950

Caesar and Cleopatra
was first published in 1901 in
Three Plays for Puritans

Revised version, 1931

Caesar and Cleopatra is reprinted by permission of the Society
of Authors, London, for the Bernard Shaw Estate. Permission
to quote from letters and holograph notes on the play has been
granted by The Society of Authors; Henry W. and Albert A.
Berg Collection, the New York Public Library, Astor, Lenox
and Tilden Foundations; The University of Texas Library; The
D. Jacques Benoliel Collection in the Rare Book Department of
The Free Library of Philadelphia; Mr. Dan H. Laurence, the
editor of the Shaw letters; and Harper and Row, Publishers,
Incorporated. The photograph of Julius Caesar is reproduced
from the Berlin bust with permission of Staatliche Museen zu
Berlin, the photograph of Forbes-Robertson by permission of
the Raymond Mander & Joe Mitchenson Theatre Collection,
and the still of the Sphinx scene by courtesy of the Rank Organisation Limited.

Library of Congress Cataloging in Publication Data

Shaw, George Bernard, 1856–1950.
  Caesar and Cleopatra.

  (The Bobbs-Merrill Shaw series)
  Bibliography: p.
  1. Caesar, C. Julius—Drama.   2. Cleopatra, Queen of
Egypt, d. 30 B.C.—Drama.   I. Larson, Gale K., ed.   II.
Title.
PR5363.C15 1973   822'.9'12   73–1609
ISBN 0-672-61154-6

Contents

Illustrations

Introduction

Bernard Shaw, the third child and only son of George Carr Shaw and Elizabeth Curly Shaw, was born July 26, 1856, in Dublin, Ireland. Mrs. Shaw, determined to have no more children, moved out of the master bedroom shortly after the birth of her son. The relationship between the Shaws had always been strained. Mrs. Shaw had not loved her husband but had accepted his proposal of marriage as a refuge from a tyrannical aunt. How could she go wrong marrying an Irish Protestant teetotaler who boasted of a £60-a-year sinecure and aristocratic connections (a distant cousin, Sir Robert Shaw, was made a baronet in 1821)? But she could, and one of the boasts was empty. Shaw's father was a secret tippler, and the sinecure was in fact only £44 a year. He sold the sinecure and invested in a wholesale corn business that was always near bankruptcy. His personal salvation was his extraordinary sense of humor, a trait not in the least appreciated by his wife but one of enduring influence upon his son. Mrs. Shaw's own salvation was to ignore her husband, neglect her children, and to retreat into the world of music. Shaw and his older sisters, Lucy and Agnes, were left to the company of nurses and servants. Shaw later recalled that "when I was troublesome a servant thumped me on the head until one day, greatly daring, I rebelled, and, on finding her collapse abjectly, became thenceforth uncontrollable." The lack of affectionate and dependent interaction in the family resulted in Shaw's intense individualism, self-sufficiency, and self-determination; he became, he says "a Freethinker before I knew how to think." In school he balked at anything that did not interest him, maintaining later that "pressing people to learn things they do not want to know is as unwholesome and disastrous as feeding them on sawdust."

Shaw had only contempt for his formal schooling, which he terminated at the early age of fifteen when he became a clerk in a real estate office. His own intense interest in music, art, and literature continued unabated. He had been surrounded by music at home. Operas, concerts, and oratorios were constantly being rehearsed, and before he was fifteen Shaw knew by heart many of the works of the great masters. Later he taught himself to play the piano, beginning his lessons with the overture to Mozart's *Don Giovanni*. With the same dogged determination he pursued the study of art, sometimes buying but mostly borrowing books on painting and prowling the National Gallery of Ireland. He was also a voracious reader of literature. "I was saturated," he writes, "with the Bible and with Shakespear before I was ten years old."

In the meantime, his mother's interest in music as well as her disgust at her husband's continued drinking and commercial failure led to her departure to London, where she and Vandaleur Lee, her impresario, established themselves as music teachers. She took her daughters with her and left young Shaw behind with his father. It was a separation for economic reasons, not for reasons of passion. Shaw was fond of pointing out that anyone who could have seduced his mother could have seduced the Virgin at Nuremburg and that she could have boarded and lodged the Three Musketeers and D'Artagnan and would have taken no notice of their sex—unless they smoked in the living room.

Six years later Shaw, by now totally disgusted with his commercial employment and with Ireland, embarked for London, where for nine years, he unashamedly boasted, "I steadily wrote my five pages a day and made a man of myself (at my mother's expense) instead of a slave." During these years of apprenticeship, Shaw wrote five novels for which he collected sixty rejection slips. At the same time he assiduously trained himself in public speaking. He jumped at every opportunity to speak, from Hyde Park Corner to the learned debating societies of the day. In time his ability as a public orator assured him of a platform.

Closely aligned to his development as speaker was his interest in social philosophy. One night in September 1882, he wandered into Memorial Hall where Henry George was speaking on Land Nationalization and the single tax. "Until I heard George that night," Shaw confessed, "I had been chiefly interested, as an atheist, in the conflict between science and religion." Now Shaw's interest turned toward economics, Karl Marx, and eventually to that distinctive brand of British socialism known as Fabianism. He joined the Fabian Society September 5, 1884, and subsequently brought into the organization the indefatigable investigator, Sidney Webb, who along with Shaw, Sydney Olivier, and Graham Wallas soon dominated the Society in their common effort to make a better human society than capitalism had provided. Shaw's temperament and his own participation in the Bloody Sunday riots in Trafalgar Square led to his rejection of violence as a necessary contingency for social change, a position advocated by the more revolutionary groups of English Socialism, Hyndman's Social-Democratic Federation and Morris's Socialist League. Of these groups, only the Fabian Society, which still exists, survived its founders.

Shaw's serious career as a journalist began in 1885, the year his father died. For the next thirteen years he playfully needled the British public with his reviews and criticisms of art, music, and literature in the *Pall Mall Gazette, The World, The Star,* and the *Saturday Review.* William Archer, who had helped launch Shaw as a reviewer, also interested him in Ibsen and the "New Drama." Thereafter, Shaw's energies, like those of Archer, were directed toward getting Ibsen's plays produced on the English stages. When the Fabian Society reluctantly agreed to a series of lectures under the general heading of "Socialism in Contemporary Literature" for its summer meetings, Shaw was urged by Annie Besant to "take Ibsen." His paper was read at St. James's Restaurant on July 8, 1890, and was subsequently published as *The Quintessence of Ibsenism,* an outspoken analysis of Ibsen as moral philosopher and social thinker. Later, J. T. Grein, the founder of the Independent Theatre and producer of Ibsen's plays, stated that the New Drama was without a single original piece of any importance by an English author. Shaw was aghast. "This was not to be endured," Shaw wrote. "I had rashly taken up the case; and rather than let it collapse, I manufactured the evidence." The "evidence" was *Widowers' Houses*, a play Shaw had begun with William Archer in 1884. The most notable of Shaw's many careers was finally launched.

In 1892 Shaw wrote *The Philanderer* and *Mrs. Warren's Profession*, both of which fired up the moral indignation of the critics and public alike. Shaw himself called *The Philanderer* a "nasty play," explaining that it was a "combination of mechanical farce with realistic filth," but *Mrs. Warren's Profession* he defended as a faithful presentation of the "economic basis of modern commercial prostitution." The play was, however, banned from public performance, not because of the peculiarity of Mrs. Warren's profession but because of an incidental reference to the possibility of incest. Shaw continued to write controversial plays, and at the end of that decade he had added seven more to his repertoire: *Arms and the Man, The Man of Destiny, Candida, You Never Can Tell, The Devil's Disciple, Caesar and Cleopatra,* and *Captain Brassbound's Conversion.* Shaw had indeed found his creative milieu in the drama, and for the next fifty years he continued to write plays that delighted and angered the British and world audiences alike.

BIRTH OF THE PLAY

Shaw's interest in Caesar and Cleopatra as possible subjects for a play of his own may be seen emerging during his years as drama critic for the *Saturday Review.* In March of 1897 Louis Calvert and Janet Achurch performed *Antony and Cleopatra* at the Queen's Theatre in Manchester. Shaw was appalled with the latter's inability to interpret the Egyptian queen's character. He declared the production a failure in characterization since "there is not a stroke of Cleopatra in it." Shaw again saw the production when it came to London at the Olympic Theatre on May 24, 1897, under the auspices of the Independent Theatre. He described it as "an afternoon of lacerating anguish, spent partly in contemplating

Miss Achurch's overpowering experiments in rhetoric, and partly in wishing I had never been born."

Janet Achurch's acting was only a partial explanation for Shaw's "lacerating anguish," for Shaw had severe reservations about Shakespeare's play. In his Preface, "Better than Shakespear?" in *Three Plays for Puritans*, he scored Shakespeare for making "sexual infatuation a tragic theme." And once, when an interviewer attempted to ascribe moral value to the play, Shaw exclaimed, "Moral value! It has no moral value whatever. I always think of what Dr. Johnson said: 'Sir, the long and short of it is, the woman's a whore!' "

Shaw had only disgust for Shakespeare's *Julius Caesar;* he bluntly called it "an admitted failure." He expressed his views of the play in the *Saturday Review* after he had seen the Beerbohm Tree production of the play at Her Majesty's Theatre on January 22, 1898. He scored Shakespeare for his delineation of Caesar, noting that

> . . . when we turn to Julius Caesar, the most splendidly written political melodrama we possess, we realize the apparently immortal author of Hamlet as a man, not for all time, but for an age only, and that, too, in all solidly wise and heroic aspects, the most despicable of all the ages in our history. It is impossible for even the most judicially minded critic to look without a revulsion of indignant contempt at his travestying of a great man as a silly braggart, whilst the pitiful gang of mischief-makers who destroyed him are lauded as statesmen and patriots.

Since Shakespeare's dramatic rendering of these two historical figures was unsatisfactory to Shaw, he was determined to challenge his predecessor and set forth a Caesar and a Cleopatra that would be more compatible with the modern historical *Zeitgeist*. Moreover, he had already promised Forbes-Robertson and Mrs. Patrick Campbell, two leading actors in the London theaters, a classical play worthy of their acting abilities.

He finally commenced writing the play on April 23, 1898, and finished the first act, the courtyard scene and the meeting at the

Sphinx, five days later. During that same month his health broke down, a trivial injury to his foot developed into necrosis of the bone and required two operations. His foot injury, his marriage to Charlotte Payne-Townshend, and his decision to write a book on Wagner delayed the completion of *Caesar and Cleopatra*.

It was not until September 9, 1898, that Shaw resumed work on the play, finishing it some time in December of that year. On January 2, 1899, he wrote Mrs. Mansfield, wife of the actor-manager Richard Mansfield, "I had hoped to send to you, by way of a New Year's call, a new play called 'Caesar and Cleopatra,' . . . But I have not been able to get the prompt copies typed in time; so you must for the moment take the promise for the deed."

The play was first presented at a special matinee performance for copyright at the Theatre Royal, Newcastle-on-Tyne, on Wednesday, March 15, 1899. Mr. Nutcombe Gould played Caesar to Mrs. Patrick Campbell's Cleopatra. Mrs. Shaw attended that copyright performance and was quite disgruntled with Mrs. Campbell's interpretation of the role. Cleopatra had come across, Mrs. Shaw complained, as a vampire instead of a child being moulded into a queen through the wise and patient guidance of Caesar. Mrs. Campbell never played Shaw's Cleopatra again. She had ended her partnership in acting with Forbes-Robertson, so Shaw's vision of these two classical actors impersonating his Cleopatra and Caesar was never to be realized.

In 1899 Shaw finished writing *Captain Brassbound's Conversion* and started working on the Preface and Notes to the three plays that would be published together as *Three Plays for Puritans*. Early in May of 1900 he wrote Golding Bright, "I have not yet written any more prefaces; so it only remains to say that the book will conclude with an appendix consisting of the three plays —The Devil's Disciple, Caesar & Cleopatra, and Captain Brassbound's Conversion." The plays were published in January 1901 by Grant Richards.

Because of the great length of the play, many of the early productions were staged with various omissions. Prior to the Berlin production in 1906, Shaw had written to Siegfried Trebitsch, his German translator, suggesting that Max Reinhardt omit the third act, the lighthouse scene. Reinhardt, instead, shortened the play by omitting other scenes, which, according to Shaw, ruined the entire play. "The secret of Caesar's failure is out at last," Shaw wrote to Trebitsch, "and never again shall Reinhardt have a play of mine to ruin." That failure, Shaw felt, was the result of injudicious cuttings:

> *They have cut out the first scene of the 4th Act!!!* Of course that meant utter failure. It is in that scene that the change in Cleopatra's character is shewn, and the audience prepared for the altered atmosphere and deeper seriousness of the later scene. To omit it is such a hopeless artistic stupidity that the man who would do it would do anything.
>
> He has also cut out the burning of the library, which must make the end of the second act unintelligible. I told him what to do—to omit the third act. He was too clever to do that; so he spoiled the 2nd, 3rd, & 4th acts instead, and wrecked the play. May his soul perish for it.

When Forbes-Robertson finally got around to doing "his" play, he first presented it at the Grand Theatre, Leeds, September 16, 1907, for three performances. In November of that year, the play moved to the Savoy Theatre, London, and had a run of forty performances. Both of these productions were staged without the third act. Forbes-Robertson had objected strongly to cutting this act, but the length of the play had forced the omission. When Forbes-Robertson decided to include *Caesar and Cleopatra* in his farewell performances in 1912, Shaw wrote the Ra Prologue so that the third act could be restored. That production, first seen at the Shakespeare Theatre, Liverpool, and later at Forbes-Robertson's farewell season at Drury Lane, London, included the new prologue, the restored third act, and omitted Act One, Scene One, presently entitled "An Alternative to the Prologue."

Other notable productions of the play include that staged by Barry Jackson in April 1925 at Kingsway Theatre, London. Since the Ra Prologue was not incorporated into the printed edition of the play until 1929, Shaw sent the Prologue script to Jackson, who then staged the entire play, including both Prologues. In that production, Sir Cedric Hardwicke played Caesar, a role to which

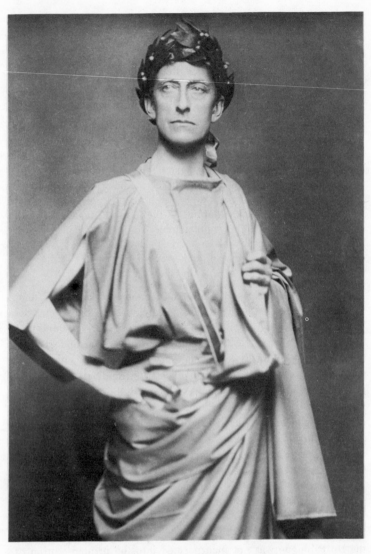

Mr. Forbes-Robertson as Caesar (1907).
From the Raymond Mander and
Joe Mitchenson Theatre Collection.

he returned in December 1940 for 151 performances in New York, with Lilli Palmer as Cleopatra.

Gabriel Pascal produced and directed the film of the play at Denham Studios, England, for the Rank Organisation. Starring Claude Rains and Vivien Leigh, the film was first shown in London at the Odeon, Marble Arch, on December 13, 1945. Shaw was consulted throughout the filming, often writing in new scenes for transitional purposes.

Six years later, Vivien Leigh, joined by Sir Laurence Olivier, acted in a stage production, first in London and then in New York, that alternated with Shakespeare's *Antony and Cleopatra*. Today the play remains as popular as ever.

THE PLAY AS HISTORY

Throughout his life, Shaw continued to defend *Caesar and Cleopatra* against the critics, especially those who dismissed it as having no real value as history. He stubbornly insisted that the play was historically accurate, maintaining that "a boy brought to see the play could pass an examination next day on the Alexandrian expedition without losing a mark." But critics and readers in general, especially those schooled in Shakespearean Roman history, have been bewildered by Shaw's alleged historicity and have summarily dismissed the play as "historical extravaganza" or "pure fantasy." Shaw's view of history and his use of historical sources will provide some answers to this persistent question of the play's historicity.

In a letter to Gilbert Murray, Shaw called his Caesar "authentic to the last comma." That claim for authenticity is based upon his knowledge and understanding of the pro-Caesar tradition of the nineteenth century. Early writers of that period such as Goethe, Niebuhr, and Hegel wrote in praise of Caesar. Goethe had referred to Caesar's assassination as "the most absurd act that ever was committed"; Niebuhr viewed Caesar's sovereignty as the first step in the revitalization of the Roman state; and Hegel looked upon Caesar as the "single will [that] could guide the Roman state." Such views as these laid the foundation for Theodor

Mommsen's historical reevaluation of Caesar. Mommsen's influence was felt in England in the Caesar biographies of James
Froude and W. Warde-Fowler, sources which we know were familiar to Shaw. Shaw told Hesketh Pearson, "I found Mommsen
conceived Caesar as I wished to present him." Mommsen and his
followers viewed the Roman Republic as an oligarchy of selfish,
partisan interests, which had degenerated into an instrument of
tyranny and injustice. They accordingly viewed Caesar as the
great political reformer whose vigorous leadership and consummate statesmanship were geared to the reconstruction of the Empire on a more humane and progressive basis. He was a political
reformer in the tradition of the Gracchi brothers, whose reforms
had been practically cancelled by Sulla, a reactionary who returned power in Rome to the hands of the aristocracy. At the time
of Caesar, Rome was in name a Republic; in reality it was an oligarchy. Shaw shared Mommsen's view, having rejected Shakespeare's Plutarchan bias. Plutarch had exalted Cato and Brutus as
the ideal heroes of Rome and, conversely, denigrated Caesar as
the ambitious destroyer of the status quo. Shakespeare's Brutus, in
turn, represented the triumph of honor and conscience over a
great but demogogic Caesar. In contrast, Shaw, a believer in social democratic principles, admired Caesar, for he saw in him the
practical statesman and popular hero in whom rested the hope of
the Roman populace and subject nations of the Empire. He thus
delineated a Caesar who was "genuinely original" and "naturally
great," a man whose destiny was synonymous with the destiny of
Rome.

In an interview with Archibald Henderson, his authorized biographer, Shaw remarked, "Then there is the chronicle play, in
which you arrange history for the stage. The value of the result
depends on your grasp of historical issues—whether your history
is big history or Little Arthur's[1] history." Thus, for Shaw, the

---

[1] "Little Arthur" was the pseudonym of Lady Maria Calcott (1785–1842),
who published *Little Arthur's History of England* (in eight volumes) in
1835.

truth of history is a matter of interpretation in which the facts must be treated imaginatively. Moreover, the interpretation itself is dependent upon a point of view that determines the selection and organization of the historical material. And finally, since that point of view changes in a period of time, history must constantly be rewritten. "Allow me," says Shaw, "to set forth Caesar in . . . [the] modern light. . . ."

Shaw's early comments on the play reveal his well-known penchant for overstating his case. When questioned whether he had "been reading up Mommsen—and people like that" in preparing for his new play, he boastfully declared, much to the chagrin of serious-minded, dry-as-dust historians:

> Not a bit of it. History is only a dramatisation of events. And if I start telling lies about Caesar it's a hundred to one that they will be just the same lies that other people have told about him. I never worry myself about historical details until the play is done; human nature is very much the same always and everywhere. And when I go over my play to put the details right I find there is surprisingly little to alter. 'Arms and the Man,' for example, was finished before I had decided where to set the scene, and then it only wanted a word here and there to put matters straight. You see, I know human nature. Given Caesar, and a certain set of circumstances, I know what would happen, and when I have finished the play you will find I have written history.

Shaw referred his critics to numerous historical sources in the elaborate playbill he drew up for the March 15, 1899, copyright performance of the play. That program contained the following directive:

> The play follows history as closely as stage exigencies permit. Critics should consult Manetho and the Egyptian Monuments, Herodotus, Diodorus, Strabo (Book 17), Plutarch, Pomponius Mela, Pliny, Tacitus, Appian of Alexandria, and, perhaps, Amianus Marcellinus.
> Ordinary spectators, if unfamiliar with the ancient tongues, may refer to Mommsen, Warde-Fowler, Mr. St. George Stock's introduction to the 1898 Clarendon Press edition of Caesar's Gallic Wars, and Murray's Handbook for Egypt. Many of these authorities have

consulted their imaginations, more or less. The author has done the same.

While Shaw at least acknowledges historical sources here, he does so indiscriminately. Of the ancient historians, only Plutarch and Appian of Alexandria contain historical material of particular pertinence to Caesar and his Alexandrian campaign. Shaw's omission of Suetonius' account of Caesar is certainly strange. Compelling evidence of his acquaintance with Suetonius is contained in a three-page, unpublished manuscript in the University of Texas Shaw collection, written in Mrs. Shaw's hand, that is an excerpt of a French translation of Suetonius. That excerpt is taken precisely from Suetonius' account of Caesar's relationship with Cleopatra and includes Curio's accusation that Caesar was "le mari de tantes les femmes, et la femme de tous les maris," the very phrase Shaw refers to in his 1913 *New Statesman* article where he acknowledges that "enemies in the Senate accused him [Caesar] of being every woman's husband and something worse to boot." Among the modern sources, Shaw had neglected to include James Froude's *Caesar: A Sketch* (1879), John Pentland Mahaffy's *Empire of the Ptolemies* (1895), and Sir J. Gardner Wilkinson's *The Manners and Customs of the Ancient Egyptians* (1878).

Crompton has suggested in *Shaw the Dramatist* that Shaw's characterization of Cleopatra closely parallels Mahaffy's dynastic view of her. Mahaffy tells his readers that the fratricidal side of Cleopatra was not something new and strange, for

> . . . she was one of a race in which almost every reigning princess for the last 200 years had been swayed by like storms of passion, or had been guilty of like daring violations of common humanity. . . . What Cleopatra, from the first to the last, had hesitated to murder a brother or a husband, to assume the throne, to raise and command armies, to discard or adopt a partner of her throne from caprice in policy or policy of caprice? Therefore it is that this last Cleopatra, probably no more than an average specimen of the beauty, talent, daring, and cruelty of her ancestors, has taken a unique place . . . in the imagination of the world. . . .

Mahaffy also calls Cleopatra's father, Ptolemy Auletes, "the most idle and worthless of the Ptolemies" and adds that he was "tyrannical and ruthless when in power, taking little account of human life when it thwarted his interest or even baulked his pleasure." Cleopatra is, in Shaw's words, "a chip of the old block."

Shaw had mentioned Froude by name in a letter to Golding Bright (December 15, 1898) as the historian who had rejected the reputed sexual liaison between Caesar and Cleopatra on the grounds that she was a mere child of sixteen when Caesar met her. Moreover, Shaw's reference in the fourth act to the study of Pythagoras as an indispensable criterion for musical proficiency as well as his incorporation into the play of various Egyptian practices in the receiving of guests are strikingly similar to Wilkinson's account of ancient Egyptian manners and customs.

That Shaw used definite historical sources to buttress his theory and treatment of history is indisputable, but somewhere between his flippant claim of "historical divination" and a scrupulous use of historical sources lies his actual method in writing a chronicle play. Shaw argued that as a playwright he "simply takes what the chronicler brings him and puts it on the stage just as it is said to have happened." Of course he is exaggerating here, but then he did not look upon history as an exact science, for under such an assumption no playwright could possibly claim to have written history. To Shaw history is an art in which the playwright is at liberty to imagine the details and accessories in order to make a scene visual, a character alive, and a conflict dynamic.

If the playwright must be allowed his imagination, so too the chronicler, who according to Mommsen, cannot present truth without fiction. I do not mean to imply that Shaw has simply ignored the facts of history. His own notes paraphrasing Mommsen's account of Caesar's Alexandrian campaign underscore his concern for historical detail; furthermore, his acknowledged consultation with the noted classicist Gilbert Murray on the play's background further supports his historical concern. The simple truth is that the facts of history cannot be realized as they are. Historians and dramatists alike would be less than mortal if those facts gathered nothing in their transcription of them. When asked by an interviewer of *To-Day* whether an historical play should be substantially accurate as to the facts, Shaw replied:

> Not more so than any other sort of play. Historical facts are not a bit more sacred than any other class of facts. In making a play out of them you must adapt them to the stage; and that alters them at once, more or less. Why, you cannot even write a history without adapting the facts to the conditions of representation on the stage. Things do not happen in the form of stories or dramas; and since they must be told in some such form, all reports, even by eyewitnesses, all histories, all stories, all dramatic representations, are only attempts to arrange the facts in a thinkable, intelligible, interesting form—that is, when they are not more or less intentional efforts to hide the truth, as they very often are.

Is Shaw's characterization of Cleopatra as a young girl of sixteen a factual distortion with an "intentional effort to hide the truth"? I think not. Shaw stubbornly maintained that Cleopatra was only a child when Caesar appeared in Alexandria. He had in mind not only her chronological age but also her basic childishness, an attribute of her character, not a matter of age only. In effect, Shaw conceived her as suffering a kind of arrested development. While he recognized the greatness of Shakespeare's Cleopatra as an artistic achievement, he judged her differently, seeing the real Cleopatra as having been "the genius of worthlessness." He had no intention of glamorizing such uselessness so as to persuade foolish spectators that the world was well lost for love.

Many critics have suggested that Shaw made Cleopatra sixteen through a misreading of Mommsen. Such may, of course, be the case, but the confusion is not unique to Shaw; many historians give conflicting information about her age. James Froude states categorically that Cleopatra was a girl of sixteen when Caesar was besieged in Alexandria. G. B. Niebuhr places Ptolemy Auletes' death after the battle of Pharsalia, Caesar's decisive victory over Pompey, which would make her sixteen. Theodore Dodge states that Pompey, who had fled to Egypt after Pharsalia, "found the ten-year-old Ptolemy, son of Ptolemy Auletes, engaged in war with his sister Cleopatra, who was seventeen, for the possession of the Egyptian throne." In *The Land of the Sphinx* (1895), a garrulous and rambling travelogue, G. Montbard has one of his disputants hotly disparage Cleopatra as "that dissolute creature who disguised herself at nighttime to frequent places of ill-repute with her Antony, after having married her young rascal of a brother at fifteen, and thrown herself into Caesar's arms a year later."

Regardless of the nature of Shaw's confusion or, for that matter, that of the above mentioned sources, a childish Cleopatra was ideal for Shaw, for he had no intention of making sexual infatuation the essence of their relationship. One reason he did not present an erotic Caesar, says Shaw, is that "Caesar was not Antony." Shaw's point is well taken; he has not gone beyond his acknowledged source. Mommsen writes that "however much . . . he [Caesar] enjoyed the society of women, he only amused himself with them, and allowed them no manner of influence over him; even his much-censured relation to queen Cleopatra was only contrived to mask a weak point in his political position." Mommsen's view was shared by such English historians as Froude, Warde-Fowler, and Merivale, all of whom wrote on Caesar prior to Shaw's play. Most twentieth-century historians, it should be pointed out, agree that Cleopatra was twenty-one at the time of Caesar's sojourn in Egypt.

Another purported distortion of historical fact is Shaw's treatment of the slaying of Pothinus. Gordon Couchman rightly points out that Mommsen is silent concerning Pothinus' death and that that may account for Shaw's "freer hand than usual." Be that as it may, Shaw's decision to have Cleopatra order Pothinus' death is based primarily upon the exigencies of Shaw's dramatic narrative, the result of which is *not* an horrendous distortion of history. The death of Pothinus serves as the climax of the play in its attempt to dramatize the theme of vengeance. Adverse and sympathetic historians, ancient and modern, have praised Caesar for his clemency. Nineteenth-century pro-Caesar writers in particular stressed Caesar's lack of vengeance and his growth in statesmanship after the period of the ruthless Gallic Wars. The scene in the second act in which reference is made to the vindictive killing of

Vercingetorix, an unintentional anachronism, is there to indicate the growth of Caesar from a ruthless general in the Gallic Wars to a statesman of heroic magnitude. That is to say, Shaw could not have involved Caesar in Pothinus' death and still maintain Caesar's rejection of vengeance.

Edwyn Bevan, a twentieth-century historian, writes that "Pothinus, convicted of being in correspondence with the enemy, was put to death by Caesar—ostensibly no doubt by order of Cleopatra." Bevan, like Mahaffy whom he updates, accepts the ferocious side of Cleopatra and can conceive of her ordering Pothinus' death. Thus, Shaw's attributing this murderous act to Cleopatra in no way violates her historically known character. Shaw has, in effect, transcended a "fact" of history so that a larger truth of historical biography would remain inviolable, that is, a delineation of a Caesar as a wise and clement ruler who was aware of the devastating consequence of unchecked vengeance.

Two pertinent implications may be drawn from these two examples of Shaw's use, or abuse, of historical fact: first, that the historical records themselves are imperfect, even contradictory; second, that Shaw valued history, not for its own sake, but for the issues or ideas at stake in any historical conflict. Like Thomas Carlyle, he looked upon history as inseparably linked with the cast of mind of the historian, whose main function is not *to record* but *to interpret*.

"Caesar," Shaw argued, "was not in Shakespear, nor in the epoch, now fast waning, which he inaugurated." He therefore delineated a Caesar commensurate with the ideals of his own epoch, the historical *Zeitgeist* of the nineteenth century, and he availed himself of those "facts" that were compatible and consistent with those ideals.

THE PERIOD OF THE PLAY

The Ra Prologue and the Alternative to the Prologue contain a minimum of historical background to set the stage for Caesar's entrance into the world of Egyptian politics. The Ptolemaic dynasty had ruled Egypt from 323 to 30 B.C., from the time of Alexander the Great to Cleopatra, the seventh Ptolemy to bear that name. When Caesar arrived, Egypt was embroiled in a dynastic struggle, a familiar state of affairs. Ptolemy XI, Cleopatra's father, had been exiled from Egypt between 58 and 55 B.C., during which time his oldest daughter Berenice ruled in his place. With the help of Rome, he was restored to power, killed his daughter, and levied excessive taxes on the people to pay his debt to Rome. He died in 51 B.C., leaving his kingdom to his son Ptolemy XII and to his daughter Cleopatra. His other two children, Arsinoe and Ptolemy XIII, were later put to death by order of Cleopatra.

The cabal behind the youthful king—Pothinus, the king's guardian, Theodotus, his tutor, and Achillas, the general of the Roman army of occupation—had gained the real power and had banished Cleopatra to Syria, where she raised an army and was preparing to wage war against her brother.

In 60 B.C. Pompey along with Caesar and Crassus had formed the First Triumvirate. Caesar had become military commander in Gaul; Pompey spent his time idly in Rome; and Crassus was military commander in Syria. Crassus was later slain in Syria, and eventually jealousies between Pompey and Caesar set in. Pompey aligned himself with the Senate and the Aristocratic party in their desire to check Caesar. Caesar, defying Roman law, crossed the Rubicon in 49 B.C., whereupon Pompey and his forces fled to Brundisium and thence to Greece. Caesar pursued him a year later, suffering a humiliating defeat at Dyrrachium, but having rallied his famous legions, he soundly defeated Pompey at Pharsalia in 48 B.C. Pompey thence fled to Egypt, where he was treacherously murdered and his head and ring later offered to Caesar upon his arrival.

Caesar remained in Alexandria from October 48 B.C. to March 47 B.C. During this time he took up Cleopatra's cause, waged war against the Alexandria army, and placed Cleopatra on the throne as coregent with her younger brother, Ptolemy XIII. The older Ptolemy had drowned at the Battle of the Nile, Caesar's decisive victory over the Alexandrians. Cleopatra then ruled Egypt jointly, first with her brother, whom she later poisoned, and then with Caesarion, officially recognized as Ptolemy XIV, her reputed son by Caesar. She was in Rome when Caesar was assassinated in 44 B.C. She then secretly returned to Egypt, became the mistress of Mark Antony, and eventually committed suicide a year after Antony's disgraceful defeat at Actium in 31 B.C. Her son Caesarion was put to death by Octavius, the victor of the Battle of Actium. With the death of Cleopatra and her son, the Ptolemaic dynasty came to an end, and Egypt became a Roman province under the rule of Octavius, the emperor Augustus Caesar.

A Bernard Shaw Chronology

1856   Born July 26, in Dublin, Ireland

1871   Began work in real estate office

1876   Left Ireland to join mother in London

1879–83   Wrote five unsuccessful novels

1884   Joined Fabian Society

1885   Book reviewer for the *Pall Mall Gazette*

1886–89   Art critic for *The World*

1888–90   Music critic for *The Star*

1889   Edited, and contributed to, *Fabian Essays in Socialism*

1890–94   Music critic for *The World*

1891   *The Quintessence of Ibsenism*

1892   *Widowers' Houses* (begun 1884) produced by Independent Theatre

1893   *The Philanderer; Mrs. Warren's Profession*

1894   *Arms and the Man; Candida*

1895–98   Drama critic for *Saturday Review* (weekly reviews published later as *Our Theatre in the Nineties*)

1896   *You Never Can Tell*

1897   *The Devil's Disciple;* began six years' service as municipal councilor in London

1898   *Caesar and Cleopatra; The Perfect Wagnerite;* married Charlotte Payne-Townshend

1899   *Captain Brassbound's Conversion;* copyright performance of *Caesar and Cleopatra* by Mrs. Patrick Campbell's Company at Theatre Royal, Newcastle-on-Tyne, March 15

1901–03   *Man and Superman*

1904–06   Vedrenne-Barker seasons at the Court Theatre specialized in Shaw plays

1904   *John Bull's Other Island*

1905   *Major Barbara*

1906   *The Doctor's Dilemma*; Max Reinhardt's production of *Caesar and Cleopatra* at the Neues Theater, Berlin, March 31

1907   *Caesar and Cleopatra* presented by Forbes-Robertson at the Grand Theatre, Leeds, September 16

1908   *Getting Married*

1910   *Misalliance*

1911   *Fanny's First Play*; *Androcles and the Lion*

1912   *Pygmalion*

1913–16   *Heartbreak House* (first conceived in 1913)

1914   *Common Sense about the War*

1918–21   *Back to Methuselah* (five-play cycle)

1923   *Saint Joan*

1926   Awarded 1925 Nobel Prize for literature

1928   *The Intelligent Woman's Guide to Socialism and Capitalism*

1929   *The Apple Cart*

1931   *Too True to Be Good*

1932   *The Adventures of the Black Girl in Her Search for God*

1933   *On the Rocks*

1934   *The Simpleton of the Unexpected Isles*

(Dates given for the plays are dates of composition, not of first performance or publication, which sometimes came several years later.)

Selected Bibliography

There is an enormous literature on the subject of Bernard Shaw. The following bibliography is highly selective and is limited, except for a few general critical works, to those studies that contain material relating to *Caesar and Cleopatra*. There is a "Continuing Checklist of Shaviana" in *The Shaw Review*, published three times a year by the Pennsylvania State University Press.

BIOGRAPHY AND LETTERS

Henderson, Archibald. *George Bernard Shaw: Man of the Century*. New York, 1956. Encyclopedic in scope, this is the third and most compendious book by Shaw's official biographer.

Laurence, Dan H. (ed.). *Collected Letters 1874–1897*. New York, 1965; *Collected Letters 1898–1910*. London, 1971. The first two volumes of a projected three-volume collection of Shaw's letters.

Pearson, Hesketh. *George Bernard Shaw: His Life and Personality*. New York, 1963. A lively narrative of Shaw's personal life for which Shaw himself provided much of the information through interviews and letters.

Weintraub, Stanley (ed.). *Shaw: An Autobiography 1856–1898; 1898–1950 (The Playwright Years)*. New York, 1969 and 1970. A compilation of scattered pieces of Shavian memoirs arranged chronologically.

CRITICAL STUDIES

Bentley, Eric. *Bernard Shaw 1856–1950*. Norfolk, Conn., 1957. A concise treatment of Shaw's ideas and career as a dramatist.

Irvine, William. *The Universe of G.B.S.* New York, 1949. A fuller account of Shaw's intellectual background than Bentley's book. Caesar is viewed as authentic history, Shavian autobiography, a vessel of the Life Force, and political spokesman for British imperial policy.

Meisel, Martin. *Shaw and the Nineteenth-Century Theater*. Princeton, N.J., 1963. An excellent account of Shaw's use of the conventions, modes, techniques, and genres of the nineteenth-century popular theater.

SPECIFIC CRITICAL WORKS

Carpenter, Charles A. *Bernard Shaw & the Art of Destroying Ideals*. Madison, Wis., 1969. A study of the early plays; the analysis of *Caesar and Cleopatra* centers around Caesar as Shaw's exemplar of greatness.

Costello, Donald P. *The Serpent's Eye: Shaw and the Cinema*. Notre Dame, Ind., 1965. A study of Shaw's plays which have been filmed by Gabriel Pascal. The author examines Shaw's hand in the motion picture script of *Caesar and Cleopatra*.

Crompton, Louis. *Shaw the Dramatist*. Lincoln, Nebr., 1969. An analysis of Shaw's major plays in the light of their Shavian ideas and intellectual milieu.

Deans, Marjorie. *Meeting at the Sphinx*. London, 1946. A beautifully illustrated memoir of the filming of the Gabriel Pascal production of *Caesar and Cleopatra*.

REVIEWS AND CRITIQUES

Baumann, Arthur A. "Mr. Shaw Run to Waste," *Saturday Review* (London), CIV (November 30, 1907), 662–63. Primarily an answer to A. B. Walkley's adverse criticism of the play.

Berst, Charles A. "The Anatomy of Greatness in *Caesar and Cleopatra*," *Journal of English and Germanic Philology*, LXVIII (January 1969), 74–91. An analysis of the various artistic elements used to convey Caesar's greatness.

Couchman, Gordon W. "Shaw, Caesar, and the Critics," *Speech Monographs*, XXIII (1956), 262–71. Evaluates the early and later critical reactions to the play.

————. "Here Was a Caesar: Shaw's Comedy Today," PMLA, LXXII (1957), 272–85. Examines Shaw's use of historical sources, and concludes that Shaw went beyond those sources in his idealization of Caesar.

Larson, Gale K. *"Caesar and Cleopatra:* The Making of a History Play," *The Shaw Review*, XIV (May 1971), 73–89. Examines the origin, the sources, and the historicity of the play.

Lüdeke, H. "Some Remarks on Shaw's History Plays," *English Studies*, XXXVI (1955), 239–46. Believes that Shaw's intent was to delineate truthfully the historical portrait of Caesar, but that forces within Shaw's own soul colored that portrait.

MacCarthy, Desmond. "Bernard Shaw's 'Julius Caesar,' " *The New Statesman*, I (April 26, 1913), 82–83. A vigorous criticism of Shaw's treatment of history which resulted in a rejoinder from Shaw.

————. "Caesar Again," *The New Statesman*, I (May 10, 1913), 149–50. A reply to Shaw's rejoinder of May 3, 1913.

Massingham, J. W. *Nation* (London), II (December 7, 1907), 338. One of the early, favorable reviews which looks upon the play as a serious and valid statement on an historical epoch.

Reardon, Joan. *"Caesar and Cleopatra* and the Commedia dell' Arte," *The Shaw Review*, XIV (September 1971), 120–36. Demonstrates Shaw's capture of the spirit of the "comedy of skill" without slavishly imitating its form.

Reinert, Otto. "Old History and New: Anachronism in *Caesar and Cleopatra*," *Modern Drama*, III (May 1960), 37–41. An analysis of Shaw's use of anachronism to demolish the myth of progress.

Walkley, A. B. The [London] *Times* (November 26, 1907), p. 5. Derides Shaw's contemporaneous use of history and likens the play to the burlesque of Meilhac and Halévy.

————. The [London] *Times* (April 15, 1913), p. 10. Calls the play an extravaganza, Shaw an incorrigible wag, and scores

Shaw for confusing historical drama with historical document.
Weintraub, Stanley. "Shaw's Mommsenite Caesar," *Anglo-German and American-German Cross Currents,* II (1962), 257–72. Demonstrates Shaw's fidelity to Mommsen's conception of Caesar, thereby answering Couchman's charge that Shaw had gone beyond his source in idealizing Caesar.

RECORDS AND FILMS

Caesar and Cleopatra. The Theatre Recording Society: A Caedman Production, TRS304M. The recording, directed by Anthony Quayle, features Max Adrian and Claire Bloom in the lead roles and Judith Anderson as Ftatateeta.

Shaw vs. Shakespeare. Part I: "The Character of Caesar," 47734; Part II: "The Tragedy of Julius Caesar," 47735; Part III: "Caesar and Cleopatra," 47736. Humanities Series. Encyclopaedia Britannica Educational Corporation, 1971. These films, each approximately one half hour in length, contrast the two playwrights' attitudes toward Caesar and his times. Donald Moffat plays Shaw and Richard Kiley plays Caesar in this combination of lecture and dramatic portrayal.

Note on the Text

The present edition is based on the text of *Caesar and Cleopatra* in the revised standard Constable edition prepared by Shaw in 1931. Shaw's idiosyncratic spelling and punctuation have been retained. The play was first published in 1901 by Grant Richards under the general title, *Three Plays for Puritans; The Devil's Disciple* and *Captain Brassbound's Conversion* rounded out the volume. Besides appending Notes to all three of these plays, Shaw also wrote a lengthy Preface to the collection in 1900. He arranged the Preface under the following headings: "Why for Puritans?" "On Diabolonian Ethics," and "Better than Shakespear?" The latter essay, included in this edition, is a companion piece to this play. Shaw made a few revisions to the Preface in 1931. He deleted "Mr" from the names of Forbes-Robertson, Stuart-Glennie, Swinburne, and "Sir" from Henry Irving. Other revisions included such changes as "Thackeray . . . is still baying" to "was," "genuine criticism of" to "serious attention to," "dramatists" to "playwrights," "selfish hound" and "brawny brute" to "spoilt child" and "brawny fool," "Shakespear" to "Cervantes," "the same liberty with Shakespear as he with Homer" to "platform from Shakespear as he from Homer," and "Board Schools" to "Free Schools."

Two minor emendations within the play occurred after its 1901 publication. Prior to the Berlin production, Shaw realized he had not got Apollodorus off the stage in the fourth act, so he added an exit line for him. Later, when Forbes-Robertson produced the play, he felt that the big scene with Septimius in the second act required some additional preparatory ferment, so Shaw obliged him and wrote in more dialogue for Caesar, Pothinus, and Theodotus prior to Septimius' entrance. Shaw incorporated these changes and added the Ra Prologue, written in 1912, to the printings of the play after 1929.

From the Preface to
Three Plays for Puritans

BETTER THAN SHAKESPEAR?

As to the other plays in this volume, the application of my title is less obvious, since neither Julius Caesar, Cleopatra, nor Lady Cicely Waynflete[1] have any external political connexion with Puritanism. The very name of Cleopatra suggests at once a tragedy of Circe, with the horrible difference that whereas the ancient myth rightly represents Circe as turning heroes into hogs, the modern romantic convention would represent her as turning hogs into heroes. Shakespear's Antony and Cleopatra must needs be as intolerable to the true Puritan as it is vaguely distressing to the ordinary healthy citizen, because, after giving a faithful picture of the soldier broken down by debauchery, and the typical wanton in whose arms such men perish, Shakespear finally strains all his huge command of rhetoric and stage pathos to give a theatrical sublimity to the wretched end of the business, and to persuade foolish spectators that the world was well lost by the twain. Such falsehood is not to be borne except by the real Cleopatras and Antonys (they are to be found in every public house) who would no doubt be glad enough to be transfigured by some poet as immortal lovers. Woe to the poet who stoops to such folly! The lot of the man who sees life truly and thinks about it romantically is Despair. How well we know the cries of that despair! Vanity of vanities, all is vanity! moans the Preacher,[2] when life has at last

---

[1] Lady Cicely Waynflete, the heroine in *Captain Brassbound's Conversion*, was a role Shaw wrote expressedly for Ellen Terry, a well-known Shakespearean actress.

[2] Ecclesiastes 1:2. The Preacher is later referred to in the Preface as "Koheleth," the Hebrew equivalent of the Greek "Ecclesiastes."

1

taught him that Nature will not dance to his moralist-made tunes. Thackeray, scores of centuries later, was still baying the moon in the same terms. Out, out, brief candle![3] cries Shakespear, in his tragedy of the modern literary man as murderer and witch consulter. Surely the time is past for patience with writers who, having to choose between giving up life in despair and discarding the trumpery moral kitchen scales in which they try to weigh the universe, superstitiously stick to the scales, and spend the rest of the lives they pretend to despise in breaking men's spirits. But even in pessimism there is a choice between intellectual honesty and dishonesty. Hogarth drew the rake and the harlot without glorifying their end. Swift, accepting our system of morals and religion, delivered the inevitable verdict of that system on us through the mouth of the king of Brobdingnag,[4] and described Man as the Yahoo, shocking his superior the horse by his every action. Strindberg, the only genuinely Shakespearean modern dramatist, shews that the female Yahoo, measured by romantic standards, is viler than her male dupe and slave.[5] I respect these resolute tragi-comedians: they are logical and faithful: they force you to face the fact that you must either accept their conclusions as valid (in which case it is cowardly to continue living) or admit that their way of judging conduct is absurd. But when your Shakespears and Thackerays huddle up the matter at the end by killing somebody and covering your eyes with the undertaker's handkerchief, duly onioned with some pathetic phrase, as The flight of angels sing thee to thy rest,[6] or Adsum,[7] or the like, I

[3] *Macbeth*, V, v, 23.

[4] The verdict given by the King of Brobdingnag in the second book of *Gulliver's Travels* after he had been apprised of English customs and affairs was, "The bulk of your natives are the most pernicious race of little odious vermin that Nature ever suffered to crawl upon the surface of the earth."

[5] Shaw perhaps has in mind Strindberg's *The Father*, a pessimistic play in which the wife ruthlessly destroys her husband in a domestic struggle. Shaw donated his Nobel Prize money for the translation of Strindberg's works into English.

[6] Hamlet, V, ii, 385–6.

[7] The Latin word for "I am present."

have no respect for them at all: such maudlin tricks may impose on tea-drunkards, not on me.

Besides, I have a technical objection to making sexual infatuation a tragic theme. Experience proves that it is only effective in the comic spirit. We can bear to see Mrs Quickly[8] pawning her plate for love of Falstaff, but not Antony running away from the battle of Actium for love of Cleopatra. Let realism have its demonstration, comedy its criticism, or even bawdry its horselaugh at the expense of sexual infatuation, if it must; but to ask us to subject our souls to its ruinous glamor, to worship it, deify it, and imply that it alone makes our life worth living, is nothing but folly gone mad erotically—a thing compared to which Falstaff's unbeglamored drinking and drabbing is respectable and right-minded. Whoever, then, expects to find Cleopatra a Circe and Caesar a hog in these pages, had better lay down my book and be spared a disappointment.

In Caesar, I have used another character with which Shakespear has been beforehand. But Shakespear, who knew human weakness so well, never knew human strength of the Caesarian type. His Caesar is an admitted failure: his Lear is a masterpiece. The tragedy of disillusion and doubt, of the agonized struggle for a foothold on the quicksand made by an acute observation striving to verify its vain attribution of morality and respectability to Nature, of the faithless will and the keen eyes that the faithless will is too weak to blind: all this will give you a Hamlet or a Macbeth, and win you great applause from literary gentlemen; but it will not give you a Julius Caesar. Caesar was not in Shakespear, nor in the epoch, now fast waning, which he inaugurated. It cost Shakespear no pang to write Caesar down for the merely technical purpose of writing Brutus up. And what a Brutus! A perfect Girondin,[9] mirrored in Shakespear's art two hundred years before

[8] Mrs. Quickly is the hostess of the Boar's Head Tavern in Shakespeare's *Henry IV*.

[9] The Girondins were moderate republicans during the early stages of the French Revolution whose social background inclined them to political but

the real thing came to maturity and talked and stalked and had its head duly cut off by the coarser Antonys and Octaviuses of its time, who at least knew the difference between life and rhetoric.[10]

It will be said that these remarks can bear no other construction than an offer of my Caesar to the public as an improvement on Shakespear's. And in fact, that is their precise purport. But here let me give a friendly warning to those scribes who have so often exclaimed against my criticisms of Shakespear as blasphemies against a hitherto unquestioned Perfection and Infallibility. Such criticisms are no more new than the creed of my Diabolonian Puritan[11] or my revival of the humors of Cool as a Cucumber.[12] Too much surprise at them betrays an acquaintance with Shakespear criticism so limited as not to include even the prefaces of Dr. Johnson and the utterances of Napoleon.[13] I have merely repeated in the dialect of my own time and in the light of its philosophy what they said in the dialect and light of theirs. Do not be misled by the Shakespear fanciers who, ever since his own time, have delighted in his plays just as they might have delighted in a particular breed of pigeons if they had never learnt to read. His genuine critics, from Ben Jonson to Mr Frank Harris,[14] have always kept as far on this side idolatry as I.

As to our ordinary uncritical citizens, they have been slowly

---

not social democracy; they wanted political institutions to protect wealth and to favor ability.

[10] Shaw's critical assessment here of Shakespeare's characterization of Caesar and Brutus closely parallels that of Georg Brandes in his two-volume work, *William Shakespeare: A Critical Study* (1895–96).

[11] The Diabolonian Puritan is Dick Dudgeon, the protagonist of *The Devil's Disciple*, the first play of *Three Plays for Puritans*, whose creed is an inversion of the conventional moral order.

[12] *Cool as a Cucumber* is a nineteenth-century dramatic farce by W. B. Jerrold.

[13] The utterance of Napoleon that Shaw refers to is that France need not envy England, particularly Shakespeare, since Corneille and Racine were superior playwrights.

[14] Frank Harris (1854–1931), novelist, critic, editor, and a friend of Shaw's, wrote *The Man Shakespeare* (1909).

trudging forward these three centuries to the point which Shakespear reached at a bound in Elizabeth's time. Today most of them have arrived there or thereabouts, with the result that his plays are at last beginning to be performed as he wrote them; and the long line of disgraceful farces, melodramas, and stage pageants which actor-managers, from Garrick and Cibber to our own contemporaries, have hacked out of his plays as peasants have hacked huts out of the Coliseum, are beginning to vanish from the stage. It is a significant fact that the mutilators of Shakespear, who never could be persuaded that Shakespear knew his business better than they, have ever been the most fanatical of his worshippers. The late Augustin Daly thought no price too extravagant for an addition to his collection of Shakespear relics; but in arranging Shakespear's plays for the stage, he proceeded on the assumption that Shakespear was a botcher and he an artist. I am far too good a Shakespearean ever to forgive Henry Irving[15] for producing a version of King Lear so mutilated that the numerous critics who had never read the play could not follow the story of Gloster. Both these idolators of the Bard must have thought Forbes Robertson[16] mad because he restored Fortinbras to the stage and played as much of Hamlet as there was time for instead of as little. And the instant success of the experiment probably altered their minds no further than to make them think the public mad. Mr Benson[17] actually gives the play complete at two sittings, causing the aforesaid numerous critics to remark with naïve surprise that Polonius is a complete and interesting character. It was the age of gross ignorance of Shakespear and incapacity for his works that produced the indiscriminate eulogies with which we are familiar. It

[15] David Garrick (1717–1779), Colly Cibber (1671–1757), Augustin Daly (1831–1899), and Henry Irving (1838–1905) were all actor-managers who produced mutilated versions of Shakespeare's plays.

[16] Shaw's admiration for Forbes-Robertson's role as Hamlet is expressed in his review of the play, 2 October 1897, *Our Theatres in the Nineties*, III, 200–207.

[17] Sir Frank Benson (1858–1939), also an actor-manager, formed a Shakespearean company which went on tour throughout England.

was the revival of serious attention to those works that coincided with the movement for giving genuine instead of spurious and silly representations of his plays. So much for Bardolatry!

It does not follow, however, that the right to criticize Shakespear involves the power of writing better plays. And in fact—do not be surprised at my modesty—I do not profess to write better plays. The writing of practicable stage plays does not present an infinite scope to human talent; and the playwrights who magnify its difficulties are humbugs. The summit of their art has been attained again and again. No man will ever write a better tragedy than Lear, a better comedy than Le Festin de Pierre[18] or Peer Gynt, a better opera than Don Giovanni, a better music drama than The Niblung's Ring, or, for the matter of that, better fashionable plays and melodramas than are now being turned out by writers whom nobody dreams of mocking with the word immortal. It is the philosophy, the outlook on life, that changes, not the craft of the playwright. A generation that is thoroughly moralized and patriotized, that conceives virtuous indignation as spiritually nutritious, that murders the murderer and robs the thief, that grovels before all sorts of ideals, social, military, ecclesiastical, royal and divine, may be, from my point of view, steeped in error; but it need not want for as good plays as the hand of man can produce. Only, those plays will be neither written nor relished by men in whose philosophy guilt and innocence, and consequently revenge and idolatry, have no meaning. Such men must rewrite all the old plays in terms of their own philosophy; and that is why, as Stuart-Glennie[19] has pointed out, there can be no new drama without a new philosophy. To which I may add that there can be no Shakespear or Goethe without one either, nor two Shakespears in one philosophic epoch, since, as I have said, the first great comer in that epoch reaps the whole harvest and reduces those who come after to the rank of mere gleaners, or, worse than that, fools who

---

[18] Molière's play about Don Juan.

[19] John Stuart-Glennie was a learned Scottish historian and barrister whom Shaw met in 1879.

go laboriously through all the motions of the reaper and binder in an empty field. What is the use of writing plays or painting frescoes if you have nothing more to say or shew than was said and shewn by Shakespear, Michael Angelo, and Raphael? If these had not seen things differently, for better or worse, from the dramatic poets of the Townley mysteries, or from Giotto,[20] they could not have produced their works: no, not though their skill of pen and hand had been double what it was. After them there was no need (and *need* alone nerves men to face the persecution in the teeth of which new art is brought to birth) to redo the already done, until in due time, when their philosophy wore itself out, a new race of nineteenth century poets and critics, from Byron to William Morris, began, first to speak coldly of Shakespear and Raphael, and then to rediscover, in the medieval art which these Renascence masters had superseded, certain forgotten elements which were germinating again for the new harvest. What is more, they began to discover that the technical skill of the masters was by no means superlative. Indeed, I defy anyone to prove that the great epoch makers in fine art have owed their position to their technical skill. It is true that when we search for examples of a prodigious command of language and of graphic line, we can think of nobody better than Shakespear and Michael Angelo. But both of them laid their arts waste for centuries by leading later artists to seek greatness in copying their technique. The technique was acquired, refined on, and elaborated over and over again; but the supremacy of the two great exemplars remained undisputed. As a matter of easily observable fact, every generation produces men of extraordinary special faculty, artistic, mathematical and linguistic, who for lack of new ideas, or indeed of any ideas worth mentioning, achieve no distinction outside music halls and class rooms, although they can do things easily that the great epoch makers did clumsily or not at all. The contempt of the academic

[20] The Townley mysteries were medieval religious plays performed originally at Wakefield, Yorkshire. Giotto (1276–1337) was an Italian medieval painter.

pedant for the original artist is often founded on a genuine superiority of technical knowledge and aptitude: he is sometimes a better anatomical draughtsman than Raphael, a better hand at triple counterpoint than Beethoven, a better versifier than Byron. Nay, this is true not merely of pedants, but of men who have produced works of art of some note. If technical facility were the secret of greatness in art, Swinburne would be greater than Browning and Byron rolled into one, Stevenson greater than Scott or Dickens, Mendelssohn than Wagner, Maclise than Madox Brown.[21] Besides, new ideas make their technique as water makes its channel; and the technician without ideas is as useless as the canal constructor without water, though he may do very skilfully what the Mississippi does very rudely. To clinch the argument, you have only to observe that the epoch maker himself has generally begun working professionally before his new ideas have mastered him sufficiently to insist on constant expression by his art. In such cases you are compelled to admit that if he had by chance died earlier, his greatness would have remained unachieved, although his technical qualifications would have been well enough established. The early imitative works of great men are usually conspicuously inferior to the best works of their forerunners. Imagine Wagner dying after composing Rienzi, or Shelley after Zastrozzi! Would any competent critic then have rated Wagner's technical aptitude as high as Rossini's, Spontini's, or Meyerbeer's; or Shelley's as high as Moore's? Turn the problem another way: does anyone suppose that if Shakespear had conceived Goethe's or Ibsen's ideas, he would have expressed them any worse than Goethe or Ibsen? Human faculty being what it is, is it likely that in our time any advance, except in external conditions, will take place in the arts of expression sufficient to enable an author, without making himself ridiculous, to undertake to say what he has to say better than Homer or Shakespear? But the humblest author, and much more

[21] Daniel Maclise (1806–1870), an Irish painter of portraits and historical frescoes, was an illustrator of Dickens' novels; Ford Madox Brown (1821–1893) was a painter who was a leader of the Pre-Raphaelite movement in England.

a rather arrogant one like myself, may profess to have something
to say by this time that neither Homer nor Shakespear said. And
the playgoer may reasonably ask to have historical events and persons presented to him in the light of his own time, even though
Homer and Shakespear have already shewn them in the light of
their time. For example, Homer presented Achilles and Ajax as
heroes to the world in the Iliads. In due time came Shakespear,
who said, virtually: I really cannot accept this spoilt child and
this brawny fool as great men merely because Homer flattered
them in playing to the Greek gallery. Consequently we have, in
Troilus and Cressida, the verdict of Shakespear's epoch (our own)
on the pair. This did not in the least involve any pretence on
Shakespear's part to be a greater poet than Homer.

When Shakespear in turn came to deal with Henry V and Julius
Caesar, he did so according to his own essentially knightly conception of a great statesman-commander. But in the XIX century
comes the German historian Mommsen,[22] who also takes Caesar
for his hero, and explains the immense difference in scope between
the perfect knight Vercingetorix[23] and his great conqueror Julius
Caesar. In this country, Carlyle,[24] with his vein of peasant inspiration, apprehended the sort of greatness that places the true hero of
history so far beyond the mere *preux chevalier*, whose fanatical
personal honor, gallantry, and self-sacrifice, are founded on a passion for death born of inability to bear the weight of a life that
will not grant ideal conditions to the liver. This one ray of percep-
tion became Carlyle's whole stock-in-trade; and it sufficed to make
a literary master of him. In due time, when Mommsen is an old
man, and Carlyle dead, come I, and dramatize the by-this-time fa-

[22] See editor's Introduction, pp. xv–xxii.

[23] Vercingetorix was the last of the chieftains who rose against Caesar
during the Roman subjugation of Gaul. He was led in captive bonds through
the streets of Rome where he was later executed in 46 B.C.

[24] Shaw's reference here is to Carlyle's *On Heroes, Hero Worship, and the
Heroic in History* (1841). *Preux Chevalier* is a French title that means
"brave knight."

miliar distinction in Arms and the Man,[25] with its comedic conflict between the knightly Bulgarian and the Mommsenite Swiss captain. Whereupon a great many playgoers who have not yet read Cervantes, much less Mommsen and Carlyle, raise a shriek of concern for their knightly ideal as if nobody had ever questioned its sufficiency since the middle ages. Let them thank me for educating them so far. And let them allow me to set forth Caesar in the same modern light, taking the platform from Shakespear as he from Homer, and with no thought of pretending to express the Mommsenite view of Caesar any better than Shakespear expressed a view which was not even Plutarchian, and must, I fear, be referred to the tradition in stage conquerors established by Marlowe's Tamerlane as much as to the chivalrous conception of heroism dramatized in Henry V.

For my own part, I can avouch that such powers of invention, humor and stage ingenuity as I have been able to exercise in Plays Pleasant and Unpleasant,[26] and in these Three Plays for Puritans, availed me not at all until I saw the old facts in a new light. Technically, I do not find myself able to proceed otherwise than as former playwrights have done. True, my plays have the latest mechanical improvements: the action is not carried on by impossible soliloquys and asides; and my people get on and off the stage without requiring four doors to a room which in real life would have only one. But my stories are the old stories; my characters are the familiar harlequin and columbine, clown and pantaloon (note the harlequin's leap in the third act of Caesar and Cleopatra); my stage tricks and suspenses and thrills and jests are the ones in vogue when I was a boy, by which time my grandfather was tired of them. To the young people who make their acquaintance for the first time in my plays, they may be as novel

---

25 *Arms and the Man* (1894) is an early play of Shaw's in which he satirized romanticized heroism, much in the manner of Cervantes (1547–1616) in *Don Quixote*.

26 *Plays Pleasant and Unpleasant*, published in two volumes in 1898, contain the first seven plays written by Shaw.

as Cyrano's nose to those who have never seen Punch;[27] whilst to older playgoers the unexpectedness of my attempt to substitute natural history for conventional ethics and romantic logic may so transfigure the eternal stage puppets and their inevitable dilemmas as to make their identification impossible for the moment. If so, so much the better for me: I shall perhaps enjoy a few years of immortality. But the whirligig of time will soon bring my audiences to my own point of view; and then the next Shakespear that comes along will turn these petty tentatives of mine into masterpieces final for their epoch. By that time my twentieth century characteristics will pass unnoticed as a matter of course, whilst the eighteenth century artificiality that marks the work of every literary Irishman of my generation will seem antiquated and silly. It is a dangerous thing to be hailed at once, as a few rash admirers have hailed me, as above all things original: what the world calls originality is only an unaccustomed method of tickling it. Meyerbeer seemed prodigiously original to the Parisians when he first burst on them. Today, he is only the crow who followed Beethoven's plough. I am a crow who have followed many ploughs. No doubt I seem prodigiously clever to those who have never hopped, hungry and curious, across the fields of philosophy, politics, and art. Karl Marx said of Stuart Mill that his eminence was due to the flatness of the surrounding country. In these days of Free Schools, universal reading, cheap newspapers, and the inevitable ensuing demand for notabilities of all sorts, literary, military, political and fashionable, to write paragraphs about, that sort of eminence is within the reach of very moderate ability. Reputations are cheap nowadays. Even were they dear, it would still be impossible for any public-spirited citizen of the world to hope that his reputation might endure; for this would be to hope that the flood of general enlightenment may never rise above his

[27] Like Cyrano de Bergerac (1619–1655), a French soldier, playwright, and novelist, Punch, the chief character in the puppet show "Punch and Judy," is characterized as having a large nose. Cyrano was the subject of a play by Edmond Rostand in 1898.

miserable high-watermark. I hate to think that Shakespear has lasted 300 years, though he got no further than Koheleth the Preacher, who died many centuries before him; or that Plato, more than 2000 years old, is still ahead of our voters. We must hurry on: we must get rid of reputations: they are weeds in the soil of ignorance. Cultivate that soil, and they will flower more beautifully, but only as annuals. If this preface will at all help to get rid of mine, the writing of it will have been well worth the pains.

SURREY, 1900.

CAESAR AND CLEOPATRA

A History

1898

The Sun God Ra

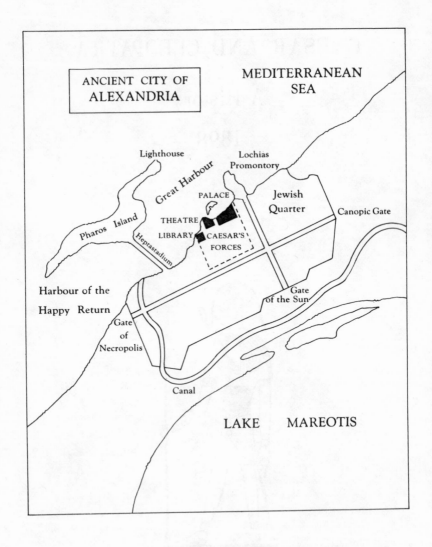

ANCIENT CITY OF
ALEXANDRIA

MEDITERRANEAN
SEA

Lighthouse

Great Harbour

Lochias
Promontory

Pharos Island

Heptastadium

PALACE

THEATRE

LIBRARY

CAESAR'S
FORCES

Jewish
Quarter

Canopic Gate

Harbour of the
Happy Return

Gate
of the Sun

Gate
of
Necropolis

Canal

LAKE   MAREOTIS

Caesar and Cleopatra

PROLOGUE

In the doorway of the temple of Ra in Memphis. Deep gloom. An august personage with a hawk's head is mysteriously visible by his own light in the darkness within the temple. He surveys the modern audience with great contempt; and finally speaks the following words to them.

Peace! Be silent and hearken unto me, ye quaint little islanders. Give ear, ye men with white paper on your breasts and nothing written thereon (to signify the innocency of your minds). Hear me, ye women who adorn yourselves alluringly and conceal your thoughts from your men, leading them to believe that ye deem them wondrous strong and masterful whilst in truth ye hold them in your hearts as children without judgment. Look upon my hawk's head; and know that I am Ra,[1] who was once in Egypt a mighty god. Ye cannot kneel nor prostrate yourselves; for ye are packed in rows without freedom to move, obstructing one another's vision; neither do any of ye regard it as seemly to do ought until ye see all the rest do so too; wherefore it commonly happens that in great emergencies ye do nothing, though each telleth his fellow that something must be done. I ask you not for worship, but for silence. Let not your men speak nor your women cough; for I am come to draw you back two thousand years over the graves of sixty generations. Ye poor posterity, think not that ye are the first. Other fools before ye have seen the sun rise and

---

[1] Ra, in Egyptian mythology, is the midday sun god and supreme deity, generally represented as a hawk-headed man bearing on his head the solar disk and the uraeus, or sacred asp.

set, and the moon change her shape and her hour. As they were so ye are; and yet not so great; for the pyramids my people built stand to this day; whilst the dustheaps on which ye slave, and which ye call empires, scatter in the wind even as ye pile your dead sons' bodies on them to make yet more dust.

Hearken to me then, oh ye compulsorily educated ones. Know that even as there is an old England and a new, and ye stand perplexed between the twain; so in the days when I was worshipped was there an old Rome and a new, and men standing perplexed between them. And the old Rome was poor and little, and greedy and fierce, and evil in many ways; but because its mind was little and its work was simple, it knew its own mind and did its own work; and the gods pitied it and helped it and strengthened it and shielded it; for the gods are patient with littleness. Then the old Rome, like the beggar on horseback, presumed on the favor of the gods, and said, "Lo! there is neither riches nor greatness in our littleness: the road to riches and greatness is through robbery of the poor and slaughter of the weak." So they robbed their own poor until they became great masters of that art, and knew by what laws it could be made to appear seemly and honest. And when they had squeezed their own poor dry, they robbed the poor of other lands, and added those lands to Rome until there came a new Rome, rich and huge. And I, Ra, laughed; for the minds of the Romans remained the same size whilst their dominion spread over the earth.

Now mark me, that ye may understand what ye are presently to see. Whilst the Romans still stood between the old Rome and the new, there arose among them a mighty soldier: Pompey the Great. And the way of the soldier is the way of death; but the way of the gods is the way of life; and so it comes that a god at the end of his way is wise and a soldier at the end of his way is a fool. So Pompey held by the old Rome, in which only soldiers could become great; but the gods turned to the new Rome, in which any man with wit enough could become what he would. And Pompey's friend Julius Caesar was on the side of the gods; for he saw that Rome had passed beyond the control of the little old

Romans. This Caesar was a great talker and a politician: he bought men with words and with gold, even as ye are bought. And when they would not be satisfied with words and gold, and demanded also the glories of war, Caesar in his middle age[2] turned his hand to that trade; and they that were against him when he sought their welfare, bowed down before him when he became a slayer and a conqueror; for such is the nature of you mortals. And as for Pompey, the gods grew tired of his triumphs and his airs of being himself a god; for he talked of law and duty and other matters that concerned not a mere human worm.[3] And the gods smiled on Caesar; for he lived the life they had given him boldly, and was not forever rebuking us for our indecent ways of creation, and hiding our handiwork as a shameful thing. Ye know well what I mean; for this is one of your own sins.

And thus it fell out between the old Rome and the new, that Caesar said, "Unless I break the law of old Rome, I cannot take my share in ruling her; and the gift of ruling that the gods gave me will perish without fruit." But Pompey said, "The law is above all; and if thou break it thou shalt die." Then said Caesar, "I will break it: kill me who can." And he broke it. And Pompey went for him, as ye say, with a great army to slay him and uphold the old Rome. So Caesar fled across the Adriatic sea; for the high gods had a lesson to teach him, which lesson they shall also teach you in due time if ye continue to forget them and to worship that cad among gods, Mammon. Therefore before they raised Caesar to be master of the world, they were minded to throw him down

[2] Caesar was forty-two when he became military commander of the Roman legions in Gaul. For ten years he conducted brilliant campaigns against the rebellious Gallic tribes, all of which he recorded in his *Commentaries on the Gallic Wars*.

[3] This characterization of Pompey follows Mommsen, who describes him as a man who "would doubtless gladly have placed himself beyond the law if only he could have done so without forsaking legal ground," but who "trembled at the mere thought of undertaking anything unconstitutional," and "who for want of faith in himself and in his star timidly clung in public life to formal right."

into the dust, even beneath the feet of Pompey, and blacken his face before the nations.[4] And Pompey they raised higher than ever, he and his laws and his high mind that aped the gods, so that his fall might be the more terrible. And Pompey followed Caesar, and overcame him with all the majesty of old Rome, and stood over him and over the whole world even as ye stand over it with your fleet that covers thirty miles of the sea. And when Caesar was brought down to utter nothingness, he made a last stand to die honorably, and did not despair; for he said, "Against me there is Pompey, and the old Rome, and the law and the legions: all all against me; but high above these are the gods; and Pompey is a fool." And the gods laughed and approved; and on the field of Pharsalia[5] the impossible came to pass; the blood and iron ye pin your faith on fell before the spirit of man; for the spirit of man is the will of the gods; and Pompey's power crumbled in his hand, even as the power of imperial Spain[6] crumbled when it was set against your fathers in the days when England was little, and knew her own mind, and had a mind to know instead of a circulation of newspapers. Wherefore look to it, lest some little people whom ye would enslave rise up and become in the hand of God the scourge of your boastings and your injustices and your lusts and stupidities.[7]

And now, would ye know the end of Pompey, or will ye sleep while a god speaks? Heed my words well; for Pompey went where ye have gone, even to Egypt, where there was a Roman occupation

---

[4] Caesar's first serious engagement with Pompey was at Dyrrhachium, where he was soundly beaten, but when Pompey failed to follow-up with pursuit, Caesar, according to Suetonius, remarked, "He does not know how to win wars."

[5] At Pharsalia, on the plains of Thessaly, Caesar was greatly outnumbered, yet he won a decisive victory over Pompey, who fled to Egypt and to death.

[6] The English defeat of the allegedly invincible Spanish Armada in 1588 was as amazing as Caesar's victory at Pharsalia in 48 B.C.

[7] Shaw undoubtedly has in mind here the Boer War in which a group of unskilled and ill-equipped natives routed the British army.

even as there was but now a British one.[8] And Caesar pursued
Pompey to Egypt: a Roman fleeing, and a Roman pursuing: dog
eating dog. And the Egyptians said, "Lo: these Romans which
have lent money to our kings and levied a distraint upon us with
their arms, call for ever upon us to be loyal to them by betraying
our own country to them. But now behold two Romes! Pompey's
Rome and Caesar's Rome! To which of the twain shall we pretend
to be loyal?" So they turned in their perplexity to a soldier that
had once served Pompey, and that knew the ways of Rome and
was full of her lusts. And they said to him, "Lo: in thy country
dog eats dog; and both dogs are coming to eat us: what counsel
hast thou to give us?" And this soldier, whose name was Lucius
Septimius, and whom ye shall presently see before ye, replied,
"Ye shall diligently consider which is the bigger dog of the two;
and ye shall kill the other dog for his sake and thereby earn his
favor." And the Egyptians said, "Thy counsel is expedient; but if
we kill a man outside the law we set ourselves in the place of the
gods; and this we dare not do. But thou, being a Roman, art
accustomed to this kind of killing; for thou hast imperial instincts. Wilt thou therefore kill the lesser dog for us?" And he
said, "I will; for I have made my home in Egypt; and I desire
consideration and influence among you." And they said, "We
knew well thou wouldst not do it for nothing: thou shalt have thy
reward." Now when Pompey came, he came alone in a little galley,
putting his trust in the law and the constitution. And it was plain
to the people of Egypt that Pompey was now but a very small dog.
So when he set his foot on the shore he was greeted by his old
comrade Lucius Septimius, who welcomed him with one hand and
with the other smote off his head, and kept it as it were a pickled
cabbage to make a present to Caesar. And mankind shuddered;
but the gods laughed; for Septimius was but a knife that Pompey
had sharpened; and when it turned against his own throat they
said that Pompey had better have made Septimius a ploughman

---

[8] In 1881, when British forces crushed a general uprising in Alexandria,
Egypt became a virtual possession of Great Britain.

than so brave and readyhanded a slayer. Therefore again I bid you beware, ye who would all be Pompeys if ye dared; for war is a wolf that may come to your own door.

Are ye impatient with me? Do ye crave for a story of an unchaste woman? Hath the name of Cleopatra tempted ye hither? Ye foolish ones; Cleopatra is as yet but a child that is whipped by her nurse.[9] And what I am about to shew you for the good of your souls is how Caesar, seeking Pompey in Egypt, found Cleopatra; and how he received that present of a pickled cabbage that was once the head of Pompey; and what things happened between the old Caesar and the child queen before he left Egypt and battled his way back to Rome to be slain there as Pompey was slain, by men in whom the spirit of Pompey still lived. All this ye shall see; and ye shall marvel, after your ignorant manner, that men twenty centuries ago were already just such as you, and spoke and lived as ye speak and live, no worse and no better, no wiser and no sillier. And the two thousand years that have past are to me, the god Ra, but a moment; nor is this day any other than the day in which Caesar set foot in the land of my people. And now I leave you; for ye are a dull folk, and instruction is wasted on you; and I had not spoken so much but that it is in the nature of a god to struggle for ever with the dust and the darkness, and to drag from them, by the force of his longing for the divine, more life and more light. Settle ye therefore in your seats and keep silent; for ye are about to hear a man speak, and a great man he was, as ye count greatness. And fear not that I shall speak to you again: the rest of the story must ye learn from them that lived it. Farewell; and do not presume to applaud me. [*The temple vanishes in utter darkness*].

[1912].

---

[9] See editor's Introduction, pp. xx–xxi.

AN ALTERNATIVE TO THE PROLOGUE

An October night on the Syrian border of Egypt towards the end of the XXXIII Dynasty,[10] in the year 706 by Roman computation, afterwards reckoned by Christian computation as 48 B.C. A great radiance of silver fire, the dawn of a moonlit night, is rising in the east. The stars and the cloudless sky are our own contemporaries, nineteen and a half centuries younger than we know them; but you would not guess that from their appearance. Below them are two notable drawbacks of civilization: a palace, and soldiers. The palace, an old, low, Syrian building of whitened mud, is not so ugly as Buckingham Palace; and the officers in the courtyard are more highly civilized than modern English officers: for example, they do not dig up the corpses of their dead enemies and mutilate them, as we dug up Cromwell and the Mahdi.[11] They are in two groups: one intent on the gambling of their captain Belzanor, a warrior of fifty, who, with his spear on the ground beside his knee, is stooping to throw dice with a sly-looking young Persian recruit; the other gathered about a guardsman who has just finished telling a naughty story (still current in English barracks) at which they are laughing uproariously. They are about a dozen in number, all highly aristocratic young Egyptian guardsmen, handsomely equipped with weapons and armor, very unEnglish in point of not being ashamed of and uncomfortable in their profes-

10 The XXXIII Dynasty was the Ptolemaic, named after a general in the forces of Alexander the Great. The Ptolemies ruled Egypt for nearly 300 years, beginning in 323 B.C. until the death of Cleopatra and her son in 30 B.C.

11 Mohammed Ahmed, or the Mahdi (1844–1885) led an insurrection against the British Government in the Sudan in 1881; he captured Khartoum in January of 1885, killing General Gordon, and died the following June. Later his body was dug up and mutilated in revenge by Lord Kitchener's British forces at his express command.

sional dress; on the contrary, rather ostentatiously and arrogantly warlike, as valuing themselves on their military caste.

Belzanor is a typical veteran, tough and wilful; prompt, capable and crafty where brute force will serve; helpless and boyish when it will not: an effective sergeant, an incompetent general, a deplorable dictator. Would, if influentially connected, be employed in the two last capacities by a modern European State on the strength of his success in the first.[12] Is rather to be pitied just now in view of the fact that Julius Caesar is invading his country. Not knowing this, is intent on his game with the Persian, whom, as a foreigner, he considers quite capable of cheating him.

His subalterns are mostly handsome young fellows whose interest in the game and the story symbolize with tolerable completeness the main interests in life of which they are conscious. Their spears are leaning against the walls, or lying on the ground ready to their hands. The corner of the courtyard forms a triangle of which one side is the front of the palace, with a doorway, the other a wall with a gateway. The storytellers are on the palace side: the gamblers, on the gateway side. Close to the gateway, against the wall, is a stone block high enough to enable a Nubian sentinel, standing on it, to look over the wall. The yard is lighted by a torch stuck in the wall. As the laughter from the group round the storyteller dies away, the kneeling Persian, winning the throw, snatches up the stake from the ground.

BELZANOR. By Apis,[13] Persian, thy gods are good to thee.
PERSIAN. Try yet again, O captain. Double or quits![14]
BELZANOR. No more. I am not in the vein.

---

[12] Belzanor is described here in the terms that Mommsen uses for Pompey: "Neither a bad nor an incapable man, but a man thoroughly ordinary, created by nature to be a good sergeant, called by circumstances to be a general and statesman."

[13] Apis, in Egyptian mythology, is the sacred bull represented with the disk of the sun between his horns.

[14] An English phrase used in tossing a coin to decide whether a debt is "quitted" or "doubled."

THE SENTINEL [*poising his javelin as he peers over the wall*] Stand. Who goes there?

They all start, listening. A strange voice replies from without.

VOICE. The bearer of evil tidings.

BELZANOR [*calling to the sentry*] Pass him.

THE SENTINEL [*grounding his javelin*] Draw near, O bearer of evil tidings.

BELZANOR [*pocketing the dice and picking up his spear*] Let us receive this man with honor. He bears evil tidings.

The guardsmen seize their spears and gather about the gate, leaving a way through for the new comer.

PERSIAN [*rising from his knee*] Are evil tidings, then, so honorable?

BELZANOR. O barbarous Persian, hear my instruction. In Egypt the bearer of good tidings is sacrificed to the gods as a thank offering; but no god will accept the blood of the messenger of evil. When we have good tidings, we are careful to send them in the mouth of the cheapest slave we can find. Evil tidings are borne by young noblemen who desire to bring themselves into notice. [*They join the rest at the gate*].

THE SENTINEL. Pass. O young captain; and bow the head in the House of the Queen.

VOICE. Go anoint thy javelin with fat of swine, O Blackamoor; for before morning the Romans will make thee eat it to the very butt.

The owner of the voice, a fairhaired dandy, dressed in a different fashion from that affected by the guardsmen, but no less extravagantly, comes through the gateway laughing. He is somewhat battlestained; and his left forearm, bandaged, comes through a torn sleeve. In his right hand he carries a Roman sword in its sheath. He swaggers down the courtyard, the Persian on his right, Belzanor on his left, and the guardsmen crowding down behind him.

BELZANOR. Who are thou that laughest in the House of Cleopatra the Queen, and in the teeth of Belzanor, the captain of her guard?

THE NEW COMER. I am Bel Affris, descended from the gods.

BELZANOR [*ceremoniously*] Hail, cousin!

ALL [*except the Persian*] Hail, cousin!

PERSIAN. All the Queen's guards are descended from the gods, O stranger, save myself. I am Persian, and descended from many kings.

BEL AFFRIS [*to the guardsmen*] Hail, cousins! [*To the Persian, condescendingly*] Hail, mortal!

BELZANOR. You have been in battle, Bel Affris; and you are a soldier among soldiers. You will not let the Queen's women have the first of your tidings.

BEL AFFRIS. I have no tidings, except that we shall have our throats cut presently, women, soldiers, and all.

PERSIAN [*to Belzanor*] I told you so.

THE SENTINEL [*who has been listening*] Woe, alas!

BEL AFFRIS [*calling to him*] Peace, peace, poor Ethiop: destiny is with the gods who painted thee black. [*To Belzanor*] What has this mortal [*indicating the Persian*] told you?

BELZANOR. He says that the Roman Julius Caesar, who has landed on our shores with a handful of followers, will make himself master of Egypt. He is afraid of the Roman soldiers. [*The guardsmen laugh with boisterous scorn*]. Peasants, brought up to scare crows and follow the plough! Sons of smiths and millers and tanners! And we nobles, consecrated to arms, descended from the gods!

PERSIAN. Belzanor: the gods are not always good to their poor relations.

BELZANOR [*hotly, to the Persian*] Man to man, are we worse than the slaves of Caesar?

BEL AFFRIS [*stepping between them*] Listen, cousin. Man to man, we Egyptians are as gods above the Romans.

THE GUARDSMEN [*exultantly*] Aha!

BEL AFFRIS. But this Caesar does not pit man against man: he throws a legion at you where you are weakest as he throws a stone from a catapult; and that legion is as a man with one head, a thousand arms, and no religion. I have fought against them; and I know.

BELZANOR [*derisively*] Were you frightened, cousin?

The guardsmen roar with laughter, their eyes sparkling at the wit of their captain.

BEL AFFRIS. No, cousin; but I was beaten. They were frightened (perhaps); but they scattered us like chaff.

The guardsmen, much damped, utter a growl of contemptuous disgust.

BELZANOR. Could you not die?

BEL AFFRIS. No: that was too easy to be worthy of a descendant of the gods. Besides, there was no time: all was over in a moment. The attack came just where we least expected it.

BELZANOR. That shews that the Romans are cowards.

BEL AFFRIS. They care nothing about cowardice, these Romans: they fight to win. The pride and honor of war are nothing to them.

PERSIAN. Tell us the tale of the battle. What befell?

THE GUARDSMEN [*gathering eagerly round Bel Affris*] Ay: the tale of the battle.

BEL AFFRIS. Know then, that I am a novice in the guard of the temple of Ra in Memphis, serving neither Cleopatra nor her brother Ptolemy, but only the high gods. We went a journey to inquire of Ptolemy why he had driven Cleopatra into Syria, and how we of Egypt should deal with the Roman Pompey, newly come to our shores after his defeat by Caesar at Pharsalia. What, think ye, did we learn? Even that Caesar is coming also in hot pursuit of his foe, and that Ptolemy has slain Pompey, whose severed head he holds in readiness to present to the conqueror. [*Sensation among the guardsmen*]. Nay, more: we found that Caesar is already come; for we had not made half a day's journey on our way back when we came upon a city rabble flying from his legions, whose landing they had gone out to withstand.

BELZANOR. And ye, the temple guard! did ye not withstand these legions?

BEL AFFRIS. What man could, that we did. But there came the sound of a trumpet whose voice was as the cursing of a black mountain. Then saw we a moving wall of shields coming towards us. You know how the heart burns when you charge a fortified wall; but how if the fortified wall were to charge you?

PERSIAN [*exulting in having told them so*] Did I not say it?

BEL AFFRIS. When the wall came nigh, it changed into a line of men—common fellows enough, with helmets, leather tunics, and breastplates. Every man of them flung his javelin: the one that came my way drove through my shield as through a papyrus—lo there! [*he points to the bandage on his left arm*] and would have gone through my neck had I not stooped. They were charging at the double then, and were upon us with short swords almost as soon as their javelins. When a man is close to you with such a sword, you can do nothing with our weapons: they are all too long.

PERSIAN. What did you do?

BEL AFFRIS. Doubled my fist and smote my Roman on the sharpness of his jaw. He was but mortal after all: he lay down in a stupor; and I took his sword and laid it on. [*Drawing the sword*] Lo! a Roman sword with Roman blood on it!

THE GUARDSMEN [*approvingly*] Good! [*They take the sword and hand it round, examining it curiously*].

PERSIAN. And your men?

BEL AFFRIS. Fled. Scattered like sheep.

BELZANOR [*furiously*] The cowardly slaves! Leaving the descendants of the gods to be butchered!

BEL AFFRIS [*with acid coolness*] The descendants of the gods did not stay to be butchered, cousin. The battle was not to the strong; but the race was to the swift.[15] The Romans who have no chariots, sent a cloud of horsemen in pursuit, and slew multitudes. Then our high priest's captain rallied a dozen descendants of the gods and exhorted us to die fighting. I said to myself: surely it is safer to stand than to lose my breath and be stabbed in the back; so I joined our captain and stood. Then the Romans treated us with respect; for no man attacks a lion when the field is full of sheep, except for the pride and honor of war, of which these Ro-

15 Shaw's expression here is a modification of the proverb in Ecclesiastes: "The race is not to the swift, nor the battle to the strong" (9:11).

mans know nothing. So we escaped with our lives; and I am come to warn you that you must open your gates to Caesar; for his advance guard is scarce an hour behind me; and not an Egyptian warrior is left standing between you and his legions.

THE SENTINEL. Woe, alas! [*He throws down his javelin and flies into the palace*].

BELZANOR. Nail him to the door, quick! [*The guardsmen rush for him with their spears; but he is too quick for them*]. Now this news will run through the palace like fire through stubble.

BEL AFFRIS. What shall we do to save the women from the Romans?

BELZANOR. Why not kill them?

PERSIAN. Because we should have to pay blood money for some of them. Better let the Romans kill them: it is cheaper.

BELZANOR [*awestruck at his brain power*] O subtle one! O serpent!

BEL AFFRIS. But your Queen?

BELZANOR. True: we must carry off Cleopatra.

BEL AFFRIS. Will ye not await her command?

BELZANOR. Command! a girl of sixteen! Not we. At Memphis ye deem her a Queen: here we know better. I will take her on the crupper of my horse. When we soldiers have carried her out of Caesar's reach, then the priests and the nurses and the rest of them can pretend she is a queen again, and put their commands into her mouth.

PERSIAN. Listen to me, Belzanor.

BELZANOR. Speak, O subtle beyond thy years.

PERSIAN. Cleopatra's brother Ptolemy is at war with her. Let us sell her to him.

THE GUARDSMEN. O subtle one! O serpent!

BELZANOR. We dare not. We are descended from the gods; but Cleopatra is descended from the river Nile; and the lands of our fathers will grow no grain if the Nile rises not to water them. Without our father's gifts we should live the lives of dogs.

PERSIAN. It is true: the Queen's guard cannot live on its pay. But hear me further, O ye kinsmen of Osiris.

THE GUARDSMEN. Speak, O subtle one. Hear the serpent begotten!

PERSIAN. Have I heretofore spoken truly to you of Caesar, when you thought I mocked you?

THE GUARDSMEN. Truly, truly.

BELZANOR [*reluctantly admitting it*] So Bel Affris says.

PERSIAN. Hear more of him, then. This Caesar is a great lover of women: he makes them his friends and counsellors.

BELZANOR. Faugh! This rule of women will be the ruin of Egypt.

PERSIAN. Let it rather be the ruin of Rome! Caesar grows old now: he is past fifty and full of labors and battles. He is too old for the young women; and the old women are too wise to worship him.

BEL AFFRIS. Take heed, Persian. Caesar is by this time almost within earshot.

PERSIAN. Cleopatra is not yet a woman: neither is she wise. But she already troubles men's wisdom.

BELZANOR. Ay: that is because she is descended from the river Nile and a black kitten of the sacred White Cat. What then?

PERSIAN. Why, sell her secretly to Ptolemy, and then offer ourselves to Caesar as volunteers to fight for the overthrow of her brother and the rescue of our Queen, the Great Granddaughter of the Nile.

THE GUARDSMEN. O serpent!

PERSIAN. He will listen to us if we come with her picture in our mouths. He will conquer and kill her brother, and reign in Egypt with Cleopatra for his Queen. And we shall be her guard.

THE GUARDSMEN. O subtlest of all the serpents! O admiration! O wisdom!

BEL AFFRIS. He will also have arrived before you have done talking, O word spinner.

BELZANOR. That is true. [*An affrighted uproar in the palace interrupts him*]. Quick: the flight has begun: guard the door. [*They rush to the door and form a cordon before it with their spears. A mob of women-servants and nurses surges out. Those in front recoil from the spears, screaming to those behind to keep back. Belzanor's voice dominates the disturbance as he shouts]* Back there. In again, unprofitable cattle.

THE GUARDSMEN. Back, unprofitable cattle.

BELZANOR. Send us out Ftatateeta, the Queen's chief nurse.

THE WOMEN [*calling into the palace*] Ftatateeta, Ftatateeta. Come, come. Speak to Belzanor.

A WOMAN. Oh, keep back. You are thrusting me on the spearheads.

A huge grim woman, her face covered with a network of tiny wrinkles, and her eyes old, large, and wise; sinewy handed, very tall, very strong; with the mouth of a bloodhound and the jaws of a bulldog, appears on the threshold. She is dressed like a person of consequence in the palace, and confronts the guardsmen insolently.

FTATATEETA. Make way for the Queen's chief nurse.

BELZANOR [*with solemn arrogance*] Ftatateeta: I am Belzanor, the captain of the Queen's guard, descended from the gods.

FTATATEETA [*retorting his arrogance with interest*] Belzanor: I am Ftatateeta, the Queen's chief nurse; and your divine ancestors were proud to be painted on the wall in the pyramids of the kings whom my fathers served.

The women laugh triumphantly.

BELZANOR [*with grim humor*] Ftatateeta: daughter of a long-tongued, swivel-eyed chameleon, the Romans are at hand. [*A cry of terror from the women: they would fly but for the spears*]. Not even the descendants of the gods can resist them; for they have each man seven arms, each carrying seven spears. The blood in their veins is boiling quicksilver; and their wives become mothers in three hours, and are slain and eaten the next day.

A shudder of horror from the women. Ftatateeta, despising them and scorning the soldiers, pushes her way through the crowd and confronts the spear points undismayed.

FTATATEETA. Then fly and save yourselves, O cowardly sons of the cheap clay gods that are sold to fish porters; and leave us to shift for ourselves.

BELZANOR. Not until you have first done our bidding, O terror of manhood. Bring out Cleopatra the Queen to us; and then go whither you will.

FTATATEETA [*with a derisive laugh*] Now I know why the gods have taken her out of our hands. [*The guardsmen start and look at one another*]. Know, thou foolish soldier, that the Queen has been missing since an hour past sundown.

BELZANOR [*furiously*] Hag: you have hidden her to sell to Caesar or her brother. [*He grasps her by the left wrist, and drags her, helped by a few of the guard, to the middle of the courtyard, where, as they fling her on her knees, he draws a murderous looking knife*]. Where is she? Where is she? or—[*He threatens to cut her throat*].

FTATATEETA [*savagely*] Touch me, dog; and the Nile will not rise on your fields for seven times seven years of famine.

BELZANOR [*frightened, but desperate*] I will sacrifice: I will pay. Or stay. [*To the Persian*] You, O subtle one: your father's lands lie far from the Nile. Slay her.

PERSIAN [*threatening her with his knife*] Persia has but one god; yet he loves the blood of old women. Where is Cleopatra?

FTATATEETA. Persian: as Osiris lives, I do not know. I chid her for bringing evil days upon us by talking to the sacred cats of the priests, and carrying them in her arms. I told her she would be left alone here when the Romans came as a punishment for her disobedience. And now she is gone—run away—hidden. I speak the truth. I call Osiris to witness—

THE WOMEN [*protesting officiously*] She speaks the truth, Belzanor.

BELZANOR. You have frightened the child: she is hiding. Search —quick—into the palace—search every corner.

The guards, led by Belzanor, shoulder their way into the palace through the flying crowd of women, who escape through the courtyard gate.

FTATATEETA [*screaming*] Sacrilege! Men in the Queen's chambers! Sa— [*Her voice dies away as the Persian puts his knife to her throat*].

BEL AFFRIS [*laying a hand on Ftatateeta's left shoulder*] Forbear her yet a moment, Persian. [*To Ftatateeta, very signifi-cantly*] Mother: your gods are asleep or away hunting; and the sword is at your throat. Bring us to where the Queen is hid, and you shall live.

FTATATEETA [*contemptuously*] Who shall stay the sword in the hand of a fool, if the high gods put it there? Listen to me, ye young men without understanding. Cleopatra fears me; but she fears the Romans more. There is but one power greater in her eyes than the wrath of the Queen's nurse and the cruelty of Caesar; and that is the power of the Sphinx that sits in the desert watching the way to the sea. What she would have it know, she tells into the ears of the sacred cats; and on her birthday she sacrifices to it and decks it with poppies. Go ye therefore into the desert and seek Cleopatra in the shadow of the Sphinx; and on your heads see to it that no harm comes to her.

BEL AFFRIS [*to the Persian*] May we believe this, O subtle one?

PERSIAN. Which way come the Romans?

BEL AFFRIS. Over the desert, from the sea, by this very Sphinx.

PERSIAN [*to Ftatateeta*] O mother of guile! O aspic's tongue! You have made up this tale so that we two may go into the desert and perish on the spears of the Romans. [*Lifting his knife*] Taste death.

FTATATEETA. Not from thee, baby. [*She snatches his ankle from under him and flies stooping along the palace wall, vanishing in the darkness within its precinct. Bel Affris roars with laughter as the Persian tumbles. The guardsmen rush out of the palace with Belzanor and a mob of fugitives, mostly carrying bundles*].

PERSIAN. Have you found Cleopatra?

BELZANOR. She is gone. We have searched every corner.

THE NUBIAN SENTINEL [*appearing at the door of the palace*] Woe! Alas! Fly, fly!

BELZANOR. What is the matter now?

THE NUBIAN SENTINEL. The sacred white cat has been stolen.

ALL. Woe! woe! [*General panic. They all fly with cries of con-sternation. The torch is thrown down and extinguished in the rush. The noise of the fugitives dies away. Darkness and dead silence*].

ACT I

The same darkness into which the temple of Ra and the Syrian palace vanished. The same silence. Suspense. Then the blackness and stillness break softly into silver mist and strange airs as the wind-swept harp of Memnon plays at the dawning of the moon.[16] It rises full over the desert; and a vast horizon comes into relief, broken by a huge shape which soon reveals itself in the spreading radiance as a Sphinx pedestalled on the sands. The light still clears, until the upraised eyes of the image are distinguished looking straight forward and upward in infinite fearless vigil, and a mass of color between its great paws defines itself as a heap of red poppies on which a girl lies motionless, her silken vest heaving gently and regularly with the breathing of a dreamless sleeper, and her braided hair glittering in a shaft of moonlight like a bird's wing.

Suddenly there comes from afar a vaguely fearful sound (it might be the bellow of a Minotaur[17] softened by great distance) and Memnon's music stops. Silence: then a few faint high-ringing trumpet notes. Then silence again. Then a man comes from the south with stealing steps, ravished by the mystery of the night, all wonder, and halts, lost in contemplation, opposite the left flank of

---

[16] Of the two statues representing King Amenhotep III in a sitting position, located in Upper Egypt near the ancient site of Thebes, Henry Brugsch-Bey records in *A History of Egypt under the Pharaohs* (1881) that "the northern one is that which the Greeks and Romans celebrated in poetry and prose by the name of the Vocal Statue of Memnon." In 27 B.C., in consequence of an earthquake, the upper half of the statue was knocked to the ground. It is from that time until Emperor Septimius Serverus repaired the statue that travellers recorded their assurances of having heard Memnon sing. The sound was perhaps caused by a sudden change in temperature in which pressure was exerted on the cracked rocks. Shaw's reference is therefore anachronistic.

[17] A mythical creature with the body of a man and the head of a bull.

the Sphinx,[18] *whose bosom, with its burden, is hidden from him by its massive shoulder.*

THE MAN. Hail, Sphinx: salutation from Julius Caesar! I have wandered in many lands, seeking the lost regions from which my birth into this world exiled me, and the company of creatures such as I myself. I have found flocks and pastures, men and cities, but no other Caesar, no air native to me, no man kindred to me, none who can do my day's deed, and think my night's thought. In the little world yonder, Sphinx, my place is as high as yours in this great desert; only I wander, and you sit still; I conquer, and you endure; I work and wonder, you watch and wait; I look up and am dazzled, look down and am darkened, look round and am puzzled, whilst your eyes never turn from looking out—out of the world—to the lost region—the home from which we have strayed. Sphinx, you and I, strangers to the race of men, are no strangers to one another: have I not been conscious of you and of this place since I was born? Rome is a madman's dream: this is my Reality. These starry lamps of yours I have seen from afar in Gaul, in Britain, in Spain, in Thessaly, signalling great secrets to some eternal sentinel below, whose post I never could find. And here at last is their sentinel—an image of the constant and immortal part of my life, silent, full of thoughts, alone in the silver desert. Sphinx, Sphinx: I have climbed mountains at night to hear in the distance the stealthy footfall of the winds that chase your sands in forbidden play—our invisible children, O Sphinx, laughing in whispers. My way hither was the way of destiny; for I am he of whose genius you are the symbol: part brute, part woman, and part god—nothing of man in me at all. Have I read your riddle, Sphinx?

THE GIRL [*who has wakened, and peeped cautiously from her nest to see who is speaking*] Old gentleman.

---

[18] The Egyptian Sphinx, unlike its Greek counterpart, was usually a male creature, representing the God Horus. Thousands of these figures existed in varying sizes, but the most famous Sphinx is the one near the Great Pyramid at Ghizeh.

CAESAR [*starting violently, and clutching his sword*] Immortal gods!

THE GIRL. Old gentleman: dont run away.

CAESAR [*stupefied*] "Old gentleman: dont run away"!!! This! to Julius Caesar!

THE GIRL [*urgently*] Old gentleman.

CAESAR. Sphinx: you presume on your centuries. I am younger than you, though your voice is but a girl's voice as yet.

THE GIRL. Climb up here, quickly; or the Romans will come and eat you.

CAESAR [*running forward past the Sphinx's shoulder, and seeing her*] A child at its breast! a divine child!

THE GIRL. Come up quickly. You must get up at its side and creep round.

CAESAR [*amazed*] Who are you?

THE GIRL. Cleopatra, Queen of Egypt.

CAESAR. Queen of the Gypsies, you mean.

CLEOPATRA. You must not be disrespectful to me, or the Sphinx will let the Romans eat you. Come up. It is quite cosy here.

CAESAR [*to himself*] What a dream! What a magnificent dream! Only let me not wake, and I will conquer ten continents to pay for dreaming it out to the end. [*He climbs to the Sphinx's flank, and presently reappears to her on the pedestal, stepping round its right shoulder*].

CLEOPATRA. Take care. Thats right. Now sit down: you may have its other paw. [*She seats herself comfortably on its left paw*]. It is very powerful and will protect us; but [*shivering, and with plaintive loneliness*] it would not take any notice of me or keep me company. I am glad you have come: I was very lonely. Did you happen to see a white cat anywhere?

CAESAR [*sitting slowly down on the right paw in extreme wonderment*] Have you lost one?

CLEOPATRA. Yes: the sacred white cat: is it not dreadful? I brought him here to sacrifice him to the Sphinx; but when we got a little way from the city a black cat called him, and he jumped

*Vivien Leigh and Claude Rains as Cleopatra and
Caesar in the Gabriel Pascal film production of*
Caesar and Cleopatra, *1945*

out of my arms and ran away to it. Do you think that the black cat can have been my great-great-great-grandmother?

CAESAR [*staring at her*] Your great-great-great-grandmother! Well, why not? Nothing would surprise me on this night of nights.

CLEOPATRA. I think it must have been. My great-grandmother's great-grandmother was a black kitten of the sacred white cat; and the river Nile made her his seventh wife. That is why my hair is so wavy. And I always want to be let do as I like, no matter whether it is the will of the gods or not: that is because my blood is made with Nile water.

CAESAR. What are you doing here at this time of night? Do you live here?

CLEOPATRA. Of course not: I am the Queen; and I shall live in the palace at Alexandria when I have killed my brother, who drove me out of it. When I am old enough I shall do just what I like. I shall be able to poison the slaves and see them wriggle, and pretend to Ftatateeta that she is going to be put into the fiery furnace.

CAESAR. Hm! Meanwhile why are you not at home and in bed?

CLEOPATRA. Because the Romans are coming to eat us all. You are not at home and in bed either.

CAESAR [*with conviction*] Yes I am. I live in a tent; and I am now in that tent, fast asleep and dreaming. Do you suppose that I believe you are real, you impossible little dream witch?

CLEOPATRA [*giggling and leaning trustfully towards him*] You are a funny old gentleman. I like you.

CAESAR. Ah, that spoils the dream. Why dont you dream that I am young?

CLEOPATRA. I wish you were; only I think I should be more afraid of you. I like men, especially young men with round strong arms; but I am afraid of them. You are old and rather thin and stringy; but you have a nice voice; and I like to have somebody to talk to, though I think you are a little mad. It is the moon that makes you talk to yourself in that silly way.

CAESAR. What! you heard that, did you? I was saying my prayers to the great Sphinx.

CLEOPATRA. But this isnt the great Sphinx.[19]

CAESAR [*much disappointed, looking up at the statue*] What!

CLEOPATRA. This is only a dear little kitten of a Sphinx. Why, the Great Sphinx is so big that it has a temple between its paws. This is my pet Sphinx. Tell me: do you think the Romans have any sorcerers who could take us away from the Sphinx by magic?

CAESAR. Why? Are you afraid of the Romans?

CLEOPATRA [*very seriously*] Oh, they would eat us if they caught us. They are barbarians. Their chief is called Julius Caesar. His father was a tiger and his mother a burning mountain; and his nose is like an elephant's trunk. [*Caesar involuntarily rubs his nose*]. They all have long noses, and ivory tusks, and little tails, and seven arms with a hundred arrows in each; and they live on human flesh.

CAESAR. Would you like me to shew you a real Roman?

CLEOPATRA [*terrified*] No. You are frightening me.

CAESAR. No matter: this is only a dream—

CLEOPATRA [*excitedly*] It is not a dream: it is not a dream. See, see. [*She plucks a pin from her hair and jabs it repeatedly into his arm*].

CAESAR. Ffff—Stop. [*Wrathfully*] How dare you?

CLEOPATRA [*abashed*] You said you were dreaming. [*Whimpering*] I only wanted to shew you—

CAESAR [*gently*] Come, come: dont cry. A queen mustnt cry. [*He rubs his arm, wondering at the reality of the smart*]. Am I awake? [*He strikes his hand against the Sphinx to test its solidity. It feels so real that he begins to be alarmed, and says perplexedly*] Yes, I— [*quite panicstriken*] no: impossible: madness, madness! [*Desperately*] Back to camp—to camp. [*He rises to spring down from the pedestal*].

CLEOPATRA [*flinging her arms in terror round him*] No: you shant leave me. No, no, no: dont go. I'm afraid—afraid of the Romans.

[19] See note 18, p. 33.

CAESAR [*as the conviction that he is really awake forces itself on him*] Cleopatra: can you see my face well?

CLEOPATRA. Yes. It is so white in the moonlight.

CAESAR. Are you sure it is the moonlight that makes me look whiter than an Egyptian? [*Grimly*] Do you notice that I have a rather long nose?

CLEOPATRA [*recoiling, paralysed by a terrible suspicion*] Oh!

CAESAR. It is a Roman nose, Cleopatra.

CLEOPATRA. Ah! [*With a piercing scream she springs up; darts round the left shoulder of the Sphinx; scrambles down to the sand; and falls on her knees in frantic supplication, shrieking*] Bite him in two, Sphinx: bite him in two. I meant to sacrifice the white cat—I did indeed—I [*Caesar, who has slipped down from the pedestal, touches her on the shoulder*]—Ah! [*She buries her head in her arms*].

CAESAR. Cleopatra: shall I teach you a way to prevent Caesar from eating you?

CLEOPATRA [*clinging to him piteously*] Oh do, do, do. I will steal Ftatateeta's jewels and give them to you. I will make the river Nile water your lands twice a year.

CAESAR. Peace, peace, my child. Your gods are afraid of the Romans: you see the Sphinx dare not bite me, nor prevent me carrying you off to Julius Caesar.

CLEOPATRA [*in pleading murmurings*] You wont, you wont. You said you wouldnt.

CAESAR. Caesar never eats women.

CLEOPATRA [*springing up full of hope*] What!

CAESAR [*impressively*] But he eats girls [*she relapses*] and cats. Now you are a silly little girl; and you are descended from the black kitten. You are both a girl and a cat.

CLEOPATRA [*trembling*] And will he eat me?

CAESAR. Yes; unless you make him believe that you are a woman.

CLEOPATRA. Oh, you must get a sorcerer to make a woman of me. Are you a sorcerer?

CAESAR. Perhaps. But it will take a long time; and this very night you must stand face to face with Caesar in the palace of your fathers.

CLEOPATRA. No, no. I darent.

CAESAR. Whatever dread may be in your soul—however terrible Caesar may be to you—you must confront him as a brave woman and a great queen; and you must feel no fear. If your hand shakes: if your voice quavers; then—night and death! [*She moans*]. But if he thinks you worthy to rule, he will set you on the throne by his side and make you the real ruler of Egypt.

CLEOPATRA [*despairingly*] No: he will find me out: he will find me out.

CAESAR [*rather mournfully*] He is easily deceived by women. Their eyes dazzle him; and he sees them not as they are, but as he wishes them to appear to him.

CLEOPATRA [*hopefully*] Then we will cheat him. I will put on Ftatateeta's head-dress; and he will think me quite an old woman.

CAESAR. If you do that he will eat you at one mouthful.

CLEOPATRA. But I will give him a cake with my magic opal and seven hairs of the white cat baked in it; and—

CAESAR [*abruptly*] Pah! you are a little fool. He will eat your cake and you too. [*He turns contemptuously from her*].

CLEOPATRA [*running after him and clinging to him*] Oh please, please! I will do whatever you tell me. I will be good. I will be your slave. [*Again the terrible bellowing note sounds across the desert, now closer at hand. It is the bucina, the Roman war trumpet*].

CAESAR. Hark!

CLEOPATRA [*trembling*] What was that?

CAESAR. Caesar's voice.

CLEOPATRA [*pulling at his hand*] Let us run away. Come. Oh, come.

CAESAR. You are safe with me until you stand on your throne to receive Caesar. Now lead me thither.

CLEOPATRA [*only too glad to get away*] I will, I will. [*Again the bucina*]. Oh come, come, come: the gods are angry. Do you feel the earth shaking?

CAESAR. It is the tread of Caesar's legions.

CLEOPATRA [*drawing him away*] This way, quickly. And let us look for the white cat as we go. It is he that has turned you into a Roman.

CAESAR. Incorrigible, oh, incorrigible! Away! [*He follows her, the bucina sounding louder as they steal across the desert. The moonlight wanes: the horizon again shews black against the sky, broken only by the fantastic silhouette of the Sphinx. The sky itself vanishes in darkness, from which there is no relief until the gleam of a distant torch falls on great Egyptian pillars supporting the roof of a majestic corridor. At the further end of this corridor a Nubian slave appears carrying the torch. Caesar, still led by Cleopatra, follows him. They come down the corridor, Caesar peering keenly about at the strange architecture, and at the pillar shadows between which, as the passing torch makes them hurry noiselessly backwards, figures of men with wings and hawks' heads, and vast black marble cats, seem to flit in and out of ambush. Further along, the wall turns a corner and makes a spacious transept in which Caesar sees, on his right, a throne, and behind the throne a door. On each side of the throne is a slender pillar with a lamp on it*].

CAESAR. What place is this?

CLEOPATRA. This is where I sit on the throne when I am allowed to wear my crown and robes. [*The slave holds his torch to shew the throne*].

CAESAR. Order the slave to light the lamps.

CLEOPATRA [*shyly*] Do you think I may?

CAESAR. Of course. You are the Queen. [*She hesitates*]. Go on.

CLEOPATRA [*timidly, to the slave*] Light all the lamps.

FTATATEETA [*suddenly coming from behind the throne*] Stop. [*The slave stops. She turns sternly to Cleopatra, who quails like a naughty child*]. Who is this you have with you; and how dare you order the lamps to be lighted without my permission? [*Cleopatra is dumb with apprehension*].

CAESAR. Who is she?

CLEOPATRA. Ftatateeta.

FTATATEETA [*arrogantly*] Chief nurse to—

CAESAR [*cutting her short*] I speak to the Queen. Be silent. [*To Cleopatra*] Is this how your servants know their places? Send her away; and do you [*to the slave*] do as the Queen has bidden. [*The slave lights the lamps. Meanwhile Cleopatra stands hesitating, afraid of Ftatateeta*]. You are the Queen: send her away.

CLEOPATRA [*cajoling*] Ftatateeta, dear: you must go away—just for a little.

CAESAR. You are not commanding her to go away: you are begging her. You are no Queen. You will be eaten. Farewell. [*He turns to go*].

CLEOPATRA [*clutching him*] No, no, no. Dont leave me.

CAESAR. A Roman does not stay with queens who are afraid of their slaves.

CLEOPATRA. I am not afraid. Indeed I am not afraid.

FTATATEETA. We shall see who is afraid here. [*Menacingly*] Cleopatra—

CAESAR. On your knees, woman: am I also a child that you dare trifle with me? [*He points to the floor at Cleopatra's feet. Ftatateeta, half cowed, half savage, hesitates. Caesar calls to the Nubian*] Slave. [*The Nubian comes to him*]. Can you cut off a head? [*The Nubian nods and grins ecstatically, showing all his teeth. Caesar takes his sword by the scabbard, ready to offer the hilt to the Nubian, and turns again to Ftatateeta, repeating his gesture*]. Have you remembered yourself, mistress?

Ftatateeta, crushed, kneels before Cleopatra, who can hardly believe her eyes.

FTATATEETA [*hoarsely*] O Queen, forget not thy servant in the days of thy greatness.

CLEOPATRA [*blazing with excitement*] Go. Begone. Go away. [*Ftatateeta rises with stooped head, and moves backwards towards the door. Cleopatra watches her submission eagerly, almost clapping her hands, which are trembling. Suddenly she cries*] Give me something to beat her with. [*She snatches a snake-skin from the throne and dashes after Ftatateeta, whirling it like a scourge in the air. Caesar makes a bound and manages to catch her and hold her while Ftatateeta escapes*].

CAESAR. You scratch, kitten, do you?

CLEOPATRA [*breaking from him*] I will beat somebody. I will beat him. [*She attacks the slave*]. There, there, there! [*The slave flies for his life up the corridor and vanishes. She throws the snakeskin away and jumps on the step of the throne with her arms waving, crying*] I am a real Queen at last—a real, real Queen! Cleopatra the Queen! [*Caesar shakes his head dubiously, the advantage of the change seeming open to question from the point of view of the general welfare of Egypt. She turns and looks at him exultantly. Then she jumps down from the steps, runs to him, and flings her arms round him rapturously, crying*] Oh, I love you for making me a Queen.

CAESAR. But queens love only kings.

CLEOPATRA. I will make all the men I love kings. I will make you a king. I will have many young kings, with round, strong arms; and when I am tired of them I will whip them to death; but you shall always be my king: my nice, kind, wise, good old king.

CAESAR. Oh, my wrinkles, my wrinkles! And my child's heart! You will be the most dangerous of all Caesar's conquests.

CLEOPATRA [*appalled*] Caesar! I forgot Caesar. [*Anxiously*] You will tell him that I am a Queen, will you not?—a real Queen. Listen! [*stealthily coaxing him*]: let us run away and hide until Caesar is gone.

CAESAR. If you fear Caesar, you are no true queen; and though you were to hide beneath a pyramid, he would go straight to it and lift it with one hand. And then—! [*He chops his teeth together*].

CLEOPATRA [*trembling*] Oh!

CAESAR. Be afraid if you dare. [*The note of the bucina resounds again in the distance. She moans with fear. Caesar exults in it, exclaiming*] Aha! Caesar approaches the throne of Cleopatra. Come: take your place. [*He takes her hand and leads her to the throne. She is too downcast to speak*]. Ho, there, Teetatota. How do you call your slaves?

CLEOPATRA [*spiritlessly, as she sinks on the throne and cowers there, shaking*] Clap your hands.

He claps his hands. Ftatateeta returns.

CAESAR. Bring the Queen's robes, and her crown, and her women; and prepare her.

CLEOPATRA [*eagerly—recovering herself a little*] Yes, the crown, Ftatateeta: I shall wear the crown.

FTATATEETA. For whom must the Queen put on her state?

CAESAR. For a citizen of Rome. A king of kings, Totateeta.

CLEOPATRA [*stamping at her*] How dare you ask questions? Go and do as you are told. [*Ftatateeta goes out with a grim smile. Cleopatra goes on eagerly, to Caesar*] Caesar will know that I am a Queen when he sees my crown and robes, will he not?

CAESAR. No. How shall he know that you are not a slave dressed up in the Queen's ornaments?

CLEOPATRA. You must tell him.

CAESAR. He will not ask me. He will know Cleopatra by her pride, her courage, her majesty, and her beauty. [*She looks very doubtful*]. Are you trembling?

CLEOPATRA [*shivering with dread*] No, I—I— [*in a very sickly voice*] No.

Ftatateeta and three women come in with the regalia.

FTATATEETA. Of all the Queen's women, these three alone are left. The rest are fled. [*They begin to deck Cleopatra, who submits, pale and motionless*].

CAESAR. Good, good. Three are enough. Poor Caesar generally has to dress himself.

FTATATEETA [*contemptuously*] The queen of Egypt is not a Roman barbarian. [*To Cleopatra*] Be brave, my nursling. Hold up your head before this stranger.

CAESAR [*admiring Cleopatra, and placing the crown on her head*] Is it sweet or bitter to be a Queen, Cleopatra?

CLEOPATRA. Bitter.

CAESAR. Cast out fear; and you will conquer Caesar. Tota: are the Romans at hand?

FTATATEETA. They are at hand; and the guard has fled.

THE WOMEN [*wailing subduedly*] Woe to us!

The Nubian comes running down the hall.

NUBIAN. The Romans are in the courtyard. [*He bolts through the door. With a shriek, the women fly after him. Ftatateeta's jaw expresses savage resolution: she does not budge. Cleopatra can hardly restrain herself from following them. Caesar grips her wrist, and looks steadfastly at her. She stands like a martyr*].

CAESAR. The Queen must face Caesar alone. Answer "So be it."

CLEOPATRA [*white*] So be it.

CAESAR [*releasing her*] Good.

A tramp and tumult of armed men is heard. Cleopatra's terror increases. The bucina sounds close at hand, followed by a formidable clangor of trumpets. This is too much for Cleopatra: she utters a cry and darts towards the door. Ftatateeta stops her ruthlessly.

FTATATEETA. You are my nursling. You have said "So be it"; and if you die for it, you must make the Queen's word good. [*She hands Cleopatra to Caesar, who takes her back, almost beside herself with apprehension, to the throne*].

CAESAR. Now, if you quail—! [*He seats himself on the throne*].

She stands on the step, all but unconscious, waiting for death. The Roman soldiers troop in tumultuously through the corridor, headed by their ensign with his eagle, and their bucinator,[20] a burly fellow with his instrument coiled round his body, its brazen bell shaped like the head of a howling wolf. When they reach the transept, they stare in amazement at the throne; dress into ordered rank opposite it; draw their swords and lift them in the air with a shout of Hail, Caesar. *Cleopatra turns and stares wildly at Caesar; grasps the situation; and with a great sob of relief, falls into his arms.*

[20] The soldier in the Roman army whose duty it was to sound the bucina, or war trumpet.

ACT II

Alexandria. A hall on the first floor of the Palace, ending in a loggia approached by two steps. Through the arches of the loggia the Mediterranean can be seen, bright in the morning sun. The clean lofty walls, painted with a procession of the Egyptian theocracy, presented in profile as flat ornament, and the absence of mirrors, sham perspectives, stuffy upholstery and textiles, make the place handsome, wholesome, simple and cool, or, as a rich English manufacturer would express it, poor, bare, ridiculous and unhomely. For Tottenham Court Road civilization is to this Egyptian civilization as glass bead and tattoo civilization is to Tottenham Court Road.[21]

The young king Ptolemy Dionysus (aged ten) is at the top of the steps, on his way in through the loggia, led by his guardian Pothinus, who has him by the hand. The court is assembled to receive him. It is made up of men and women (some of the women being officials) of various complexions and races, mostly Egyptians; some of them, comparatively fair, from lower Egypt, some, much darker, from upper Egypt; with a few Greeks and Jews. Prominent in a group on Ptolemy's right hand is Theodotus, Ptolemy's tutor. Another group, on Ptolemy's left, is headed by Achillas, the general of Ptolemy's troops. Theodotus is a little old man, whose features are as cramped and wizened as his limbs, except his tall straight forehead, which occupies more space than all the rest of his face. He maintains an air of magpie keenness and profundity, listening to what the others say with the sarcastic vigilance of a philosopher listening to the exercises of his disciples. Achillas is a tall handsome man of thirty-five, with a fine black beard curled like the coat of a poodle. Apparently not a clever man, but distinguished and dignified. Pothinus is a vigorous

---

[21] Tottenham Court Road in London is known for its shops dealing in cheap furniture and bric-a-brac.

man of fifty, a eunuch, passionate, energetic and quick witted, but of common mind and character; impatient and unable to control his temper. He has fine tawny hair, like fur. Ptolemy, the King, looks much older than an English boy of ten; but has the childish air, the habit of being in leading strings, the mixture of impotence and petulance, the appearance of being excessively washed, combed and dressed by other hands, which is exhibited by court-bred princes of all ages.

All receive the King with reverences. He comes down the steps to a chair of state which stands a little to his right, the only seat in the hall. Taking his place before it, he looks nervously for instructions to Pothinus, who places himself at his left hand.

POTHINUS. The king of Egypt has a word to speak.

THEODOTUS [in a squeak which he makes impressive by sheer self-opinionativeness] Peace for the King's word!

PTOLEMY [without any vocal inflexions: he is evidently repeating a lesson] Take notice of this all of you. I am the first-born son of Auletes the Flute Blower who was your King. My sister Berenice drove him from his throne and reigned in his stead but —but—[he hesitates]—

POTHINUS [stealthily prompting]—but the gods would not suffer—

PTOLEMY. Yes—the gods would not suffer—not suffer—[He stops; then, crestfallen] I forgot what the gods would not suffer.

THEODOTUS. Let Pothinus, the King's guardian, speak for the King.

POTHINUS [suppressing his impatience with difficulty] The King wished to say that the gods would not suffer the impiety of his sister to go unpunished.

PTOLEMY [hastily] Yes: I remember the rest of it. [He resumes his monotone]. Therefore the gods sent a stranger one Mark Antony a Roman captain of horsemen across the sands of the desert and he set my father again upon the throne. And my father took Berenice my sister and struck her head off. And now that my father is dead yet another of his daughters my sister Cleopatra would snatch the kingdom from me and reign in my place. But the gods would not suffer—[*Pothinus coughs admonitorily*]—the gods—the gods would not suffer—

POTHINUS [*prompting*]—will not maintain—

PTOLEMY. Oh yes—will not maintain such iniquity they will give her head to the axe even as her sister's. But with the help of the witch Ftatateeta she hath cast a spell on the Roman Julius Caesar to make him uphold her false pretence to rule in Egypt. Take notice then that I will not suffer—that I will not suffer— [*pettishly, to Pothinus*] What is it that I will not suffer?

POTHINUS [*suddenly exploding with all the force and emphasis of political passion*] The King will not suffer a foreigner to take from him the throne of our Egypt. [*A shout of applause*]. Tell the King, Achillas, how many soldiers and horsemen follow the Roman?

THEODOTUS. Let the King's general speak!

ACHILLAS. But two Roman legions, O King. Three thousand soldiers and scarce a thousand horsemen.

The court breaks into derisive laughter; and a great chattering begins, amid which Rufio, a Roman officer, appears in the loggia. He is a burly, black-bearded man of middle age, very blunt, prompt and rough, with small clear eyes, and plump nose and cheeks, which, however, like the rest of his flesh, are in ironhard condition.

RUFIO [*from the steps*] Peace, ho! [*The laughter and chatter cease abruptly*]. Caesar approaches.

THEODOTUS [*with much presence of mind*] The King permits the Roman commander to enter!

Caesar, plainly dressed, but wearing an oak wreath to conceal his baldness,[22] enters from the loggia, attended by Britannus, his secretary, a Briton, about forty, tall, solemn, and already slightly bald, with a heavy, drooping, hazel-colored moustache trained so

---

[22] Suetonius records that of all the honors bestowed on Caesar the wearing of the laurel wreath on all occasions pleased him the most since it enabled him to conceal his baldness.

as to lose its ends in a pair of trim whiskers. He is carefully dressed in blue, with portfolio, inkhorn, and reed pen at his girdle. His serious air and sense of the importance of the business in hand is in marked contrast to the kindly interest of Caesar, who looks at the scene, which is new to him, with the frank curiosity of a child, and then turns to the king's chair: Britannus and Rufio posting themselves near the steps at the other side.

CAESAR [*looking at Pothinus and Ptolemy*] Which is the King? the man or the boy?

POTHINUS. I am Pothinus, the guardian of my lord the King.

CAESAR [*patting Ptolemy kindly on the shoulder*] So you are the King. Dull work at your age, eh? [*To Pothinus*] Your servant, Pothinus. [*He turns away unconcernedly and comes slowly along the middle of the hall, looking from side to side at the courtiers until he reaches Achillas*]. And this gentleman?

THEODOTUS. Achillas, the King's general.

CAESAR [*to Achillas, very friendly*] A general, eh? I am a general myself. But I began too old, too old. Health and many victories, Achillas!

ACHILLAS. As the gods will, Caesar.

CAESAR [*turning to Theodotus*] And you, sir, are—?

THEODOTUS. Theodotus, the King's tutor.

CAESAR. You teach men how to be kings, Theodotus. That is very clever of you. [*Looking at the gods on the walls as he turns away from Theodotus and goes up again to Pothinus*] And this place?

POTHINUS. The council chamber of the chancellors of the King's treasury, Caesar.

CAESAR. Ah! that reminds me. I want some money.

POTHINUS. The King's treasury is poor, Caesar.

CAESAR. Yes: I notice that there is but one chair in it.

RUFIO [*shouting gruffly*] Bring a chair there, some of you, for Caesar.

PTOLEMY [*rising shyly to offer his chair*] Caesar—

CAESAR [*kindly*] No, no, my boy: that is your chair of state. Sit down.

He makes Ptolemy sit down again. Meanwhile Rufio, looking about him, sees in the nearest corner an image of the god Ra, represented as a seated man with the head of a hawk. Before the image is a bronze tripod, about as large as a three-legged stool, with a stick of incense burning on it. Rufio, with Roman resourcefulness and indifference to foreign superstitions, promptly seizes the tripod; shakes off the incense; blows away the ash; and dumps it down behind Caesar, nearly in the middle of the hall.

RUFIO. Sit on that, Caesar.

A shiver runs through the court, followed by a hissing whisper of Sacrilege!

CAESAR [*seating himself*] Now, Pothinus, to business. I am badly in want of money.

BRITANNUS [*disapproving of these informal expressions*] My master would say that there is a lawful debt due to Rome by Egypt, contracted by the King's deceased father to the Triumvirate; and that it is Caesar's duty to his country to require immediate payment.[23]

CAESAR [*blandly*] Ah, I forgot. I have not made my companions known here. Pothinus: this is Britannus, my secretary. He is an islander from the western end of the world, a day's voyage from Gaul. [*Britannus bows stiffly*]. This gentleman is Rufio, my comrade in arms. [*Rufio nods*]. Pothinus: I want 1,600 talents.

The courtiers, appalled, murmur loudly, and Theodotus and Achillas appeal mutely to one another against so monstrous a demand.

POTHINUS [*aghast*] Forty million sesterces! Impossible. There is not so much money in the King's treasury.

CAESAR [*encouragingly*] Only sixteen hundred talents, Pothinus.

[23] The banished Ptolemy Auletes, Cleopatra's father, purchased in 59 B.C. Roman support for his recognition as king of Egypt for 6000 talents or about 3½ million dollars. Later, at the Conference of Luca, the Triumvirate got a promise of an extra 10,000 talents from Auletes if he were reinstated. Aulus Gabinius, the Roman governor of Syria, was ordered to restore him to the Egyptian throne.

Why count it in sesterces? A sestertius is only worth a loaf of bread.

POTHINUS. And a talent is worth a racehorse. I say it is impossible. We have been at strife here, because the King's sister Cleopatra falsely claims his throne. The King's taxes have not been collected for a whole year.

CAESAR. Yes they have, Pothinus. My officers have been collecting them all morning. [*Renewed whisper and sensation, not without some stifled laughter, among the courtiers*].

RUFIO [*bluntly*] You must pay, Pothinus. Why waste words? You are getting off cheaply enough.

POTHINUS [*bitterly*] Is it possible that Caesar, the conqueror of the world, has time to occupy himself with such a trifle as our taxes?

CAESAR. My friend: taxes are the chief business of a conqueror of the world.

POTHINUS. Then take warning, Caesar. This day, the treasures of the temple and the gold of the King's treasury shall be sent to the mint to be melted down for our ransom in the sight of the people. They shall see us sitting under bare walls and drinking from wooden cups. And their wrath be on your head, Caesar, if you force us to this sacrilege!

CAESAR. Do not fear, Pothinus: the people know how well wine tastes in wooden cups. In return for your bounty, I will settle this dispute about the throne for you, if you will. What say you?

POTHINUS. If I say no, will that hinder you?

RUFIO [*defiantly*] No.

CAESAR. You say the matter has been at issue for a year, Pothinus. May I have ten minutes at it?

POTHINUS. You will do your pleasure, doubtless.

CAESAR. Good! But first, let us have Cleopatra here.

THEODOTUS. She is not in Alexandria: she is fled into Syria.

CAESAR. I think not. [*To Rufio*] Call Totateeta.

RUFIO [*calling*] Ho there, Teetatota.

Ftatateeta enters the loggia, and stands arrogantly at the top of the steps.

FTATATEETA. Who pronounces the name of Ftatateeta, the Queen's chief nurse?

CAESAR. Nobody can pronounce it, Tota, except yourself. Where is your mistress?

Cleopatra, who is hiding behind Ftatateeta, peeps out at them laughing. Caesar rises.

CAESAR. Will the Queen favor us with her presence for a moment?

CLEOPATRA [*pushing Ftatateeta aside and standing haughtily on the brink of the steps*] Am I to behave like a Queen?

CAESAR. Yes.

Cleopatra immediately comes down to the chair of state; seizes Ptolemy; drags him out of his seat; then takes his place in the chair. Ftatateeta seats herself on the step of the loggia, and sits there, watching the scene with sibylline intensity.

PTOLEMY [*mortified, and struggling with his tears*] Caesar: this is how she treats me always. If I am a king why is she allowed to take everything from me?

CLEOPATRA. You are not to be King, you little cry-baby. You are to be eaten by the Romans.

CAESAR [*touched by Ptolemy's distress*] Come here, my boy, and stand by me.

Ptolemy goes over to Caesar, who, resuming his seat on the tripod, takes the boy's hand to encourage him. Cleopatra, furiously jealous, rises and glares at them.

CLEOPATRA [*with flaming cheeks*] Take your throne: I dont want it. [*She flings away from the chair, and approaches Ptolemy, who shrinks from her*]. Go this instant and sit down in your place.

CAESAR. Go, Ptolemy. Always take a throne when it is offered to you.

RUFIO. I hope you will have the good sense to follow your own advice when we return to Rome, Caesar.

Ptolemy slowly goes back to the throne, giving Cleopatra a wide berth, in evident fear of her hands. She takes his place beside Caesar.

CAESAR. Pothinus—

CLEOPATRA [*interrupting him*] Are you not going to speak to me?

CAESAR. Be quiet. Open your mouth again before I give you leave; and you shall be eaten.

CLEOPATRA. I am not afraid. A queen must not be afraid. Eat my husband there, if you like: he is afraid.

CAESAR [*starting*] Your husband! What do you mean?[24]

CLEOPATRA [*pointing to Ptolemy*] That little thing.

The two Romans and the Briton stare at one another in amazement.

THEODOTUS. Caesar: you are a stranger here, and not conversant with our laws. The kings and queens of Egypt may not marry except with their own royal blood. Ptolemy and Cleopatra are born king and consort just as they are born brother and sister.

BRITANNUS [*shocked*] Caesar: this is not proper.

THEODOTUS [*outraged*] How!

CAESAR [*recovering his self-possession*] Pardon him, Theodotus: he is a barbarian, and thinks that the customs of his tribe and island are the laws of nature.

BRITANNUS. On the contrary, Caesar, it is these Egyptians who are barbarians; and you do wrong to encourage them. I say it is a scandal.

CAESAR. Scandal or not, my friend, it opens the gate of peace. [*He addresses Pothinus seriously*]. Pothinus: hear what I propose.

RUFIO. Hear Caesar there.

CAESAR. Ptolemy and Cleopatra shall reign jointly in Egypt.

ACHILLAS. What of the King's younger brother and Cleopatra's younger sister?

RUFIO [*explaining*] There is another little Ptolemy, Caesar: so they tell me.

---

[24] Diodorus of Sicily writes that Egyptians permitted marriage between brothers and sisters within the royal family, having as their precedent the marriage between the gods Isis and Osiris.

CAESAR. Well, the little Ptolemy can marry the other sister; and we will make them both a present of Cyprus.[25]

POTHINUS [*impatiently*] Cyprus is of no use' to anybody.

CAESAR. No matter: you shall have it for the sake of peace.

BRITANNUS [*unconsciously anticipating a later statesman*] Peace with honor,[26] Pothinus.

POTHINUS [*mutinously*] Caesar: be honest. The money you demand is the price of our freedom. Take it; and leave us to settle our own affairs.

THE BOLDER COURTIERS [*encouraged by Pothinus's tone and Caesar's quietness*] Yes, yes. Egypt for the Egyptians![27]

The conference now becomes an altercation, the Egyptians becoming more and more heated. Caesar remains unruffled; but Rufio grows fiercer and doggeder, and Britannus haughtily indignant.

RUFIO [*contemptuously*] Egypt for the Egyptians! Do you forget that there is a Roman army of occupation here, left by Aulus Gabinius[28] when he set up your toy king for you?

ACHILLAS [*suddenly asserting himself*] And now under my command. *I* am the Roman general here, Caesar.

CAESAR [*tickled by the humor of the situation*] And also the Egyptian general, eh?

POTHINUS [*triumphantly*] That is so, Caesar.

CAESAR [*to Achillas*] So you can make war on the Egyptians in

[25] Cyprus was seized by the Romans from Ptolemy of Cyprus, the brother of Ptolemy Auletes, without resistance in 58 B.C.

[26] "Peace with honor" was the comment used by the Earl of Beaconsfield, Benjamin Disraeli, British Prime Minister, after the Berlin Congress of 1878 in the settlement of the Russo-Turkish War. Shaw is suggesting here the hypocrisy with which the British covered up their selfish action.

[27] In January 1882, there appeared in the London *Times* a manifesto with the slogan "Egypt for the Egyptians." It was generally believed that the document was written or suggested by Ahmed Pasha Arabi (1839–1911), popular leader of Egyptian nationalism.

[28] Aulus Gabinius, Roman governor of Syria, routed the Egyptian army near Pelusium, with the help of Mark Antony, and restored Ptolemy Auletes to his throne in 55 B.C.

the name of Rome, and on the Romans—on me, if necessary—in the name of Egypt?

ACHILLAS. That is so, Caesar.

CAESAR. And which side are you on at present, if I may presume to ask, general?

ACHILLAS. On the side of the right and of the gods.

CAESAR. Hm! How many men have you?

ACHILLAS. That will appear when I take the field.

RUFIO [*truculently*] Are your men Romans? If not, it matters not how many there are, provided you are no stronger than 500 to ten.

POTHINUS. It is useless to try to bluff us, Rufio. Caesar has been defeated before and may be defeated again. A few weeks ago Caesar was flying for his life before Pompey: a few months hence he may be flying for his life before Cato and Juba of Numidia, the African King.[29]

ACHILLAS [*following up Pothinus's speech menacingly*] What can you do with 4,000 men?

THEODOTUS [*following up Achillas's speech with a raucous squeak*] And without money? Away with you.

ALL THE COURTIERS [*shouting fiercely and crowding towards Caesar*] Away with you. Egypt for the Egyptians! Begone.

Rufio bites his beard, too angry to speak. Caesar sits as comfortably as if he were at breakfast, and the cat were clamoring for a piece of Finnan-haddie.

CLEOPATRA. Why do you let them talk to you like that, Caesar? Are you afraid?

CAESAR. Why, my dear, what they say is quite true.

CLEOPATRA. But if you go away, I shall not be Queen.

CAESAR. I shall not go away until you are Queen.

---

[29] Cato the Younger, a fugitive from the battle of Pharsalia, had rallied his forces in Africa under the protection of Juba of Numidia. Caesar defeated those forces at the battle of Thapsus in 46 B.C. Both Cato and Juba chose to die by their own swords.

POTHINUS. Achillas: if you are not a fool, you will take that girl whilst she is under your hand.

RUFIO [*daring them*] Why not take Caesar as well, Achillas?

POTHINUS [*retorting the defiance with interest*] Well said, Rufio. Why not?

RUFIO. Try, Achillas. [*Calling*] Guard there.

The loggia immediately fills with Caesar's soldiers, who stand, sword in hand, at the top of the steps, waiting the word to charge from their centurion, who carries a cudgel. For a moment the Egyptians face them proudly: then they retire sullenly to their former places.

BRITANNUS. You are Caesar's prisoners, all of you.

CAESAR [*benevolently*] Oh no, no, no. By no means. Caesar's guests, gentlemen.

CLEOPATRA. Wont you cut their heads off?

CAESAR. What! Cut off your brother's head?

CLEOPATRA. Why not? He would cut off mine, if he got the chance. Wouldnt you, Ptolemy?

PTOLEMY [*pale and obstinate*] I would. I will, too, when I grow up.

Cleopatra is rent by a struggle between her newly-acquired dignity as a queen, and a strong impulse to put out her tongue at him. She takes no part in the scene which follows, but watches it with curiosity and wonder, fidgeting with the restlessness of a child, and sitting down on Caesar's tripod when he rises.

POTHINUS. Caesar: if you attempt to detain us—

RUFIO. He will succeed, Egyptian: make up your mind to that. We hold the palace, the beach, and the eastern harbor. The road to Rome is open; and you shall travel it if Caesar chooses.

CAESAR [*courteously*] I could do no less, Pothinus, to secure the retreat of my own soldiers. I am accountable for every life among them. But you are free to go. So are all here, and in the palace.

RUFIO [*aghast at this clemency*] What! Renegades and all?

CAESAR [*softening the expression*] Roman army of occupation and all, Rufio.

POTHINUS [*bewildered*] But—but—but—

CAESAR. Well, my friend?

POTHINUS. You are turning us out of our own palace into the streets; and you tell us with a grand air that we are free to go! It is for you to go.

CAESAR. Your friends are in the street, Pothinus. You will be safer there.

POTHINUS. This is a trick. I am the king's guardian: I refuse to stir. I stand on my right here. Where is your right?

CAESAR. It is in Rufio's scabbard, Pothinus. I may not be able to keep it there if you wait too long.

Sensation.

POTHINUS [*bitterly*] And this is Roman justice!

THEODOTUS. But not Roman gratitude, I hope.

CAESAR. Gratitude! Am I in your debt for any service, gentlemen?

THEODOTUS. Is Caesar's life of so little account to him that he forgets that we have saved it?

CAESAR. My life! Is that all?

THEODOTUS. Your life. Your laurels. Your future.

POTHINUS. It is true. I can call a witness to prove that but for us, the Roman army of occupation, led by the greatest soldier in the world, would now have Caesar at its mercy. [*Calling through the loggia*] Ho, there, Lucius Septimius [*Caesar starts, deeply moved*]: if my voice can reach you, come forth and testify before Caesar.

CAESAR [*shrinking*] No, no.

THEODOTUS. Yes, I say. Let the military tribune bear witness.

Lucius Septimius, a clean shaven, trim athlete of about 40, with symmetrical features, resolute mouth, and handsome, thin Roman nose, in the dress of a Roman officer, comes in through the loggia and confronts Caesar, who hides his face with his robe for a moment; then, mastering himself, drops it, and confronts the tribune with dignity.

POTHINUS. Bear witness, Lucius Septimius. Caesar came hither in pursuit of his foe. Did we shelter his foe?

LUCIUS. As Pompey's foot touched the Egyptian shore, his head fell by the stroke of my sword.

THEODOTUS [*with viperish relish*] Under the eyes of his wife and child! Remember that, Caesar! They saw it from the ship he had just left. We have given you a full and sweet measure of vengeance.

CAESAR [*with horror*] Vengeance!

POTHINUS. Our first gift to you, as your galley came into the roadstead, was the head of your rival for the empire of the world. Bear witness, Lucius Septimius: is it not so?

LUCIUS. It is so. With this hand, that slew Pompey, I placed his head at the feet of Caesar.

CAESAR. Murderer! So would you have slain Caesar, had Pompey been victorious at Pharsalia.

LUCIUS. Woe to the vanquished, Caesar! When I served Pompey, I slew as good men as he, only because he conquered them. His turn came at last.

THEODOTUS [*flatteringly*] The deed was not yours, Caesar, but ours—nay, mine; for it was done by my counsel. Thanks to us, you keep your reputation for clemency, and have your vengeance too.

CAESAR. Vengeance! Vengeance!! Oh, if I could stoop to vengeance, what would I not exact from you as the price of this murdered man's blood? [*They shrink back, appalled and disconcerted*]. Was he not my son-in-law, my ancient friend, for 20 years the master of great Rome, for 30 years the compeller of victory? Did not I, as a Roman, share his glory? Was the Fate that forced us to fight for the mastery of the world, of our making? Am I Julius Caesar, or am I a wolf, that you fling to me the grey head of the old soldier, the laurelled conqueror, the mighty Roman, treacherously struck down by this callous ruffian, and then claim my gratitude for it! [*To Lucius Septimius*] Begone: you fill me with horror.

LUCIUS [*cold and undaunted*] Pshaw! You have seen severed heads before, Caesar, and severed right hands too, I think; some thousands of them, in Gaul, after you vanquished Vercingetorix.[30] Did you spare him, with all your clemency? Was that vengeance?

CAESAR. No, by the gods! would that it had been! Vengeance at least is human. No, I say: those severed right hands, and the brave Vercingetorix basely strangled in a vault beneath the Capitol, were [*with shuddering satire*] a wise severity, a necessary protection to the commonwealth, a duty of statesmanship—follies and fictions ten times bloodier than honest vengeance! What a fool was I then! To think that men's lives should be at the mercy of such fools! [*Humbly*] Lucius Septimius, pardon me: why should the slayer of Vercingetorix rebuke the slayer of Pompey? You are free to go with the rest. Or stay if you will: I will find a place for you in my service.

LUCIUS. The odds are against you, Caesar. I go. [*He turns to go out through the loggia*].

RUFIO [*full of wrath at seeing his prey escaping*] That means that he is a Republican.

LUCIUS [*turning defiantly on the loggia steps*] And what are you?

RUFIO. A Caesarian, like all Caesar's soldiers.

CAESAR [*courteously*] Lucius: believe me, Caesar is no Caesarian. Were Rome a true republic, then were Caesar the first of Republicans. But you have made your choice. Farewell.

LUCIUS. Farewell. Come, Achillas, whilst there is yet time.

Caesar, seeing that Rufio's temper threatens to get the worse of him, puts his hand on his shoulder and brings him down the hall out of harm's way, Britannus accompanying them and posting himself on Caesar's right hand. This movement brings the three in a little group to the place occupied by Achillas, who moves

---

[30] Vercingetorix, king of the Arverni, a Celtic tribe in Gaul, surrendered himself to Caesar in 52 B.C. outside the gates of Alesia. He was led to Rome a captive, where, according to Dio Cassius, he was executed in 46 B.C., two years after Caesar's sojourn in Egypt. The end of Gallic independence came not with his surrender but with the fall of Uxellodunum in 51 B.C. Caesar dealt harshly with the insurgents: he ordered the severing of their right hands.

haughtily away and joins Theodotus on the other side. Lucius Septimius goes out through the soldiers in the loggia. Pothinus, Theodotus and Achillas follow him with the courtiers, very mistrustful of the soldiers, who close up in their rear and go out after them, keeping them moving without much ceremony. The King is left in his chair, piteous, obstinate, with twitching face and fingers. During these movements Rufio maintains an energetic grumbling, as follows:—

RUFIO [*as Lucius departs*] Do you suppose he would let us go if he had our heads in his hands?

CAESAR. I have no right to suppose that his ways are any baser than mine.

RUFIO. Psha!

CAESAR. Rufio: if I take Lucius Septimius for my model, and become exactly like him, ceasing to be Caesar, will you serve me still?

BRITANNUS. Caesar: this is not good sense. Your duty to Rome demands that her enemies should be prevented from doing further mischief. [*Caesar, whose delight in the moral eye-to-business of his British secretary is inexhaustible, smiles indulgently*].

RUFIO. It is no use talking to him, Britannus: you may save your breath to cool your porridge. But mark this, Caesar. Clemency is very well for you; but what is it for your soldiers, who have to fight tomorrow the men you spared yesterday? You may give what orders you please; but I tell you that your next victory will be a massacre, thanks to your clemency. *I*, for one, will take no prisoners. I will kill my enemies in the field; and then you can preach as much clemency as you please: I shall never have to fight them again. And now, with your leave, I will see these gentry off the premises. [*He turns to go*].

CAESAR [*turning also and seeing Ptolemy*] What! have they left the boy alone! Oh shame, shame!

RUFIO [*taking Ptolemy's hand and making him rise*] Come, your majesty!

PTOLEMY [*to Caesar, drawing away his hand from Rufio*] Is he turning me out of my palace?

RUFIO [*grimly*] You are welcome to stay if you wish.

CAESAR [*kindly*] Go, my boy. I will not harm you; but you will be safer away, among your friends. Here you are in the lion's mouth.

PTOLEMY [*turning to go*] It is not the lion I fear, but [*looking at Rufio*] the jackal. [*He goes out through the loggia*].

CAESAR [*laughing approvingly*] Brave boy!

CLEOPATRA [*jealous of Caesar's approbation, calling after Ptolemy*] Little silly. You think that very clever.

CAESAR. Britannus: attend the King. Give him in charge to that Pothinus fellow. [*Britannus goes out after Ptolemy*].

RUFIO [*pointing to Cleopatra*] And this piece of goods? What is to be done with her? However, I suppose I may leave that to you. [*He goes out through the loggia*].

CLEOPATRA [*flushing suddenly and turning on Caesar*] Did you mean me to go with the rest?

CAESAR [*a little preoccupied, goes with a sigh to Ptolemy's chair, whilst she waits for his answer with red cheeks and clenched fists*] You are free to do just as you please, Cleopatra.

CLEOPATRA. Then you do not care whether I stay or not?

CAESAR [*smiling*] Of course I had rather you stayed.

CLEOPATRA. Much, much rather?

CAESAR [*nodding*] Much, much rather.

CLEOPATRA. Then I consent to stay, because I am asked. But I do not want to, mind.

CAESAR. That is quite understood. [*Calling*] Totateeta.

Ftatateeta, still seated, turns her eyes on him with a sinister expression, but does not move.

CLEOPATRA [*with a splutter of laughter*] Her name is not Totateeta: it is Ftatateeta. [*Calling*] Ftatateeta. [*Ftatateeta instantly rises and comes to Cleopatra*].

CAESAR [*stumbling over the name*] Tfatafeeta will forgive the erring tongue of a Roman. Tota: the Queen will hold her state here in Alexandria. Engage women to attend upon her; and do all that is needful.

FTATATEETA. Am I then the mistress of the Queen's household?

CLEOPATRA [*sharply*] No: *I* am the mistress of the Queen's household. Go and do as you are told, or I will have you thrown into the Nile this very afternoon, to poison the poor crocodiles.

CAESAR [*shocked*] Oh no, no.

CLEOPATRA. Oh yes, yes. You are very sentimental, Caesar; but you are clever; and if you do as I tell you, you will soon learn to govern.

Caesar, quite dumbfounded by this impertinence, turns in his chair and stares at her.

Ftatateeta, smiling grimly, and shewing a splendid set of teeth, goes, leaving them alone together.

CAESAR. Cleopatra: I really think I must eat you, after all.

CLEOPATRA [*kneeling beside him and looking at him with eager interest, half real, half affected to shew how intelligent she is*] You must not talk to me now as if I were a child.

CAESAR. You have been growing up since the sphinx introduced us the other night; and you think you know more than I do already.

CLEOPATRA [*taken down, and anxious to justify herself*] No: that would be very silly of me: of course I know that. But—[*suddenly*] are you angry with me?

CAESAR. No.

CLEOPATRA [*only half believing him*] Then why are you so thoughtful?

CAESAR [*rising*] I have work to do, Cleopatra.

CLEOPATRA [*drawing back*] Work! [*Offended*] You are tired of talking to me; and that is your excuse to get away from me.

CAESAR [*sitting down again to appease her*] Well, well: another minute. But then—work!

CLEOPATRA. Work! what nonsense! You must remember that you are a king now: I have made you one. Kings dont work.

CAESAR. Oh! Who told you that, little kitten? Eh?

CLEOPATRA. My father was King of Egypt; and he never worked. But he was a great king, and cut off my sister's head because she rebelled against him and took the throne from him.

CAESAR. Well; and how did he get his throne back again?

CLEOPATRA [*eagerly, her eyes lighting up*] I will tell you. A beautiful young man, with strong round arms, came over the desert with many horsemen, and slew my sister's husband[31] and gave my father back his throne. [*Wistfully*] I was only twelve then. Oh, I wish he would come again, now that I am queen. I would make him my husband.

CAESAR. It might be managed, perhaps; for it was I who sent that beautiful young man to help your father.

CLEOPATRA [*enraptured*] You know him!

CAESAR [*nodding*] I do.

CLEOPATRA. Has he come with you? [*Caesar shakes his head: she is cruelly disappointed*]. Oh, I wish he had, I wish he had. If only I were a little older; so that he might not think me a mere kitten, as you do! But perhaps that is because you are old. He is many many years younger than you, is he not?

CAESAR [*as if swallowing a pill*] He is somewhat younger.

CLEOPATRA. Would he be my husband, do you think, if I asked him?

CAESAR. Very likely.

CLEOPATRA. But I should not like to ask him. Could you not persuade him to ask me—without knowing that I wanted him to?

CAESAR [*touched by her innocence of the beautiful young man's character*] My poor child!

CLEOPATRA. Why do you say that as if you were sorry for me? Does he love anyone else?

CAESAR. I am afraid so.

CLEOPATRA [*tearfully*] Then I shall not be his first love.

CAESAR. Not quite the first. He is greatly admired by women.

CLEOPATRA. I wish I could be the first. But if he loves me, I will make him kill all the rest. Tell me: is he still beautiful? Do his strong round arms shine in the sun like marble?

---

[31] Archelaus, alleged son of Mithridates, ruled jointly with his wife Berenice during the years 56–55 B.C. Both were killed when Ptolemy Auletes was restored to his throne in 55 B.C.

CAESAR. He is in excellent condition—considering how much he eats and drinks.

CLEOPATRA. Oh, you must not say common, earthly things about him; for I love him. He is a god.

CAESAR. He is a great captain of horsemen, and swifter of foot than any other Roman.

CLEOPATRA. What is his real name?

CAESAR [*puzzled*] His real name?

CLEOPATRA. Yes. I always call him Horus, because Horus is the most beautiful of our gods. But I want to know his real name.

CAESAR. His name is Mark Antony.

CLEOPATRA [*musically*] Mark Antony, Mark Antony, Mark Antony! What a beautiful name! [*She throws her arms round Caesar's neck*]. Oh, how I love you for sending him to help my father! Did you love my father very much?

CAESAR. No, my child; but your father, as you say, never worked. I always work. So when he lost his crown he had to promise me 16,000 talents to get it back for him.

CLEOPATRA. Did he ever pay you?

CAESAR. Not in full.

CLEOPATRA. He was quite right: it was too dear. The whole world is not worth 16,000 talents.

CAESAR. That is perhaps true, Cleopatra. Those Egyptians who work paid as much of it as he could drag from them. The rest is still due. But as I most likely shall not get it, I must go back to my work. So you must run away for a little and send my secretary to me.

CLEOPATRA [*coaxing*] No: I want to stay and hear you talk about Mark Antony.

CAESAR. But if I do not get to work, Pothinus and the rest of them will cut us off from the harbor; and then the way from Rome will be blocked.

CLEOPATRA. No matter: I dont want you to go back to Rome.

CAESAR. But you want Mark Antony to come from it.

CLEOPATRA [*springing up*] Oh yes, yes, yes: I forgot. Go quickly and work, Caesar; and keep the way over the sea open for my Mark Antony. [*She runs out through the loggia, kissing her hand to Mark Antony across the sea*].

CAESAR [*going briskly up the middle of the hall to the loggia steps*] Ho, Britannus. [*He is startled by the entry of a wounded Roman soldier, who confronts him from the upper step*]. What now?

SOLDIER [*pointing to his bandaged head*] This, Caesar; and two of my comrades killed in the market place.

CAESAR [*quiet, but attending*] Ay. Why?

SOLDIER. There is an army come to Alexandria, calling itself the Roman army.

CAESAR. The Roman army of occupation. Ay?

SOLDIER. Commanded by one Achillas.

CAESAR. Well?

SOLDIER. The citizens rose against us when the army entered the gates. I was with two others in the market place when the news came. They set upon us. I cut my way out; and here I am.

CAESAR. Good. I am glad to see you alive. [*Rufio enters the loggia hastily, passing behind the soldier to look out through one of the arches at the quay beneath*]. Rufio: we are besieged.

RUFIO. What! Already?

CAESAR. Now or tomorrow: what does it matter? We shall be besieged.

Britannus runs in.

BRITANNUS. Caesar—

CAESAR [*anticipating him*] Yes: I know. [*Rufio and Britannus come down the hall from the loggia at opposite sides, past Caesar, who waits for a moment near the step to say to the soldier*] Comrade: give the word to turn out on the beach and stand by the boats. Get your wound attended to. Go. [*The soldier hurries out. Caesar comes down the hall between Rufio and Britannus*] Rufio: we have some ships in the west harbor. Burn them.

RUFIO [*staring*] Burn them!!

CAESAR. Take every boat we have in the east harbor, and seize the Pharos—that island with the lighthouse. Leave half our men behind to hold the beach and the quay outside this palace: that is the way home.

RUFIO [*disapproving strongly*] Are we to give up the city?

CAESAR. We have not got it, Rufio. This palace we have; and— what is that building next door?

RUFIO. The theatre.

CAESAR. We will have that too: it commands the strand.[32] For the rest, Egypt for the Egyptians!

RUFIO. Well, you know best, I suppose. Is that all?

CAESAR. That is all. Are those ships burnt yet?

RUFIO. Be easy: I shall waste no more time. [*He runs out*].

BRITANNUS. Caesar: Pothinus demands speech of you. In my opinion he needs a lesson. His manner is most insolent.

CAESAR. Where is he?

BRITANNUS. He waits without.

CAESAR. Ho there! admit Pothinus.

Pothinus appears in the loggia, and comes down the hall very haughtily to Caesar's left hand.

CAESAR. Well, Pothinus?

POTHINUS. I have brought you our ultimatum, Caesar.

CAESAR. Ultimatum! The door was open: you should have gone out through it before you declared war. You are my prisoner now. [*He goes to the chair and loosens his toga*].

POTHINUS [*scornfully*] I your prisoner! Do you know that you are in Alexandria, and that King Ptolemy, with an army outnumbering your little troop a hundred to one, is in possession of Alexandria?

CAESAR [*unconcernedly taking off his toga and throwing it on the chair*] Well, my friend, get out if you can. And tell your friends not to kill any more Romans in the market place. Otherwise my soldiers, who do not share my celebrated clemency, will probably kill you. Britannus: pass the word to the guard; and fetch my armor. [*Britannus runs out. Rufio returns*]. Well?

---

[32] Shaw is punning. The "Strand" in London is the main artery between the City and the West End and is noted for its numerous theaters. It also means—its first use here—the beach or shore.

RUFIO [*pointing from the loggia to a cloud of smoke drifting over the harbor*] See there! [*Pothinus runs eagerly up the steps to look out*].

CAESAR. What, ablaze already! Impossible!

RUFIO. Yes, five good ships, and a barge laden with oil grappled to each. But it is not my doing: the Egyptians have saved me the trouble. They have captured the west harbor.

CAESAR [*anxiously*] And the east harbor? The lighthouse, Rufio?

RUFIO [*with a sudden splutter of raging ill usage, coming down to Caesar and scolding him*] Can I embark a legion in five minutes? The first cohort is already on the beach. We can do no more. If you want faster work, come and do it yourself.

CAESAR [*soothing him*] Good, good. Patience, Rufio, patience.

RUFIO. Patience! Who is impatient here, you or I? Would I be here, if I could not oversee them from that balcony?

CAESAR. Forgive me, Rufio; and [*anxiously*] hurry them as much as—

He is interrupted by an outcry as of an old man in the extremity of misfortune. It draws near rapidly; and Theodotus rushes in, tearing his hair, and squeaking the most lamentable exclamations. Rufio steps back to stare at him, amazed at his frantic condition. Pothinus turns to listen.

THEODOTUS [*on the steps, with uplifted arms*] Horror unspeakable! Woe, alas! Help!

RUFIO. What now?

CAESAR [*frowning*] Who is slain?

THEODOTUS. Slain! Oh, worse than the death of ten thousand men! Loss irreparable to mankind!

RUFIO. What has happened, man?

THEODOTUS [*rushing down the hall between them*] The fire has spread from your ships. The first of the seven wonders of the world perishes. The library of Alexandria is in flames.

RUFIO. Psha! [*Quite relieved, he goes up to the loggia and watches the preparations of the troops on the beach*].

CAESAR. Is that all?

THEODOTUS [*unable to believe his senses*] All! Caesar: will you go down to posterity as a barbarous soldier too ignorant to know the value of books?

CAESAR. Theodotus: I am an author myself; and I tell you it is better that the Egyptians should live their lives than dream them away with the help of books.

THEODOTUS [*kneeling, with genuine literary emotion: the passion of the pedant*] Caesar: once in ten generations of men, the world gains an immortal book.

CAESAR [*inflexible*] If it did not flatter mankind, the common executioner would burn it.

THEODOTUS. Without history, death will lay you beside your meanest soldier.

CAESAR. Death will do that in any case. I ask no better grave.

THEODOTUS. What is burning there is the memory of mankind.

CAESAR. A shameful memory. Let it burn.

THEODOTUS [*wildly*] Will you destroy the past?

CAESAR. Ay, and build the future with its ruins. [*Theodotus, in despair, strikes himself on the temples with his fists*]. But harken, Theodotus, teacher of kings: you who valued Pompey's head no more than a shepherd values an onion, and who now kneel to me, with tears in your old eyes, to plead for a few sheepskins scrawled with errors. I cannot spare you a man or a bucket of water just now; but you shall pass freely out of the palace. Now, away with you to Achillas; and borrow his legions to put out the fire. [*He hurries him to the steps*].

POTHINUS [*significantly*] You understand, Theodotus: I remain a prisoner.

THEODOTUS. A prisoner!

CAESAR. Will you stay to talk whilst the memory of mankind is burning? [*Calling through the loggia*] Ho there! Pass Theodotus out. [*To Theodotus*] Away with you.

THEODOTUS [*To Pothinus*] I must go to save the library. [*He hurries out*].

CAESAR. Follow him to the gate, Pothinus. Bid him urge your people to kill no more of my soldiers, for your sake.

POTHINUS. My life will cost you dear if you take it, Caesar. [*He goes out after Theodotus*].

Rufio, absorbed in watching the embarkation, does not notice the departure of the two Egyptians.

RUFIO [*shouting from the loggia to the beach*] All ready, there?

A CENTURION [*from below*] All ready. We wait for Caesar.

CAESAR. Tell them Caesar is coming—the rogues! [*Calling*] Britannicus. [*This magniloquent version of his secretary's name is one of Caesar's jokes. In later years it would have meant, quite seriously and officially, Conqueror of Britain*].

RUFIO [*calling down*] Push off, all except the longboat. Stand by it to embark, Caesar's guard there. [*He leaves the balcony and comes down into the hall*]. Where are those Egyptians? Is this more clemency? Have you let them go?

CAESAR [*chuckling*] I have let Theodotus go to save the library. We must respect literature, Rufio.

RUFIO [*raging*] Folly on folly's head! I believe if you could bring back all the dead of Spain, Gaul, and Thessaly to life, you would do it that we might have the trouble of fighting them over again.

CAESAR. Might not the gods destroy the world if their only thought were to be at peace next year? [*Rufio, out of all patience, turns away in anger. Caesar suddenly grips his sleeve, and adds slyly in his ear*] Besides, my friend: every Egyptian we imprison means imprisoning two Roman soldiers to guard him. Eh?

RUFIO. Agh! I might have known there was some fox's trick behind your fine talking. [*He gets away from Caesar with an ill-humored shrug, and goes to the balcony for another look at the preparations; finally goes out*].

CAESAR. Is Britannus asleep? I sent him for my armor an hour ago. [*Calling*] Britannicus, thou British islander. Britannicus!

Cleopatra runs in through the loggia with Caesar's helmet and sword, snatched from Britannus, who follows her with a cuirass and greaves. They come down to Caesar, she to his left hand, Britannus to his right.

CLEOPATRA. I am going to dress you, Caesar. Sit down. [*He obeys*]. These Roman helmets are so becoming! [*She takes off his wreath*]. Oh! [*She bursts out laughing at him*].

CAESAR. What are you laughing at?

CLEOPATRA. Youre bald [*beginning with a big B, and ending with a splutter*].

CAESAR [*almost annoyed*] Cleopatra! [*He rises, for the convenience of Britannus, who puts the cuirass on him*].

CLEOPATRA. So that is why you wear the wreath—to hide it.

BRITANNUS. Peace, Egyptian: they are the bays of the conqueror. [*He buckles the cuirass*].

CLEOPATRA. Peace, thou: islander! [*To Caesar*] You should rub your head with strong spirits of sugar, Caesar. That will make it grow.

CAESAR [*with a wry face*] Cleopatra: do you like to be reminded that you are very young?

CLEOPATRA [*pouting*] No.

CAESAR [*sitting down again, and setting out his leg for Britannus, who kneels to put on his greaves*] Neither do I like to be reminded that I am—middle aged. Let me give you ten of my superfluous years. That will make you 26, and leave me only—no matter. Is it a bargain?

CLEOPATRA. Agreed. 26, mind. [*She puts the helmet on him*]. Oh! How nice! You look only about 50 in it!

BRITANNUS [*looking up severely at Cleopatra*] You must not speak in this manner to Caesar.

CLEOPATRA. Is it true that when Caesar caught you on that island, you were painted all over blue?[33]

BRITANNUS. Blue is the color worn by all Britons of good standing. In war we stain our bodies blue; so that though our enemies may strip us of our clothes and our lives, they cannot strip us of our respectability. [*He rises*].

---

[33] Caesar, who journeyed twice across the Channel during his Gallic campaign, described the early Britons as having dyed themselves with blue woad to give themselves a terrible appearance in war.

CLEOPATRA [*with Caesar's sword*] Let me hang this on. Now you look splendid. Have they made any statues of you in Rome?

CAESAR. Yes, many statues.

CLEOPATRA. You must send for one and give it to me.

RUFIO [*coming back into the loggia, more impatient than ever*] Now Caesar: have you done talking? The moment your foot is aboard there will be no holding our men back: the boats will race one another for the lighthouse.

CAESAR [*drawing his sword and trying the edge*] Is this well set today, Britannicus? At Pharsalia it was as blunt as a barrel-hoop.

BRITANNUS. It will split one of the Egyptian's hairs today, Caesar. I have set it myself.

CLEOPATRA [*suddenly throwing her arms in terror round Caesar*] Oh, you are not really going into battle to be killed?

CAESAR. No, Cleopatra. No man goes to battle to be killed.

CLEOPATRA. But they do get killed. My sister's husband was killed in battle. You must not go. Let him go [*pointing to Rufio. They all laugh at her*]. Oh please, please dont go. What will happen to me if you never come back?

CAESAR [*gravely*] Are you afraid?

CLEOPATRA [*shrinking*] No.

CAESAR [*with quiet authority*] Go to the balcony; and you shall see us take the Pharos. You must learn to look on battles. Go. [*She goes, downcast, and looks out from the balcony*]. That is well. Now, Rufio. March.

CLEOPATRA [*suddenly clapping her hands*] Oh, you will not be able to go!

CAESAR. Why? What now?

CLEOPATRA. They are drying up the harbor with buckets—a multitude of soldiers—over there [*pointing out across the sea to her left*]—they are dipping up the water.

RUFIO [*hastening to look*] It is true. The Egyptian army! Crawling over the edge of the west harbor like locusts. [*With sudden anger he strides down to Caesar*]. This is your accursed clemency, Caesar. Theodotus has brought them.

CAESAR [*delighted at his own cleverness*] I meant him to, Rufio. They have come to put out the fire. The library will keep them busy whilst we seize the lighthouse. Eh? [*He rushes out buoyantly through the loggia, followed by Britannus*].

RUFIO [*disgustedly*] More foxing! Agh! [*He rushes off. A shout from the soldiers announces the appearance of Caesar below*].

CENTURION [*below*] All aboard. Give way there. [*Another shout*].

CLEOPATRA [*waving her scarf through the loggia arch*] Goodbye, goodbye, dear Caesar. Come back safe. Goodbye!

ACT III

The edge of the quay in front of the palace, looking out west over the east harbor of Alexandria to Pharos island, just off the end of which, and connected with it by a narrow mole, is the famous lighthouse, a gigantic square tower of white marble diminishing in size storey by storey to the top, on which stands a cresset beacon. The island is joined to the main land by the Heptastadium, a great mole or causeway five miles long bounding the harbor on the south.

In the middle of the quay a Roman sentinel stands on guard, pilum in hand, looking out to the lighthouse with strained attention, his left hand shading his eyes. The pilum is a stout wooden shaft 4½ feet long, with an iron spit about three feet long fixed in it. The sentinel is so absorbed that he does not notice the approach from the north end of the quay of four Egyptian market porters carrying rolls of carpet, preceded by Ftatateeta and Apollodorus the Sicilian. Apollodorus is a dashing young man of about 24, handsome and debonair, dressed with deliberate aestheticism in the most delicate purples and dove greys, with ornaments of bronze, oxydized silver, and stones of jade and agate. His sword, designed as carefully as a medieval cross, has a blued blade shewing through an openwork scabbard of purple leather and filagree. The porters, conducted by Ftatateeta, pass along the quay behind the sentinel to the steps of the palace, where they put down their bales and squat on the ground. Apollodorus does not pass along with them: he halts, amused by the preoccupation of the sentinel.

APOLLODORUS [*calling to the sentinel*] Who goes there, eh?

SENTINEL [*starting violently and turning with his pilum at the charge, revealing himself as a small, wiry, sandy-haired, conscientious young man with an elderly face*] Whats this? Stand. Who are you?

72

APOLLODORUS. I am Apollodorus the Sicilian. Why, man, what are you dreaming of? Since I came through the lines beyond the theatre there, I have brought my caravan past three sentinels, all so busy staring at the lighthouse that not one of them challenged me. Is this Roman discipline?

SENTINEL. We are not here to watch the land but the sea. Caesar has just landed on the Pharos. [*Looking at Ftatateeta*] What have you here? Who is this piece of Egyptian crockery?

FTATATEETA. Apollodorus: rebuke this Roman dog; and bid him bridle his tongue in the presence of Ftatateeta, the mistress of the Queen's household.

APOLLODORUS. My friend: this is a great lady, who stands high with Caesar.

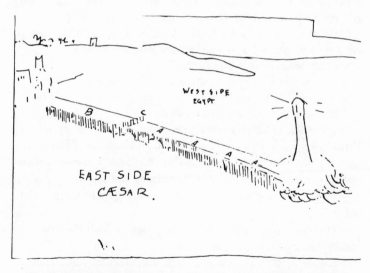

Shaw's drawing of the Heptastadium that joined Pharos Island to Alexandria. Section C, the Wall, separated the Alexandrians from the Romans, represented by B and A respectively. The Alexandrians sailed around the wall, landed close to the lighthouse, and forced the Romans into the East Harbor, including Caesar.

SENTINEL [*not at all impressed, pointing to the carpets*] And what is all this truck?

APOLLODORUS. Carpets for the furnishing of the Queen's apartments in the palace. I have picked them from the best carpets in the world; and the Queen shall choose the best of my choosing.

SENTINEL. So you are the carpet merchant?

APOLLODORUS [*hurt*] My friend: I am a patrician.

SENTINEL. A patrician! A patrician keeping a shop instead of following arms!

APOLLODORUS. I do not keep a shop. Mine is a temple of the arts. I am a worshipper of beauty. My calling is to choose beautiful things for beautiful queens. My motto is Art for Art's sake.[34]

SENTINEL. That is not the password.

APOLLODORUS. It is a universal password.

SENTINEL. I know nothing about universal passwords. Either give me the password for the day or get back to your shop.

Ftatateeta, roused by his hostile tone, steals towards the edge of the quay with the step of a panther, and gets behind him.

APOLLODORUS. How if I do neither?

SENTINEL. Then I will drive this pilum through you.

APOLLODORUS. At your service, my friend. [*He draws his sword, and springs to his guard with unruffled grace*].

FTATATEETA [*suddenly seizing the sentinel's arms from behind*] Thrust your knife into the dog's throat, Apollodorus. [*The chivalrous Apollodorus laughingly shakes his head; breaks ground away from the sentinel towards the palace; and lowers his point*].

SENTINEL [*struggling vainly*] Curse on you! Let me go. Help ho!

FTATATEETA [*lifting him from the ground*] Stab the little Roman reptile. Spit him on your sword.

A couple of Roman soldiers, with a centurion, come running along the edge of the quay from the north end. They rescue their

---

[34] Victor Cousin (1792–1867) coined this phrase to describe the work of those poets who believed that beauty is an end in itself. Shaw, a didacticist in art, was opposed to this esthetic position.

comrade, and throw off Ftatateeta, who is sent reeling away on the left hand of the sentinel.

CENTURION [*an unattractive man of fifty, short in his speech and manners, with a vinewood cudgel in his hand*] How now? What is all this?

FTATATEETA [*to Apollodorus*] Why did you not stab him? There was time!

APOLLODORUS. Centurion: I am here by order of the Queen to—

CENTURION [*interrupting him*] The Queen! Yes, yes: [*to the sentinel*] pass him in. Pass all these bazaar people in to the Queen, with their goods. But mind you pass no one out that you have not passed in—not even the Queen herself.

SENTINEL. This old woman is dangerous: she is as strong as three men. She wanted the merchant to stab me.

APOLLODORUS. Centurion: I am not a merchant. I am a patrician and a votary of art.

CENTURION. Is the woman your wife?

APOLLODORUS [*horrified*] No, no! [*Correcting himself politely*] Not that the lady is not a striking figure in her own way. But [*emphatically*] she is not my wife.

FTATATEETA [*to the centurion*] Roman: I am Ftatateeta, the mistress of the Queen's household.

CENTURION. Keep your hands off our men, mistress; or I will have you pitched into the harbor, though you were as strong as ten men. [*To his men*] To your posts: march! [*He returns with his men the way they came*].

FTATATEETA [*looking malignantly after him*] We shall see whom Isis loves best: her servant Ftatateeta or a dog of a Roman.

SENTINEL [*to Apollodorus, with a wave of his pilum towards the palace*] Pass in there; and keep your distance. [*Turning to Ftatateeta*] Come within a yard of me, you old crocodile; and I will give you this [*the pilum*] in your jaws.

CLEOPATRA [*calling from the palace*] Ftatateeta, Ftatateeta.

FTATATEETA [*looking up, scandalized*] Go from the window, go from the window. There are men here.

CLEOPATRA. I am coming down.

FTATATEETA [*distracted*] No, no. What are you dreaming of? O ye gods, ye gods! Apollodorus: bid your men pick up your bales; and in with me quickly.

APOLLODORUS. Obey the mistress of the Queen's household.

FTATATEETA [*impatiently, as the porters stoop to lift the bales*] Quick, quick: she will be out upon us. [*Cleopatra comes from the palace and runs across the quay to Ftatateeta*]. Oh that ever I was born!

CLEOPATRA [*eagerly*] Ftatateeta: I have thought of something. I want a boat—at once.

FTATATEETA. A boat! No, no: you cannot. Appollodorus: speak to the Queen.

APOLLODORUS [*gallantly*] Beautiful queen: I am Apollodorus the Sicilian, your servant, from the bazaar. I have brought you the three most beautiful Persian carpets in the world to choose from.

CLEOPATRA. I have no time for carpets today. Get me a boat.

FTATATEETA. What whim is this? You cannot go on the water except in the royal barge.

APOLLODORUS. Royalty, Ftatateeta, lies not in the barge but in the Queen [*To Cleopatra*] The touch of your majesty's foot on the gunwale of the meanest boat in the harbor will make it royal. [*He turns to the harbor and calls seaward*] Ho there, boatman! Pull in to the steps.

CLEOPATRA. Apollodorus: you are my perfect knight; and I will always buy my carpets through you. [*Apollodorus bows joyously. An oar appears above the quay; and the boatman, a bullet-headed, vivacious, grinning fellow, burned almost black by the sun, comes up a flight of steps from the water on the sentinel's right, oar in hand, and waits at the top*]. Can you row, Apollodorus?

APOLLODORUS. My oars shall be your majesty's wings. Whither shall I row my Queen?

CLEOPATRA. To the lighthouse. Come. [*She makes for the steps*].

SENTINEL [*opposing her with his pilum at the charge*] Stand. You cannot pass.

CLEOPATRA [*flushing angrily*] How dare you? Do you know that I am the Queen?

SENTINEL. I have my orders. You cannot pass.

CLEOPATRA. I will make Caesar have you killed if you do not obey me.

SENTINEL. He will do worse to me if I disobey my officer. Stand back.

CLEOPATRA. Ftatateeta: strangle him.

SENTINEL [*alarmed—looking apprehensively at Ftatateeta, and brandishing his pilum*] Keep off, there.

CLEOPATRA [*running to Apollodorus*] Apollodorus: make your slaves help us.

APOLLODORUS. I shall not need their help, lady. [*He draws his sword*]. Now, soldier: choose which weapon you will defend yourself with. Shall it be sword against pilum, or sword against sword?

SENTINEL. Roman against Sicilian, curse you. Take that. [*He hurls his pilum at Apollodorus, who drops expertly on one knee. The pilum passes whizzing over his head and falls harmless. Apollodorus, with a cry of triumph, springs up and attacks the sentinel, who draws his sword and defends himself, crying*] Ho there, guard. Help!

Cleopatra, half frightened, half delighted, takes refuge near the palace, where the porters are squatting among the bales. The boatman, alarmed, hurries down the steps out of harm's way, but stops, with his head just visible above the edge of the quay, to watch the fight. The sentinel is handicapped by his fear of an attack in the rear from Ftatateeta. His swordsmanship, which is of a rough and ready sort, is heavily taxed, as he has occasionally to strike at her to keep her off between a blow and a guard with Apollodorus. The centurion returns with several soldiers. Apollodorus springs back towards Cleopatra as this reinforcement confronts him.

CENTURION [*coming to the sentinel's right hand*] What is this? What now?

SENTINEL [*panting*] I could do well enough by myself if it

werent for the old woman. Keep her off me: that is all the help I need.

CENTURION. Make your report, soldier. What has happened?

FTATATEETA. Centurion: he would have slain the Queen.

SENTINEL [*bluntly*] I would, sooner than let her pass. She wanted to take boat, and go—so she said—to the lighthouse. I stopped her, as I was ordered to; and she set this fellow on me. [*He goes to pick up his pilum and returns to his place with it*].

CENTURION [*turning to Cleopatra*] Cleopatra: I am loth to offend you; but without Caesar's express order we dare not let you pass beyond the Roman lines.

APOLLODORUS. Well, Centurion; and has not the lighthouse been within the Roman lines since Caesar landed there?

CLEOPATRA. Yes, yes. Answer that, if you can.

CENTURION [*to Apollodorus*] As for you, Apollodorus, you may thank the gods that you are not nailed to the palace door with a pilum for your meddling.

APOLLODORUS [*urbanely*] My military friend, I was not born to be slain by so ugly a weapon. When I fall, it will be [*holding up his sword*] by this white queen of arms, the only weapon fit for an artist. And now that you are convinced that we do not want to go beyond the lines, let me finish killing your sentinel and depart with the Queen.

CENTURION [*as the sentinel makes an angry demonstration*] Peace there, Cleopatra: I must abide by my orders, and not by the subtleties of this Sicilian. You must withdraw into the palace and examine your carpets there.

CLEOPATRA [*pouting*] I will not: I am the Queen. Caesar does not speak to me as you do. Have Caesar's centurions changed manners with his scullions?

CENTURION [*sulkily*] I do my duty. That is enough for me.

APOLLODORUS. Majesty: when a stupid man is doing something he is ashamed of, he always declares that it is his duty.

CENTURION [*angry*] Apollodorus—

APOLLODORUS [*interrupting him with defiant elegance*] I will make amends for that insult with my sword at fitting time and place. Who says artist, says duellist. [*To Cleopatra*] Hear my counsel, star of the east. Until word comes to these soldiers from Caesar himself, you are a prisoner. Let me go to him with a message from you, and a present; and before the sun has stooped half way to the arms of the sea, I will bring you back Caesar's order of release.

CENTURION [*sneering at him*] And you will sell the Queen the present, no doubt.

APOLLODORUS. Centurion: the Queen shall have from me, without payment, as the unforced tribute of Sicilian taste to Egyptian beauty, the richest of these carpets for her present to Caesar.

CLEOPATRA [*exultantly, to the centurion*] Now you see what an ignorant common creature you are!

CENTURION [*curtly*] Well, a fool and his wares are soon parted. [*He turns to his men*]. Two more men to this post here; and see that no one leaves the palace but this man and his merchandize. If he draws his sword again inside the lines, kill him. To your posts. March.

He goes out, leaving two auxiliary sentinels with the other.

APOLLODORUS [*with polite goodfellowship*] My friends: will you not enter the palace and bury our quarrel in a bowl of wine? [*He takes out his purse, jingling the coins in it*]. The Queen has presents for you all.

SENTINEL [*very sulky*] You heard our orders. Get about your business.

FIRST AUXILIARY. Yes: you ought to know better. Off with you.

SECOND AUXILIARY [*looking longingly at the purse—this sentinel is a hooknosed man, unlike his comrade, who is squab faced*] Do not tantalize a poor man.

APOLLODORUS [*to Cleopatra*] Pearl of Queens: the centurion is at hand; and the Roman soldier is incorruptible when his officer is looking. I must carry your word to Caesar.

CLEOPATRA [*who has been meditating among the carpets*] Are these carpets very heavy?[35]

[35] Plutarch records Cleopatra's ruse of concealing herself in a rug so as to gain access to Caesar. George W. Whiting in "The Cleopatra Rug Scene: Another Source," *The Shaw Review*, III (January 1960), 15–17, argues that

APOLLODORUS. It matters not how heavy. There are plenty of porters.

CLEOPATRA. How do they put the carpets into boats? Do they throw them down?

APOLLODORUS. Not into small boats, majesty. It would sink them.

CLEOPATRA. Not into that man's boat, for instance? [*pointing to the boatman*].

APOLLODORUS. No. Too small.

CLEOPATRA. But you can take a carpet to Caesar in it if I send one?

APOLLODORUS. Assuredly.

CLEOPATRA. And you will have it carried gently down the steps and take great care of it?

APOLLODORUS. Depend on me.

CLEOPATRA. Great, great care?

APOLLODORUS. More than of my own body.

CLEOPATRA. You will promise me not to let the porters drop it or throw it about?

APOLLODORUS. Place the most delicate glass goblet in the palace in the heart of the roll, Queen; and if it be broken, my head shall pay for it.

CLEOPATRA. Good. Come, Ftatateeta. [*Ftatateeta comes to her. Apollodorus offers to squire them into the palace*]. No, Apollodorus, you must not come. I will choose a carpet for myself. You must wait here. [*She runs into the palace*].

APOLLODORUS [*to the porters*] Follow this lady [*indicating Ftatateeta*] and obey her.

The porters rise and take up their bales.

FTATATEETA [*addressing the porters as if they were vermin*] This way. And take your shoes off before you put your feet on those stairs.

She goes in, followed by the porters with the carpets. Meanwhile

---

Shaw was also influenced by Gérome's celebrated painting, "Cléopâtre apportée à César dans un tapis."

Apollodorus goes to the edge of the quay and looks out over the harbor. The sentinels keep their eyes on him malignantly.

APOLLODORUS [*addressing the sentinel*] My friend—

SENTINEL [*rudely*] Silence there.

FIRST AUXILIARY. Shut your muzzle, you.

SECOND AUXILIARY [*in a half whisper, glancing apprehensively towards the north end of the quay*] Cant you wait a bit?

APOLLODORUS. Patience, worthy three-headed donkey. [*They mutter ferociously; but he is not at all intimidated*]. Listen: were you set here to watch me, or to watch the Egyptians?

SENTINEL. We know our duty.

APOLLODORUS. Then why dont you do it? There is something going on over there [*pointing southwestward to the mole*].

SENTINEL [*sulkily*] I do not need to be told what to do by the like of you.

APOLLODORUS. Blockhead. [*He begins shouting*] Ho there, Centurion. Hoiho!

SENTINEL. Curse your meddling. [*Shouting*] Hoiho! Alarm! Alarm!

FIRST AND SECOND AUXILIARIES. Alarm! alarm! Hoiho!

The Centurion comes running in with his guard.

CENTURION. What now? Has the old woman attacked you again? [*Seeing Apollodorus*] Are you here still?

APOLLODORUS [*pointing as before*] See there. The Egyptians are moving. They are going to recapture the Pharos. They will attack by sea and land: by land along the great mole; by sea from the west harbor. Stir yourselves, my military friends: the hunt is up. [*A clangor of trumpets from several points along the quay*]. Aha! I told you so.

CENTURION [*quickly*] The two extra men pass the alarm to the south posts. One man keep guard here. The rest with me—quick.

The two auxiliary sentinels run off to the south. The centurion and his guard run off northward; and immediately afterwards the bucina sounds. The four porters come from the palace carrying a carpet, followed by Ftatateeta.

SENTINEL [*handling his pilum apprehensively*] You again! [*The porters stop*].

FTATATEETA. Peace, Roman fellow: you are now single-handed. Apollodorus: this carpet is Cleopatra's present to Caesar. It has rolled up in it ten precious goblets of the thinnest Iberian crystal, and a hundred eggs of the sacred blue pigeon. On your honor, let not one of them be broken.

APOLLODORUS. On my head be it! [*To the porters*] Into the boat with them carefully.

The porters carry the carpet to the steps.

FIRST PORTER [*looking down at the boat*] Beware what you do, sir. Those eggs of which the lady speaks must weigh more than a pound apiece. This boat is too small for such a load.

BOATMAN [*excitedly rushing up the steps*] Oh thou injurious porter! Oh thou unnatural son of a she-camel! [*To Apollodorus*] My boat, sir, hath often carried five men. Shall it not carry your lordship and a bale of pigeon's eggs? [*To the porter*] Thou mangey dromedary, the gods shall punish thee for this envious wickedness.

FIRST PORTER [*stolidly*] I cannot quit this bale now to beat thee; but another day I will lie in wait for thee.

APOLLODORUS [*going between them*] Peace there. If the boat were but a single plank, I would get to Caesar on it.

FTATATEETA [*anxiously*] In the name of the gods, Apollodorus, run no risks with that bale.

APOLLODORUS. Fear not, thou venerable grotesque: I guess its great worth. [*To the porters*] Down with it, I say; and gently; or ye shall eat nothing but stick for ten days.

The boatman goes down the steps, followed by the porters with the bale: Ftatateeta and Apollodorus watching from the edge.

APOLLODORUS. Gently, my sons, my children—[*with sudden alarm*] gently, ye dogs. Lay it level in the stern—so—tis well.

FTATATEETA [*screaming down at one of the porters*] Do not step on it, do not step on it. Oh thou brute beast!

FIRST PORTER [*ascending*] Be not excited, mistress: all is well.

FTATATEETA [*panting*] All well! Oh, thou hast given my heart a turn! [*She clutches her side, gasping*].

The four porters have now come up and are waiting at the stair-head to be paid.

APOLLODORUS. Here, ye hungry ones. [*He gives money to the first porter, who holds it in his hand to shew to the others. They crowd greedily to see how much it is, quite prepared, after the Eastern fashion, to protest to heaven against their patron's stinginess. But his liberality overpowers them*].

FIRST PORTER. O bounteous prince!

SECOND PORTER. O lord of the bazaar!

THIRD PORTER. O favored of the gods!

FOURTH PORTER. O father to all the porters of the market!

SENTINEL [*enviously, threatening them fiercely with his pilum*] Hence, dogs: off. Out of this. [*They fly before him northward along the quay*].

APOLLODORUS. Farewell, Ftatateeta. I shall be at the lighthouse before the Egyptians. [*He descends the steps*].

FTATATEETA. The gods speed thee and protect my nursling!

The sentry returns from chasing the porters and looks down at the boat, standing near the stairhead lest Ftatateeta should attempt to escape.

APOLLODORUS [*from beneath, as the boat moves off*] Farewell, valiant pilum pitcher.

SENTINEL. Farewell, shopkeeper.

APOLLODORUS. Ha, ha! Pull, thou brave boatman, pull. Soho-o-o-o-o! [*He begins to sing in barcarolle measure to the rhythm of the oars*]

> My heart, my heart, spread out thy wings:
> Shake off thy heavy load of love—

Give me the oars, O son of a snail.

SENTINEL [*threatening Ftatateeta*] Now mistress: back to your henhouse. In with you.

FTATATEETA [*falling on her knees and stretching her hands over the waters*] Gods of the seas, bear her safely to the shore!

SENTINEL. Bear who safely? What do you mean?

FTATATEETA [*looking darkly at him*] Gods of Egypt and of

Vengeance, let this Roman fool be beaten like a dog by his captain for suffering her to be taken over the waters.

SENTINEL. Accursed one: is she then in the boat? [*He calls over the sea*] Hoiho, there, boatman! Hoiho!

APOLLODORUS [*singing in the distance*]

> My heart, my heart, be whole and free:
> Love is thine only enemy.

Meanwhile Rufio, the morning's fighting done, sits munching dates on a faggot of brushwood outside the door of the lighthouse, which towers gigantic to the clouds on his left. His helmet, full of dates, is between his knees; and a leathern bottle of wine is by his side. Behind him the great stone pedestal of the lighthouse is shut in from the open sea by a low stone parapet, with a couple of steps in the middle to the broad coping. A huge chain with a hook hangs down from the lighthouse crane above his head. Faggots like the one he sits on lie beneath it ready to be drawn up to feed the beacon.

Caesar is standing on the step at the parapet looking out anxiously, evidently ill at ease. Britannus comes out of the lighthouse door.

RUFIO. Well, my British islander. Have you been up to the top?

BRITANNUS. I have. I reckon it at 200 feet high.

RUFIO. Anybody up there?

BRITANNUS. One elderly Tyrian to work the crane; and his son, a well conducted youth of 14.

RUFIO [*looking at the chain*] What! An old man and a boy work that! Twenty men, you mean.

BRITANNUS. Two only, I assure you. They have counterweights, and a machine with boiling water in it which I do not understand: it is not of British design. They use it to haul up barrels of oil and faggots to burn in the brazier on the roof.

RUFIO. But—

BRITANNUS. Excuse me: I came down because there are messengers coming along the mole to us from the island. I must see what their business is. [*He hurries out past the lighthouse*].

CAESAR [*coming away from the parapet, shivering and out of sorts*] Rufio: this has been a mad expedition. We shall be beaten. I wish I knew how our men are getting on with that barricade across the great mole.

RUFIO [*angrily*] Must I leave my food and go starving to bring you a report?

CAESAR [*soothing him nervously*] No, Rufio, no. Eat, my son, eat. [*He takes another turn, Rufio chewing dates meanwhile*]. The Egyptians cannot be such fools as not to storm the barricade and swoop down on us here before it is finished. It is the first time I have ever run an avoidable risk. I should not have come to Egypt.

RUFIO. An hour ago you were all for victory.

CAESAR [*apologetically*] Yes: I was a fool—rash, Rufio—boyish.

RUFIO. Boyish! Not a bit of it. Here [*offering him a handful of dates*].

CAESAR. What are these for?

RUFIO. To eat. Thats whats the matter with you. When a man comes to your age, he runs down before his midday meal. Eat and drink; and then have another look at our chances.

CAESAR [*taking the dates*] My age! [*He shakes his head and bites a date*]. Yes, Rufio: I am an old man—worn out now—true, quite true. [*He gives way to melancholy contemplation, and eats another date*]. Achillas is still in his prime: Ptolemy is a boy. [*He eats another date, and plucks up a little*]. Well, every dog has his day; and I have had mine: I cannot complain. [*With sudden cheerfulness*] These dates are not bad, Rufio. [*Britannus returns, greatly excited, with a leathern bag. Caesar is himself again in a moment*]. What now?

BRITANNUS [*triumphantly*] Our brave Rhodian mariners have captured a treasure. There! [*He throws the bag down at Caesar's feet*]. Our enemies are delivered into our hands.

CAESAR. In that bag?

BRITANNUS. Wait till you hear, Caesar. This bag contains all the letters which have passed between Pompey's party and the army of occupation here.

CAESAR. Well?

BRITANNUS [*impatient of Caesar's slowness to grasp the situation*] Well, we shall now know who your foes are. The name of every man who has plotted against you since you crossed the Rubicon may be in these papers, for all we know.

CAESAR. Put them in the fire.

BRITANNUS. Put them—[*he gasps*]!!!!

CAESAR. In the fire. Would you have me waste the next three years of my life in proscribing and condemning men who will be my friends when I have proved that my friendship is worth more than Pompey's was—than Cato's is. O incorrigible British islander: am I a bull dog, to seek quarrels merely to shew how stubborn my jaws are?

BRITANNUS. But your honor—the honor of Rome—

CAESAR. I do not make human sacrifices to my honor, as your Druids do.[36] Since you will not burn these, at least I can drown them. [*He picks up the bag and throws it over the parapet into the sea*].

BRITANNUS. Caesar: this is mere eccentricity. Are traitors to be allowed to go free for the sake of a paradox?

RUFIO [*rising*] Caesar: when the islander has finished preaching, call me again. I am going to have a look at the boiling water machine. [*He goes into the lighthouse*].

BRITANNUS [*with genuine feeling*] O Caesar, my great master, if I could but persuade you to regard life seriously, as men do in my country!

CAESAR. Do they truly do so, Britannus?

BRITANNUS. Have you not been there? Have you not seen them? What Briton speaks as you do in your moments of levity? What Briton neglects to attend the services at the sacred grove? What Briton wears clothes of many colors as you do, instead of plain blue, as all solid, well esteemed men should? These are moral questions with us.

CAESAR. Well, well, my friend: some day I shall settle down and

---

[36] Druidism was a religious system that prevailed among the ancient Celts of Gaul and Britain.

have a blue toga, perhaps. Meanwhile, I must get on as best I can in my flippant Roman way. [*Apollodorus comes past the lighthouse*]. What now?

BRITANNUS [*turning quickly, and challenging the stranger with official haughtiness*] What is this? Who are you? How did you come here?

APOLLODORUS. Calm yourself, my friend: I am not going to eat you. I have come by boat, from Alexandria, with precious gifts for Caesar.

CAESAR. From Alexandria!

BRITANNUS [*severely*] That is Caesar, sir.

RUFIO [*appearing at the lighthouse door*] Whats the matter now?

APOLLODORUS. Hail, great Caesar! I am Apollodorus the Sicilian, an artist.

BRITANNUS. An artist! Why have they admitted this vagabond?

CAESAR. Peace, man. Apollodorus is a famous patrician amateur.

BRITANNUS [*disconcerted*] I crave the gentleman's pardon. [To *Caesar*] I understood him to say that he was a professional. [*Somewhat out of countenance, he allows Apollodorus to approach Caesar, changing places with him. Rufio, after looking Apollodorus up and down with marked disparagement, goes to the other side of the platform*].

CAESAR. You are welcome, Apollodorus. What is your business?

APOLLODORUS. First, to deliver to you a present from the Queen of Queens.

CAESAR. Who is that?

APOLLODORUS. Cleopatra of Egypt.

CAESAR [*taking him into his confidence in his most winning manner*] Apollodorus: this is no time for playing with presents. Pray you, go back to the Queen, and tell her that if all goes well I shall return to the palace this evening.

APOLLODORUS. Caesar: I cannot return. As I approached the lighthouse, some fool threw a great leathern bag into the sea. It broke the nose of my boat; and I had hardly time to get myself and my charge to the shore before the poor little cockleshell sank.

CAESAR. I am sorry, Apollodorus. The fool shall be rebuked.

Well, well: what have you brought me? The Queen will be hurt if I do not look at it.

RUFIO. Have we time to waste on this trumpery? The Queen is only a child.

CAESAR. Just so: that is why we must not disappoint her. What is the present, Apollodorus?

APOLLODORUS. Caesar: it is a Persian carpet—a beauty! And in it are—so I am told—pigeons' eggs and crystal goblets and fragile precious things. I dare not for my head have it carried up that narrow ladder from the causeway.

RUFIO. Swing it up by the crane, then. We will send the eggs to the cook; drink our wine from the goblets; and the carpet will make a bed for Caesar.

APOLLODORUS. The crane! Caesar: I have sworn to tender this bale of carpet as I tender my own life.

CAESAR [cheerfully] Then let them swing you up at the same time; and if the chain breaks, you and the pigeons' eggs will perish together. [He goes to the chain and looks up along it, examining it curiously].

APOLLODORUS [to Britannus] Is Caesar serious?

BRITANNUS. His manner is frivolous because he is an Italian; but he means what he says.

APOLLODORUS. Serious or not, he spake well. Give me a squad of soldiers to work the crane.

BRITANNUS. Leave the crane to me. Go and await the descent of the chain.

APOLLODORUS. Good. You will presently see me there [turning to them all and pointing with an eloquent gesture to the sky above the parapet] rising like the sun with my treasure.

He goes back the way he came. Britannus goes into the lighthouse.

RUFIO [ill-humoredly] Are you really going to wait here for this foolery, Caesar?

CAESAR [backing away from the crane as it gives signs of working] Why not?

RUFIO. The Egyptians will let you know why not if they have the sense to make a rush from the shore end of the mole before our

barricade is finished. And here we are waiting like children to
see a carpet full of pigeons' eggs.

*The chain rattles, and is drawn up high enough to clear the
parapet. It then swings round out of sight behind the lighthouse.*

CAESAR. Fear not, my son Rufio. When the first Egyptian takes
his first step along the mole, the alarm will sound; and we two
will reach the barricade from our end before the Egyptians reach
it from their end—we two, Rufio: I, the old man, and you, his
biggest boy. And the old man will be there first. So peace; and
give me some more dates.

APOLLODORUS [*from the causeway below*] Soho, haul away.
So-ho-o-o-o! [*The chain is drawn up and comes round again from
behind the lighthouse. Apollodorus is swinging in the air with his
bale of carpet at the end of it. He breaks into song as he soars
above the parapet*]

> Aloft, aloft, behold the blue
> That never shone in woman's eyes—

Easy there: stop her. [*He ceases to rise*]. Further round! [*The
chain comes forward above the platform*].

RUFIO [*calling up*] Lower away there. [*The chain and its load
begin to descend*].

APOLLODORUS [*calling up*] Gently—slowly—mind the eggs.

RUFIO [*calling up*] Easy there—slowly—slowly.

*Apollodorus and the bale are deposited safely on the flags in
the middle of the platform. Rufio and Caesar help Apollodorus to
cast off the chain from the bale.*

RUFIO. Haul up.

*The chain rises clear of their heads with a rattle. Britannus
comes from the lighthouse and helps them to uncord the carpet.*

APOLLODORUS [*when the cords are loose*] Stand off, my friends:
let Caesar see. [*He throws the carpet open*].

RUFIO. Nothing but a heap of shawls. Where are the pigeons'
eggs?

APOLLODORUS. Approach, Caesar; and search for them among
the shawls.

RUFIO [*drawing his sword*] Ha, treachery! Keep back, Caesar: I saw the shawl move: there is something alive there.

BRITANNUS [*drawing his sword*] It is a serpent.

APOLLODORUS. Dares Caesar thrust his hand into the sack where the serpent moves?

RUFIO [*turning on him*] Treacherous dog—

CAESAR. Peace. Put up your swords. Apollodorus: your serpent seems to breathe very regularly. [*He thrusts his hand under the shawls and draws out a bare arm*]. This is a pretty little snake.

RUFIO [*drawing out the other arm*] Let us have the rest of you.

They pull Cleopatra up by the wrists into a sitting position. Britannus, scandalized, sheathes his sword with a drive of protest.

CLEOPATRA [*gasping*] Oh, I'm smothered. Oh, Caesar, a man stood on me in the boat; and a great sack of something fell upon me out of the sky; and then the boat sank; and then I was swung up into the air and bumped down.

CAESAR [*petting her as she rises and takes refuge on his breast*] Well, never mind: here you are safe and sound at last.

RUFIO. Ay; and now that she is here, what are we to do with her?

BRITANNUS. She cannot stay here, Caesar, without the companionship of some matron.

CLEOPATRA [*jealously, to Caesar, who is obviously perplexed*] Arnt you glad to see me?

CAESAR. Yes, yes; *I* am very glad. But Rufio is very angry; and Britannus is shocked.

CLEOPATRA [*contemptuously*] You can have their heads cut off, can you not?

CAESAR. They would not be so useful with their heads cut off as they are now, my sea bird.

RUFIO [*to Cleopatra*] We shall have to go away presently and cut some of your Egyptians' heads off. How will you like being left here with the chance of being captured by that little brother of yours if we are beaten?

CLEOPATRA. But you mustnt leave me alone. Caesar: you will not leave me alone, will you?

RUFIO. What! not when the trumpet sounds and all our lives

depend on Caesar's being at the barricade before the Egyptians reach it? Eh?

CLEOPATRA. Let them lose their lives: they are only soldiers.

CAESAR [*gravely*] Cleopatra: when that trumpet sounds, we must take every man his life in his hand, and throw it in the face of Death. And of my soldiers who have trusted me there is not one whose hand I shall not hold more sacred than your head. [*Cleopatra is overwhelmed. Her eyes fill with tears*]. Apollodorus: you must take her back to the palace.

APOLLODORUS. Am I a dolphin, Caesar, to cross the seas with young ladies on my back? My boat is sunk: all yours are either at the barricade or have returned to the city. I will hail one if I can: that is all I can do. [*He goes back to the causeway*].

CLEOPATRA [*struggling with her tears*] It does not matter. I will not go back. Nobody cares for me.

CAESAR. Cleopatra—

CLEOPATRA. You want me to be killed.

CAESAR [*still more gravely*] My poor child: your life matters little here to anyone but yourself. [*She gives way altogether at this, casting herself down on the faggots weeping. Suddenly a great tumult is heard in the distance, bucinas and trumpets sounding through a storm of shouting. Britannus rushes to the parapet and looks along the mole. Caesar and Rufio turn to one another with quick intelligence*].

CAESAR. Come, Rufio.

CLEOPATRA [*scrambling to her knees and clinging to him*] No no. Do not leave me, Caesar. [*He snatches his skirt from her clutch*]. Oh!

BRITANNUS [*from the parapet*] Caesar: we are cut off. The Egyptians have landed from the west harbor between us and the barricade!!!

RUFIO [*running to see*] Curses! It is true. We are caught like rats in a trap.

CAESAR [*ruthfully*] Rufio, Rufio: my men at the barricade are between the sea party and the shore party. I have murdered them.

RUFIO [*coming back from the parapet to Caesar's right hand*] Ay: that comes of fooling with this girl here.

APOLLODORUS [*coming up quickly from the causeway*] Look over the parapet, Caesar.

CAESAR. We have looked, my friend. We must defend ourselves here.

APOLLODORUS. I have thrown the ladder into the sea. They cannot get in without it.

RUFIO. Ay; and we cannot get out. Have you thought of that?

APOLLODORUS. Not get out! Why not? You have ships in the east harbor.

BRITANNUS [*hopefully, at the parapet*] The Rhodian galleys are standing in towards us already. [*Caesar quickly joins Britannus at the parapet*].

RUFIO [*to Apollodorus, impatiently*] And by what road are we to walk to the galleys, pray?

APOLLODORUS [*with gay, defiant rhetoric*] By the road that leads everywhere—the diamond path of the sun and moon. Have you never seen the child's shadow play of The Broken Bridge? "Ducks and geese with ease get over"—eh? [*He throws away his cloak and cap, and binds his sword on his back*].

RUFIO. What are you talking about?

APOLLODORUS. I will shew you. [*Calling to Britannus*] How far off is the nearest galley?

BRITANNUS. Fifty fathom.

CAESAR. No, no: they are further off than they seem in this clear air to your British eyes. Nearly quarter of a mile, Apollodorus.

APOLLODORUS. Good. Defend yourselves here until I send you a boat from that galley.

RUFIO. Have you wings, perhaps?

APOLLODORUS. Water wings, soldier. Behold!

He runs up the steps between Caesar and Britannus to the coping of the parapet; springs into the air; and plunges head foremost into the sea.

CAESAR [*like a schoolboy—wildly excited*] Bravo, bravo! [*Throwing off his cloak*] By Jupiter, I will do that too.

RUFIO. [*seizing him*] You are mad. You shall not.

CAESAR. Why not? Can I not swim as well as he?

RUFIO [*frantic*] Can an old fool dive and swim like a young one? He is twenty-five and you are fifty.

CAESAR [*breaking loose from Rufio*] Old!!!

BRITANNUS [*shocked*] Rufio: you forget yourself.

CAESAR. I will race you to the galley for a week's pay, father Rufio.

CLEOPATRA. But me! me!! me!!! what is to become of me?

CAESAR. I will carry you on my back to the galley like a dolphin. Rufio: when you see me rise to the surface, throw her in: I will answer for her. And then in with you after her, both of you.

CLEOPATRA. No, no, NO. I shall be drowned.

BRITANNUS. Caesar: I am a man and a Briton, not a fish. I must have a boat. I cannot swim.

CLEOPATRA. Neither can I.

CAESAR [*to Britannus*] Stay here, then, alone, until I recapture the lighthouse: I will not forget you. Now, Rufio.

RUFIO. You have made up your mind to this folly?

CAESAR. The Egyptians have made it up for me. What else is there to do? And mind where you jump: I do not want to get your fourteen stone in the small of my back as I come up. [*He runs up the steps and stands on the coping*].

BRITANNUS [*anxiously*] One last word, Caesar. Do not let yourself be seen in the fashionable part of Alexandria until you have changed your clothes.

CAESAR [*calling over the sea*] Ho, Apollodorus: [*he points skyward and quotes the barcarolle*]

The white upon the blue above—

APOLLODORUS [*swimming in the distance*]

Is purple on the green below—[37]

CAESAR [*exultantly*] Aha! [*He plunges into the sea*].

CLEOPATRA [*running excitedly to the steps*] Oh, let me see. He will be drowned [*Rufio seizes her*]—Ah—ah—ah—ah! [*He*

---

[37] See the Letter to Hesketh Pearson for Shaw's comments on these lines, p. 191.

pitches her screaming into the sea. Rufio and Britannus roar with laughter].

RUFIO [*looking down after her*] He has got her. [*To Britannus*] Hold the fort, Briton. Caesar will not forget you. [*He springs off*].

BRITANNUS [*running to the steps to watch them as they swim*] All safe, Rufio?

RUFIO [*swimming*] All safe.

CAESAR [*swimming further off*] Take refuge up there by the beacon; and pile the fuel on the trap door, Britannus.

BRITANNUS [*calling in reply*] I will first do so, and then commend myself to my country's gods. [*A sound of cheering from the sea. Britannus gives full vent to his excitement*]. The boat has reached him: Hip, hip, hip, hurrah!

ACT IV

Cleopatra's sousing in the east harbor of Alexandria was in October 48 B.C. In March 47 she is passing the afternoon in her boudoir in the palace, among a bevy of her ladies, listening to a slave girl who is playing the harp in the middle of the room. The harpist's master, an old musician, with a lined face, prominent brows, white beard, moustache and eyebrows twisted and horned at the ends, and a consciously keen and pretentious expression, is squatting on the floor close to her on her right, watching her performance. Ftatateeta is in attendance near the door, in front of a group of female slaves. Except the harp player all are seated: Cleopatra in a chair opposite the door on the other side of the room; the rest on the ground. Cleopatra's ladies are all young, the most conspicuous being Charmian and Iras, her favorites. Charmian is a hatchet faced, terra cotta colored little goblin, swift in her movements, and neatly finished at the hands and feet. Iras is a plump, goodnatured creature, rather fatuous, with a profusion of red hair, and a tendency to giggle on the slightest provocation.

CLEOPATRA. Can I—

FTATATEETA [*insolently, to the player*] Peace, thou! The Queen speaks. [*The player stops*].

CLEOPATRA [*to the old musician*] I want to learn to play the harp with my own hands. Caesar loves music. Can you teach me?

MUSICIAN. Assuredly I and no one else can teach the queen. Have I not discovered the lost method of the ancient Egyptians, who could make a pyramid tremble by touching a bass string? All the other teachers are quacks: I have exposed them repeatedly.

CLEOPATRA. Good: you shall teach me. How long will it take?

MUSICIAN. Not very long: only four years. Your Majesty must first become proficient in the philosophy of Pythagoras.[38]

---

[38] Music, Pythagoras felt, should be examined intellectually, that is, by the rules of harmonic proportion; it should not be submitted to the senses for one's emotional pleasure or amusement.

CLEOPATRA. Has she [*indicating the slave*] become proficient in the philosophy of Pythagoras?

MUSICIAN. Oh, she is but a slave. She learns as a dog learns.

CLEOPATRA. Well, then, I will learn as a dog learns; for she plays better than you. You shall give me a lesson every day for a fortnight. [*The musician hastily scrambles to his feet and bows profoundly*]. After that, whenever I strike a false note you shall be flogged; and if I strike so many that there is not time to flog you, you shall be thrown into the Nile to feed the crocodiles. Give the girl a piece of gold; and send them away.

MUSICIAN [*much taken aback*] But true art will not be thus forced.

FTATATEETA [*pushing him out*] What is this? Answering the Queen, forsooth. Out with you.

He is pushed out by Ftatateeta, the girl following with her harp, amid the laughter of the ladies and slaves.

CLEOPATRA. Now, can any of you amuse me? Have you any stories or any news?

IRAS. Ftatateeta—

CLEOPATRA. Oh, Ftatateeta, Ftatateeta, always Ftatateeta. Some new tale to set me against her.

IRAS. No: this time Ftatateeta has been virtuous. [*All the ladies laugh—not the slaves*]. Pothinus has been trying to bribe her to let him speak with you.

CLEOPATRA [*wrathfully*] Ha! you all sell audiences with me, as if I saw whom you please, and not whom I please. I should like to know how much of her gold piece that harp girl will have to give up before she leaves the palace.

IRAS. We can easily find out that for you.

The ladies laugh.

CLEOPATRA [*frowning*] You laugh; but take care, take care. I will find out some day how to make myself served as Caesar is served.

CHARMIAN. Old hooknose! [*They laugh again*].

CLEOPATRA [*revolted*] Silence. Charmian: do not you be a silly little Egyptian fool. Do you know why I allow you all to chatter impertinently just as you please, instead of treating you as Ftatateeta would treat you if she were Queen?

CHARMIAN. Because you try to imitate Caesar in everything; and he lets everybody say what they please to him.

CLEOPATRA. No; but because I asked him one day why he did so; and he said "Let your women talk; and you will learn something from them." What have I to learn from them? I said. "What they are," said he; and oh! you should have seen his eye as he said it. You would have curled up, you shallow things. [*They laugh. She turns fiercely on Iras*]. At whom are you laughing—at me or at Caesar?

IRAS. At Caesar.

CLEOPATRA. If you were not a fool, you would laugh at me; and if you were not a coward you would not be afraid to tell me so. [*Ftatateeta returns*]. Ftatateeta: they tell me that Pothinus has offered you a bribe to admit him to my presence.

FTATATEETA [*protesting*] Now by my father's gods—

CLEOPATRA [*cutting her short despotically*] Have I not told you not to deny things? You would spend the day calling your father's gods to witness to your virtues if I let you. Go take the bribe; and bring in Pothinus. [*Ftatateeta is about to reply*]. Dont answer me. Go.

Ftatateeta goes out; and Cleopatra rises and begins to prowl to and fro between her chair and the door, meditating. All rise and stand.

IRAS [*as she reluctantly rises*] Heigho! I wish Caesar were back in Rome.

CLEOPATRA [*threateningly*] It will be a bad day for you all when he goes. Oh, if I were not ashamed to let him see that I am as cruel at heart as my father, I would make you repent that speech! Why do you wish him away?

CHARMIAN. He makes you so terribly prosy and serious and learned and philosophical. It is worse than being religious, at our ages. [*The ladies laugh*].

CLEOPATRA. Cease that endless cackling, will you. Hold your tongues.

CHARMIAN [*with mock resignation*] Well, well: we must try to live up to Caesar.

They laugh again. Cleopatra rages silently as she continues to prowl to and fro. Ftatateeta comes back with Pothinus, who halts on the threshold.

FTATATEETA [*at the door*] Pothinus craves the ear of the—

CLEOPATRA. There, there: that will do: let him come in. [*She resumes her seat. All sit down except Pothinus, who advances to the middle of the room. Ftatateeta takes her former place*]. Well, Pothinus: what is the latest news from your rebel friends?

POTHINUS [*haughtily*] I am no friend of rebellion. And a prisoner does not receive news.

CLEOPATRA. You are no more a prisoner than I am—than Caesar is. These six months we have been besieged in this palace by my subjects. You are allowed to walk on the beach among the soldiers. Can I go further myself, or can Caesar?

POTHINUS. You are but a child, Cleopatra, and do not understand these matters.

The ladies laugh. Cleopatra looks inscrutably at him.

CHARMIAN. I see you do not know the latest news, Pothinus.

POTHINUS. What is that?

CHARMIAN. That Cleopatra is no longer a child. Shall I tell you how to grow much older, and much, much wiser in one day?

POTHINUS. I should prefer to grow wiser without growing older.

CHARMIAN. Well, go up to the top of the lighthouse; and get somebody to take you by the hair and throw you into the sea. [*The ladies laugh*].

CLEOPATRA. She is right, Pothinus: you will come to the shore with much conceit washed out of you. [*The ladies laugh. Cleopatra rises impatiently*]. Begone, all of you. I will speak with Pothinus alone. Drive them out, Ftatateeta. [*They run out laughing. Ftatateeta shuts the door on them*]. What are you waiting for?

FTATATEETA. It is not meet that the Queen remain alone with—

CLEOPATRA [*interrupting her*] Ftatateeta: must I sacrifice you to your father's gods to teach you that *I* am Queen of Egypt, and not you?

FTATATEETA [*indignantly*] You are like the rest of them. You want to be what these Romans call a New Woman.[39] [*She goes out, banging the door*].

CLEOPATRA [*sitting down again*] Now, Pothinus: why did you bribe Ftatateeta to bring you hither?

POTHINUS [*studying her gravely*] Cleopatra: what they tell me is true. You are changed.

CLEOPATRA. Do you speak with Caesar every day for six months: and you will be changed.

POTHINUS. It is the common talk that you are infatuated with this old man?

CLEOPATRA. Infatuated? What does that mean? Made foolish, is it not? Oh no: I wish I were.

POTHINUS. You wish you were made foolish! How so?

CLEOPATRA. When I was foolish, I did what I liked, except when Ftatateeta beat me; and even then I cheated her and did it by stealth. Now that Caesar has made me wise, it is no use my liking or disliking: I do what must be done, and have no time to attend to myself. That is not happiness; but it is greatness. If Caesar were gone, I think I could govern the Egyptians; for what Caesar is to me, I am to the fools around me.

POTHINUS [*looking hard at her*] Cleopatra: this may be the vanity of youth.

CLEOPATRA. No, no: it is not that I am so clever, but that the others are so stupid.

POTHINUS [*musingly*] Truly, that is the great secret.

CLEOPATRA. Well, now tell me what you came to say?

POTHINUS [*embarrassed*] I! Nothing.

CLEOPATRA. Nothing!

POTHINUS. At least—to beg for my liberty: that is all.

---

[39] At the turn of the century much discussion centered on the "New Woman," who challenged the belief that a woman's place is in the home. Ibsen, the Norwegian playwright, dramatized this theme in *A Doll's House*.

CLEOPATRA. For that you would have knelt to Caesar. No, Pothinus: you came with some plan that depended on Cleopatra being a little nursery kitten. Now that Cleopatra is a Queen, the plan is upset.

POTHINUS [*bowing his head submissively*] It is so.

CLEOPATRA [*exultant*] Aha!

POTHINUS [*raising his eyes keenly to hers*] Is Cleopatra then indeed a Queen, and no longer Caesar's prisoner and slave?

CLEOPATRA. Pothinus: we are all Caesar's slaves—all we in this land of Egypt—whether we will or no. And she who is wise enough to know this will reign when Caesar departs.

POTHINUS. You harp on Caesar's departure.

CLEOPATRA. What if I do?

POTHINUS. Does he not love you?

CLEOPATRA. Love me! Pothinus: Caesar loves no one. Who are those we love. Only those whom we do not hate: all people are strangers and enemies to us except those we love. But it is not so with Caesar. He has no hatred in him: he makes friends with everyone as he does with dogs and children. His kindness to me is a wonder: neither mother, father, nor nurse have ever taken so much care for me, or thrown open their thoughts to me so freely.

POTHINUS. Well: is not this love?

CLEOPATRA. What! when he will do as much for the first girl he meets on his way back to Rome? Ask his slave, Britannus: he has been just as good to him. Nay, ask his very horse! His kindness is not for anything in me: it is in his own nature.

POTHINUS. But how can you be sure that he does not love you as men love women?

CLEOPATRA. Because I cannot make him jealous. I have tried.

POTHINUS. Hm! Perhaps I should have asked, then, do you love him?

CLEOPATRA. Can one love a god? Besides, I love another Roman: one whom I saw long before Caesar—no god, but a man—one who can love and hate—one whom I can hurt and who would hurt me.

POTHINUS. Does Caesar know this?

CLEOPATRA. Yes.

POTHINUS. And he is not angry?

CLEOPATRA. He promises to send him to Egypt to please me!

POTHINUS. I do not understand this man.

CLEOPATRA [*with superb contempt*] You understand Caesar! How could you? [*Proudly*] I do—by instinct.

POTHINUS [*deferentially, after a moment's thought*] Your Majesty caused me to be admitted today. What message has the Queen for me?

CLEOPATRA. This. You think that by making my brother king, you will rule in Egypt, because you are his guardian and he is a little silly.

POTHINUS. The Queen is pleased to say so.

CLEOPATRA. The Queen is pleased to say this also. That Caesar will eat up you, and Achillas, and my brother, as a cat eats up mice; and that he will put on this land of Egypt as a shepherd puts on his garment. And when he has done that, he will return to Rome, and leave Cleopatra here as his viceroy.

POTHINUS [*breaking out wrathfully*] That he shall never do. We have a thousand men to his ten; and we will drive him and his beggarly legions into the sea.

CLEOPATRA [*with scorn, getting up to go*] You rant like any common fellow. Go, then, and marshal your thousands; and make haste; for Mithridates of Pergamos[40] is at hand with reinforcements for Caesar. Caesar has held you at bay with two legions: we shall see what he will do with twenty.

POTHINUS. Cleopatra—

CLEOPATRA. Enough, enough: Caesar has spoiled me for talking to weak things like you. [*She goes out. Pothinus, with a gesture of rage, is following, when Ftatateeta enters and stops him*].

POTHINUS. Let me go forth from this hateful place.

FTATATEETA. What angers you?

---

[40] Mithridates of Pergamos, a reputed son of the great Mithridates, marched through Syria, took Pelusium, and joined Caesar to defeat the Egyptians at the Battle of the Nile, March 47 B.C.

POTHINUS. The curse of all the gods of Egypt be upon her! She has sold her country to the Roman, that she may buy it back from him with her kisses.

FTATATEETA. Fool: did she not tell you that she would have Caesar gone?

POTHINUS. You listened?

FTATATEETA. I took care that some honest woman should be at hand whilst you were with her.

POTHINUS. Now by the gods—

FTATATEETA. Enough of your gods! Caesar's gods are all powerful here. It is no use you coming to Cleopatra: you are only an Egyptian. She will not listen to any of her own race: she treats us all as children.

POTHINUS. May she perish for it!

FTATATEETA [*balefully*] May your tongue wither for that wish! Go! send for Lucius Septimius, the slayer of Pompey. He is a Roman: may be she will listen to him. Begone!

POTHINUS [*darkly*] I know to whom I must go now.

FTATATEETA [*suspiciously*] To whom, then?

POTHINUS. To a greater Roman than Lucius. And mark this, mistress. You thought, before Caesar came, that Egypt should presently be ruled by you and your crew in the name of Cleopatra. I set myself against it—

FTATATEETA [*interrupting him—wrangling*] Ay; that it might be ruled by you and your crew in the name of Ptolemy.

POTHINUS. Better me, or even you, than a woman with a Roman heart; and that is what Cleopatra is now become. Whilst I live, she shall never rule. So guide yourself accordingly. [*He goes out*].

It is by this time drawing on to dinner time. The table is laid on the roof of the palace; and thither Rufio is now climbing, ushered by a majestic palace official, wand of office in hand, and followed by a slave carrying an inlaid stool. After many stairs they emerge at last into a massive colonnade on the roof. Light curtains are drawn between the columns on the north and east to soften the westering sun. The official leads Rufio to one of these shaded sections. A cord for pulling the curtains apart hangs down between the pillars.

THE OFFICIAL [*bowing*] The Roman commander will await Caesar here.

The slave sets down the stool near the southernmost column, and slips out through the curtains.

RUFIO [*sitting down, a little blown*] Pouf! That was a climb. How high have we come?

THE OFFICIAL. We are on the palace roof, O Beloved of Victory!

RUFIO. Good! the Beloved of Victory has no more stairs to get up.

A second official enters from the opposite end, walking backwards.

THE SECOND OFFICIAL. Caesar approaches.

Caesar, fresh from the bath, clad in a new tunic of purple silk, comes in, beaming and festive, followed by two slaves carrying a light couch, which is hardly more than an elaborately designed bench. They place it near the northmost of the two curtained columns. When this is done they slip out through the curtains; and the two officials, formally bowing, follow them. Rufio rises to receive Caesar.

CAESAR [*coming over to him*] Why, Rufio! [*Surveying his dress with an air of admiring astonishment*] A new baldrick! A new golden pommel to your sword! And you have had your hair cut! But not your beard—? impossible! [*He sniffs at Rufio's beard*]. Yes, perfumed, by Jupiter Olympus!

RUFIO [*growling*] Well: is it to please myself?

CAESAR [*affectionately*] No, my son Rufio, but to please me—to celebrate my birthday.

RUFIO [*contemptuously*] Your birthday! You always have a birthday when there is a pretty girl to be flattered or an ambassador to be conciliated. We had seven of them in ten months last year.

CAESAR [*contritely*] It is true, Rufio! I shall never break myself of these petty deceits.

RUFIO. Who is to dine with us—besides Cleopatra?

CAESAR. Apollodorus the Sicilian.

RUFIO. That popinjay!

CAESAR. Come! the popinjay is an amusing dog—tells a story; sings a song; and saves us the trouble of flattering the Queen. What does she care for old politicians and camp-fed bears like us? No: Apollodorus is good company, Rufio, good company.

RUFIO. Well, he can swim a bit and fence a bit: he might be worse, if he only knew how to hold his tongue.

CAESAR. The gods forbid he should ever learn! Oh, this military life! this tedious, brutal life of action! That is the worst of us Romans: we are mere doers and drudgers: a swarm of bees turned into men. Give me a good talker—one with wit and imagination enough to live without continually doing something!

RUFIO. Ay! a nice time he would have of it with you when dinner was over! Have you noticed that I am before my time?

CAESAR. Aha! I thought that meant something. What is it?

RUFIO. Can we be overheard here?

CAESAR. Our privacy invites eavesdropping. I can remedy that. [He claps his hands twice. The curtains are drawn, revealing the roof garden with a banqueting table set across in the middle for four persons, one at each end, and two side by side. The side next Caesar and Rufio is blocked with golden wine vessels and basins. A gorgeous major-domo is superintending the laying of the table by a staff of slaves. The colonnade goes round the garden at both sides to the further end, where a gap in it, like a great gateway, leaves the view open to the sky beyond the western edge of the roof, except in the middle, where a life size image of Ra, seated on a huge plinth, towers up, with hawk head and crown of asp and disk. His altar, which stands at his feet, is a single white stone]. Now everybody can see us, nobody will think of listening to us. [He sits down on the bench left by the two slaves].

RUFIO [sitting down on his stool] Pothinus wants to speak to you. I advise you to see him: there is some plotting going on here among the women.

CAESAR. Who is Pothinus?

RUFIO. The fellow with hair like squirrel's fur—the little King's bear leader, whom you kept prisoner.

CAESAR [*annoyed*] And has he not escaped?

RUFIO. No.

CAESAR [*rising imperiously*] Why not? You have been guarding this man instead of watching the enemy. Have I not told you always to let prisoners escape unless there are special orders to the contrary? Are there not enough mouths to be fed without him?

RUFIO. Yes; and if you would have a little sense and let me cut his throat, you would save his rations. Anyhow, he wont escape. Three sentries have told him they would put a pilum through him if they saw him again. What more can they do? He prefers to stay and spy on us. So would I if I had to do with generals subject to fits of clemency.

CAESAR [*resuming his seat, argued down*] Hm! And so he wants to see me.

RUFIO. Ay. I have brought him with me. He is waiting there [*jerking his thumb over his shoulder*] under guard.

CAESAR. And you want me to see him?

RUFIO [*obstinately*] I dont want anything. I daresay you will do what you like. Dont put it on to me.

CAESAR [*with an air of doing it expressly to indulge Rufio*] Well, well: let us have him.

RUFIO [*calling*] Ho there, guard! Release your man and send him up. [*Beckoning*]. Come along!

Pothinus enters and stops mistrustfully between the two, looking from one to the other.

CAESAR [*graciously*] Ah, Pothinus! You are welcome. And what is the news this afternoon?

POTHINUS. Caesar: I come to warn you of a danger, and to make you an offer.

CAESAR. Never mind the danger. Make the offer.

RUFIO. Never mind the offer. Whats the danger?

POTHINUS. Caesar: you think that Cleopatra is devoted to you.

CAESAR [*gravely*] My friend: I already know what I think. Come to your offer.

POTHINUS. I will deal plainly. I know not by what strange gods you have been enabled to defend a palace and a few yards of beach against a city and an army. Since we cut you off from Lake Mareotis, and you dug wells in the salt sea sand and brought up buckets of fresh water from them, we have known that your gods are irresistible, and that you are a worker of miracles. I no longer threaten you—

RUFIO [*sarcastically*] Very handsome of you, indeed.

POTHINUS. So be it: you are the master. Our gods sent the north west winds[41] to keep you in our hands; but you have been too strong for them.

CAESAR [*gently urging him to come to the point*] Yes, yes, my friend. But what then?

RUFIO. Spit it out, man. What have you to say?

POTHINUS. I have to say that you have a traitress in your camp. Cleopatra—

THE MAJOR-DOMO [*at the table, announcing*] The Queen! [*Caesar and Rufio rise*].

RUFIO [*aside to Pothinus*] You should have spat it out sooner, you fool. Now it is too late.

Cleopatra, in gorgeous raiment, enters in state through the gap in the colonnade, and comes down past the image of Ra and past the table to Caesar. Her retinue, headed by Ftatateeta, joins the staff at the table. Caesar gives Cleopatra his seat, which she takes.

CLEOPATRA [*quickly, seeing Pothinus*] What is he doing here?

CAESAR [*seating himself beside her, in the most amiable of tempers*] Just going to tell me something about you. You shall hear it. Proceed, Pothinus.

POTHINUS [*disconcerted*] Caesar—[*he stammers*].

CAESAR. Well, out with it.

POTHINUS. What I have to say is for your ear, not for the Queen's.

---

[41] Mommsen and others argue that the northwest winds made it impossible for Caesar to set sail for Rome and that he thus became embroiled in the politics of Egypt.

CLEOPATRA [*with subdued ferocity*] There are means of making you speak. Take care.

POTHINUS [*defiantly*] Caesar does not employ those means.

CAESAR. My friend: when a man has anything to tell in this world, the difficulty is not to make him tell it, but to prevent him from telling it too often. Let me celebrate my birthday by setting you free. Farewell: we shall not meet again.

CLEOPATRA [*angrily*] Caesar: this mercy is foolish.

POTHINUS [*to Caesar*] Will you not give me a private audience? Your life may depend on it. [*Caesar rises loftily*].

RUFIO [*aside to Pothinus*] Ass! Now we shall have some heroics.

CAESAR [*oratorically*] Pothinus—

RUFIO [*interrupting him*] Caesar: the dinner will spoil if you begin preaching your favorite sermon about life and death.

CLEOPATRA [*priggishly*] Peace, Rufio. I desire to hear Caesar.

RUFIO [*bluntly*] Your Majesty has heard it before. You repeated it to Apollodorus last week; and he thought it was all your own. [*Caesar's dignity collapses. Much tickled, he sits down again and looks roguishly at Cleopatra, who is furious. Rufio calls as before*] Ho there, guard! Pass the prisoner out. He is released. [*To Pothinus*] Now off with you. You have lost your chance.

POTHINUS [*his temper overcoming his prudence*] I will speak.

CAESAR [*to Cleopatra*] You see. Torture would not have wrung a word from him.

POTHINUS. Caesar: you have taught Cleopatra the arts by which the Romans govern the world.

CAESAR. Alas! they cannot even govern themselves. What then?

POTHINUS. What then? Are you so besotted with her beauty that you do not see that she is impatient to reign in Egypt alone, and that her heart is set on your departure?

CLEOPATRA [*rising*] Liar!

CAESAR [*shocked*] What! Protestations! Contradictions!

CLEOPATRA [*ashamed, but trembling with suppressed rage*] No. I do not deign to contradict. Let him talk. [*She sits down again*].

POTHINUS. From her own lips I have heard it. You are to be

her catspaw: you are to tear the crown from her brother's head and set it on her own, delivering us all into her hand—delivering yourself also. And then Caesar can return to Rome, or depart through the gate of death, which is nearer and surer.

CAESAR [*calmly*] Well, my friend; and is not this very natural?

POTHINUS [*astonished*] Natural! Then you do not resent treachery?

CAESAR. Resent! O thou foolish Egyptian, what have I to do with resentment? Do I resent the wind when it chills me, or the night when it makes me stumble in the darkness? Shall I resent youth when it turns from age, and ambition when it turns from servitude? To tell me such a story as this is but to tell me that the sun will rise tomorrow.

CLEOPATRA [*unable to contain herself*] But it is false—false. I swear it.

CAESAR. It is true, though you swore it a thousand times, and believed all you swore. [*She is convulsed with emotion. To screen her, he rises and takes Pothinus to Rufio, saying*] Come, Rufio: let us see Pothinus past the guard. I have a word to say to him. [*Aside to them*] We must give the Queen a moment to recover herself. [*Aloud*] Come. [*He takes Pothinus and Rufio out with him, conversing with them meanwhile*]. Tell your friends, Pothinus, that they must not think I am opposed to a reasonable settlement of the country's affairs—[*They pass out of hearing*].

CLEOPATRA [*in a stifled whisper*] Ftatateeta, Ftatateeta.

FTATATEETA [*hurrying to her from the table and petting her*] Peace, child: be comforted—

CLEOPATRA [*interrupting her*] Can they hear us?

FTATATEETA. No, dear heart, no.

CLEOPATRA. Listen to me. If he leaves the Palace alive, never see my face again.

FTATATEETA. He? Poth—

CLEOPATRA [*striking her on the mouth*] Strike his life out as I strike his name from your lips. Dash him down from the wall. Break him on the stones. Kill, kill, kill him.

FTATATEETA [*shewing all her teeth*] The dog shall perish.

CLEOPATRA. Fail in this, and you go out from before me for ever.

FTATATEETA [*resolutely*] So be it. You shall not see my face until his eyes are darkened.

Caesar comes back, with Apollodorus, exquisitely dressed, and Rufio.

CLEOPATRA [*to Ftatateeta*] Come soon—soon. [*Ftatateeta turns her meaning eyes for a moment on her mistress; then goes grimly away past Ra and out. Cleopatra runs like a gazelle to Caesar*]. So you have come back to me, Caesar. [*Caressingly*] I thought you were angry. Welcome, Apollodorus. [*She gives him her hand to kiss, with her other arm about Caesar*].

APOLLODORUS. Cleopatra grows more womanly beautiful from week to week.

CLEOPATRA. Truth, Apollodorus?

APOLLODORUS. Far, far short of the truth! Friend Rufio threw a pearl into the sea: Caesar fished up a diamond.

CAESAR. Caesar fished up a touch of rheumatism, my friend. Come: to dinner! to dinner! [*They move towards the table*].

CLEOPATRA [*skipping like a young fawn*] Yes, to dinner. I have ordered such a dinner for you, Caesar!

CAESAR. Ay? What are we to have?

CLEOPATRA. Peacocks' brains.

CAESAR [*as if his mouth watered*] Peacocks' brains, Apollodorus!

APOLLODORUS. Not for me. I prefer nightingales' tongues. [*He goes to one of the two covers set side by side*].

CLEOPATRA. Roast boar, Rufio!

RUFIO [*gluttonously*] Good! [*He goes to the seat next Apollodorus, on his left*].

CAESAR [*looking at his seat, which is at the end of the table, to Ra's left hand*] What has become of my leathern cushion?

CLEOPATRA [*at the opposite end*] I have got new ones for you.

THE MAJOR-DOMO. These cushions, Caesar, are of Maltese gauze, stuffed with rose leaves.

CAESAR. Rose leaves! Am I a caterpillar? [*He throws the cushions away and seats himself on the leather mattress underneath*].

CLEOPATRA. What a shame! My new cushions!

THE MAJOR-DOMO [*at Caesar's elbow*] What shall we serve to whet Caesar's appetite?

CAESAR. What have you got?

THE MAJOR-DOMO. Sea hedgehogs, black and white sea acorns, sea nettles, beccaficoes, purple shellfish—[42]

CAESAR. Any oysters?

THE MAJOR-DOMO. Assuredly.

CAESAR. British oysters?

THE MAJOR-DOMO [*assenting*] British oysters, Caesar.[43]

CAESAR. Oysters, then. [*The Major-Domo signs to a slave at each order; and the slave goes out to execute it*]. I have been in Britain—that western land of romance—the last piece of earth on the edge of the ocean that surrounds the world. I went there in search of its famous pearls. The British pearl was a fable; but in searching for it I found the British oyster.

APOLLODORUS. All posterity will bless you for it. [*To the Major-Domo*] Sea hedgehogs for me.

RUFIO. Is there nothing solid to begin with?

THE MAJOR-DOMO. Fieldfares with asparagus—

CLEOPATRA [*interrupting*] Fattened fowls! have some fattened fowls, Rufio.

RUFIO. Ay, that will do.

CLEOPATRA [*greedily*] Fieldfares for me.

---

[42] The menu here described is strikingly similar to the bill of fare of the banquet which Mucius Lentulus Niger gave in 63 B.C. before entering on his pontificate. Caesar was present at this banquet. Mommsen refers to this menu in his *History of Rome*.

[43] St. George Stock in his Introduction to *Caesar's Gallic Wars* comments upon Suetonius' charge that pearls had been the lure that prompted Caesar's invasion of Britain as follows: "But if the Romans were disappointed in the pearls of Britain, they were compensated by the excellence of the mollusc that produced them. The oysters of Britain became famous under the Empire, and were held to surpass in flavour even those of the Lucrine Lake."

THE MAJOR-DOMO. Caesar. will deign to choose his wine? Sicilian, Lesbian, Chian—

RUFIO [*contemptuously*] All Greek.

APOLLODORUS. Who would drink Roman wine when he could get Greek. Try the Lesbian, Caesar.

CAESAR. Bring me my barley water.

RUFIO [*with intense disgust*] Ugh! Bring me my Falernian. [*The Falernian is presently brought to him*].

CLEOPATRA [*pouting*] It is waste of time giving you dinners, Caesar. My scullions would not condescend to your diet.

CAESAR [*relenting*] Well, well: let us try the Lesbian. [*The Major-Domo fills Caesar's goblet; then Cleopatra's and Apollodorus's*]. But when I return to Rome, I will make laws against these extravagances. I will even get the laws carried out.

CLEOPATRA [*coaxingly*] Never mind. Today you are to be like other people: idle, luxurious, and kind. [*She stretches her hand to him along the table*].

CAESAR. Well, for once I will sacrifice my comfort—[*kissing her hand*] there! [*He takes a draught of wine*]. Now are you satisfied?

CLEOPATRA. And you no longer believe that I long for your departure for Rome?

CAESAR. I no longer believe anything. My brains are asleep. Besides, who knows whether I shall return to Rome?

RUFIO [*alarmed*] How? Eh? What?

CAESAR. What has Rome to shew me that I have not seen already? One year of Rome is like another, except that I grow older, whilst the crowd in the Appian Way[44] is always the same age.

APOLLODORUS. It is no better here in Egypt. The old men, when they are tired of life, say "We have seen everything except the source of the Nile."[45]

---

[44] The Appian Way, built in 312 B.C., was the chief road from Rome to Greece and the East.

[45] Herodotus had speculated on the source of the Nile in classical times. It was not until 1858, however, that John Speke discovered Lake Victoria,

CAESAR [*his imagination catching fire*] And why not see that? Cleopatra: will you come with me and track the flood to its cradle in the heart of the regions of mystery? Shall we leave Rome behind us—Rome, that has achieved greatness only to learn how greatness destroys nations of men who are not great! Shall I make you a new kingdom, and build you a holy city there in the great unknown?

CLEOPATRA [*rapturously*] Yes, yes. You shall.

RUFIO. Ay: now he will conquer Africa with two legions before we come to the roast boar.

APOLLODORUS. Come: no scoffing. This is a noble scheme: in it Caesar is no longer merely the conquering soldier, but the creative poet-artist. Let us name the holy city, and consecrate it with Lesbian wine.

CAESAR. Cleopatra shall name it herself.

CLEOPATRA. It shall be called Caesar's Gift to his Beloved.

APOLLODORUS. No, no. Something vaster than that—something universal, like the starry firmament.

CAESAR [*prosaically*] Why not simply The Cradle of the Nile?

CLEOPATRA. No: the Nile is my ancestor; and he is a god. Oh! I have thought of something. The Nile shall name it himself. Let us call upon him. [*To the Major-Domo*] Send for him. [*The three men stare at one another; but the Major-Domo goes out as if he had received the most matter-of-fact order*]. And [*to the retinue*] away with you all.

The retinue withdraws, making obeisance.

A priest enters, carrying a miniature sphinx with a tiny tripod before it. A morsel of incense is smoking in the tripod. The priest comes to the table and places the image in the middle of it. The light begins to change to the magenta purple of the Egyptian sunset, as if the god had brought a strange colored shadow with him.

---

the source of the White Nile. Whether Cleopatra actually sailed up the Nile in 47 B.C. is a moot question with historians. Some ancient writers mention a projected expedition.

The three men are determined not to be impressed; but they feel curious in spite of themselves.

CAESAR. What hocus-pocus is this?

CLEOPATRA. You shall see. And it is not hocus-pocus. To do it properly, we should kill something to please him; but perhaps he will answer Caesar without that if we spill some wine to him.

APOLLODORUS [*turning his head to look up over his shoulder at Ra*] Why not appeal to our hawkheaded friend here?

CLEOPATRA [*nervously*] Sh! He will hear you and be angry.

RUFIO [*phlegmatically*] The source of the Nile is out of his district, I expect.

CLEOPATRA. No: I will have my city named by nobody but my dear little sphinx, because it was in its arms that Caesar found me asleep. [*She languishes at Caesar then turns curtly to the priest*]. Go. I am a priestess, and have power to take your charge from you. [*The priest makes a reverence and goes out*]. Now let us call on the Nile all together. Perhaps he will rap on the table.

CAESAR. What! table rapping! Are such superstitions still believed in this year 707 of the Republic?

CLEOPATRA. It is no superstition: our priests learn lots of things from the tables. Is it not so, Apollodorus?

APOLLODORUS. Yes: I profess myself a converted man. When Cleopatra is priestess, Apollodorus is devotee. Propose the conjuration.

CLEOPATRA. You must say with me "Send us thy voice, Father Nile."

ALL FOUR [*holding their glasses together before the idol*] Send us thy voice, Father Nile.

The death cry of a man in mortal terror and agony answers them. Appalled, the men set down their glasses, and listen. Silence. The purple deepens in the sky. Caesar, glancing at Cleopatra, catches her pouring out her wine before the god, with gleaming eyes, and mute assurances of gratitude and worship. Apollodorus springs up and runs to the edge of the roof to peer down and listen.

CAESAR [*looking piercingly at Cleopatra*] What was that?

CLEOPATRA [*petulantly*] Nothing. They are beating some slave.

CAESAR. Nothing.

RUFIO. A man with a knife in him, I'll swear.

CAESAR [*rising*] A murder!

APOLLODORUS [*at the back, waving his hand for silence*] S-sh! Silence. Did you hear that?

CAESAR. Another cry?

APOLLODORUS [*returning to the table*] No, a thud. Something fell on the beach, I think.

RUFIO [*grimly, as he rises*] Something with bones in it, eh?

CAESAR [*shuddering*] Hush, hush, Rufio. [*He leaves the table and returns to the colonnade: Rufio following at his left elbow, and Apollodorus at the other side*].

CLEOPATRA [*still in her place at the table*] Will you leave me, Caesar? Apollodorus: are you going?

APOLLODORUS. Faith, dearest Queen, my appetite is gone.

CAESAR. Go down to the courtyard, Apollodorus; and find out what has happened.

Apollodorus nods and goes out, making for the staircase by which Rufio ascended.

CLEOPATRA. Your soldiers have killed somebody, perhaps. What does it matter?

The murmur of a crowd rises from the beach below. Caesar and Rufio look at one another.

CAESAR. This must be seen to. [*He is about to follow Apollodorus when Rufio stops him with a hand on his arm as Ftatateeta comes back by the far end of the roof, with dragging steps, a drowsy satiety in her eyes and in the corners of the bloodhound lips. For a moment Caesar suspects that she is drunk with wine. Not so Rufio: he knows well the red vintage that has inebriated her*].

RUFIO [*in a low tone*] There is some mischief between those two.

FTATATEETA. The Queen looks again on the face of her servant.

Cleopatra looks at her for a moment with an exultant reflection of her murderous expression. Then she flings her arms round her; kisses her repeatedly and savagely; and tears off her jewels and heaps them on her. The two men turn from the spectacle to look at one another. Ftatateeta drags herself sleepily to the altar; kneels before Ra; and remains there in prayer. Caesar goes to Cleopatra, leaving Rufio in the colonnade.

CAESAR [*with searching earnestness*] Cleopatra: what has happened?

CLEOPATRA [*in mortal dread of him, but with her utmost cajolery*] Nothing, dearest Caesar. [*With sickly sweetness, her voice almost failing*] Nothing. I am innocent. [*She approaches him affectionately*]. Dear Caesar: are you angry with me? Why do you look at me so? I have been here with you all the time. How can I know what has happened?

CAESAR [*reflectively*] That is true.

CLEOPATRA [*greatly relieved, trying to caress him*] Of course it is true. [*He does not respond to the caress*]. You know it is true, Rufio.

The murmur without suddenly swells to a roar and subsides.

RUFIO. I shall know presently. [*He makes for the altar in the burly trot that serves him for a stride, and touches Ftatateeta on the shoulder*]. Now, mistress: I shall want you. [*He orders her, with a gesture, to go before him*].

FTATATEETA [*rising and glowering at him*] My place is with the Queen.

CLEOPATRA. She has done no harm, Rufio.

CAESAR [*to Rufio*] Let her stay.

RUFIO [*sitting down on the altar*] Very well. Then my place is here too; and you can see what is the matter for yourself. The city is in a pretty uproar, it seems.

CAESAR [*with grave displeasure*] Rufio: there is a time for obedience.

RUFIO. And there is a time for obstinacy. [*He folds his arms doggedly*].

CAESAR [*to Cleopatra*] Send her away.

CLEOPATRA [*whining in her eagerness to propitiate him*] Yes, I will. I will do whatever you ask me, Caesar, always, because I love you. Ftatateeta: go away.

FTATATEETA. The Queen's word is my will. I shall be at hand for the Queen's call. [*She goes out past Ra, as she came*].

RUFIO [*following her*] Remember, Caesar, your bodyguard also is within call. [*He follows her out*].

Cleopatra, presuming upon Caesar's submission to Rufio, leaves the table and sits down on the bench in the colonnade.

CLEOPATRA. Why do you allow Rufio to treat you so? You should teach him his place.

CAESAR. Teach him to be my enemy, and to hide his thoughts from me as you are now hiding yours.

CLEOPATRA [*her fears returning*] Why do you say that, Caesar? Indeed, indeed, I am not hiding anything. You are wrong to treat me like this. [*She stifles a sob*]. I am only a child; and you turn into stone because you think some one has been killed. I cannot bear it. [*She purposely breaks down and weeps. He looks at her with profound sadness and complete coldness. She looks up to see what effect she is producing. Seeing that he is unmoved, she sits up, pretending to struggle with her emotion and to put it bravely away*]. But there: I know you hate tears: you shall not be troubled with them. I know you are not angry, but only sad; only I am so silly, I cannot help being hurt when you speak coldly. Of course you are quite right: it is dreadful to think of anyone being killed or even hurt; and I hope nothing really serious has—[*her voice dies away under his contemptuous penetration*].

CAESAR. What has frightened you into this? What have you done? [*A trumpet sounds on the beach below*]. Aha! that sounds like the answer.

CLEOPATRA [*sinking back trembling on the bench and covering her face with her hands*] I have not betrayed you, Caesar: I swear it.

CAESAR. I know that. I have not trusted you. [*He turns from her, and is about to go out when Apollodorus and Britannus drag in Lucius Septimius to him. Rufio follows. Caesar shudders*]. Again, Pompey's murderer!

RUFIO. The town has gone mad, I think. They are for tearing the palace down and driving us into the sea straight away. We laid hold of this renegade in clearing them out of the courtyard.

CAESAR. Release him. [*They let go his arms*]. What has offended the citizens, Lucius Septimius?

LUCIUS. What did you expect, Caesar? Pothinus was a favorite of theirs.

CAESAR. What has happened to Pothinus? I set him free, here, not half an hour ago. Did they not pass him out?

LUCIUS. Ay, through the gallery arch sixty feet above ground, with three inches of steel in his ribs. He is as dead as Pompey. We are quits now, as to killing—you and I.

CAESAR [*shocked*] Assassinated!—our prisoner, our guest! [*He turns reproachfully on Rufio*]. Rufio—

RUFIO [*emphatically—anticipating the question*] Whoever did it was a wise man and a friend of yours [*Cleopatra is greatly emboldened*]; but none of us had a hand in it. So it is no use to frown at me. [*Caesar turns and looks at Cleopatra*].

CLEOPATRA [*violently—rising*] He was slain by order of the Queen of Egypt. I am not Julius Caesar the dreamer, who allows every slave to insult him. Rufio has said I did well: now the others shall judge me too. [*She turns to the others*]. This Pothinus sought to make me conspire with him to betray Caesar to Achillas and Ptolemy. I refused; and he cursed me and came privily to Caesar to accuse me of his own treachery. I caught him in the act; and he insulted me—me, the Queen! to my face. Caesar would not avenge me: he spoke him fair and set him free. Was I right to avenge myself? Speak, Lucius.

LUCIUS. I do not gainsay it. But you will get little thanks from Caesar for it.

CLEOPATRA. Speak, Apollodorus. Was I wrong?

APOLLODORUS. I have only one word of blame, most beautiful. You should have called upon me, your knight; and in fair duel I should have slain the slanderer.

CLEOPATRA [*passionately*] I will be judged by your very slave, Caesar. Britannus: speak. Was I wrong?

BRITANNUS. Were treachery, falsehood, and disloyalty left unpunished, society must become like an arena full of wild beasts, tearing one another to pieces. Caesar is in the wrong.

CAESAR [*with quiet bitterness*] And so the verdict is against me, it seems.

CLEOPATRA [*vehemently*] Listen to me, Caesar. If one man in all Alexandria can be found to say that I did wrong, I swear to have myself crucified on the door of the palace by my own slaves.

CAESAR. If one man in all the world can be found, now or forever, to know that you did wrong, that man will have either to conquer the world as I have, or be crucified by it. [*The uproar in the streets again reaches them*]. Do you hear? These knockers at your gate[46] are also believers in vengeance and in stabbing. You have slain their leader: it is right that they shall slay you. If you doubt it, ask your four counsellors here. And then in the name of that right [*he emphasizes the word with great scorn*] shall I not slay them for murdering their Queen, and be slain in my turn by their countrymen as the invader of their fatherland? Can Rome do less then than slay these slayers, too, to shew the world how Rome avenges her sons and her honor.[47] And so, to the end of history, murder shall breed murder, always in the name of right and honor and peace, until the gods are tired of blood and create a race that can understand. [*Fierce uproar. Cleopatra becomes white with terror*]. Hearken, you who must not be insulted. Go near enough to catch their words: you will find them bitterer than the tongue of Pothinus. [*Loftily, wrapping himself up in an impenetrable dignity*] Let the Queen of Egypt now give her orders for vengeance, and take her measures for defence; for she has renounced Caesar. [*He turns to go*].

CLEOPATRA [*terrified, running to him and falling on her knees*] You will not desert me, Caesar. You will defend the palace.

---

46 *Macbeth*, II, iii, 1–25.

47 The particular contemporary incident Shaw had in mind here was the vengeful act of Lord Kitchener's British soldiers in digging up the body of Mohammed Ahmet, or the Mahdi, whose followers had killed General Gordon in 1885.

CAESAR. You have taken the powers of life and death upon you. I am only a dreamer.

CLEOPATRA. But they will kill me.

CAESAR. And why not?

CLEOPATRA. In pity—

CAESAR. Pity! What! has it come to this so suddenly, that nothing can save you now but pity? Did it save Pothinus?

She rises, wringing her hands, and goes back to the bench in despair. Apollodorus shews his sympathy with her by quietly posting himself behind the bench. The sky has by this time become the most vivid purple, and soon begins to change to a glowing pale orange, against which the colonnade and the great image shew darklier and darklier.

RUFIO. Caesar: enough of preaching. The enemy is at the gate.

CAESAR [*turning on him and giving way to his wrath*] Ay; and what has held him baffled at the gate all these months? Was it my folly, as you deem it, or your wisdom? In this Egyptian Red Sea of blood, whose hand has held all your heads above the waves? [*Turning on Cleopatra*] And yet, when Caesar says to such an one, "Friend, go free," you, clinging for your little life to my sword, dare steal out and stab him in the back? And you, soldiers and gentlemen, and honest servants as you forget that you are, applaud this assassination, and say "Caesar is in the wrong." By the gods, I am tempted to open my hand and let you all sink into the flood.

CLEOPATRA [*with a ray of cunning hope*] But, Caesar, if you do, you will perish yourself.

Caesar's eyes blaze.

RUFIO [*greatly alarmed*] Now, by great Jove, you filthy little Egyptian rat, that is the very word to make him walk out alone into the city and leave us here to be cut to pieces. [*Desperately, to Caesar*] Will you desert us because we are a parcel of fools? I mean no harm by killing: I do it as a dog kills a cat, by instinct. We are all dogs at your heels; but we have served you faithfully.

CAESAR [*relenting*] Alas, Rufio, my son, my son: as dogs we are like to perish now in the streets.

APOLLODORUS [*at his post behind Cleopatra's seat*] Caesar: what you say has an Olympian ring in it: it must be right; for it is fine art. But I am still on the side of Cleopatra. If we must die, she shall not want the devotion of a man's heart nor the strength of a man's arm.

CLEOPATRA [*sobbing*] But I dont want to die.

CAESAR [*sadly*] Oh, ignoble, ignoble!

LUCIUS [*coming forward between Caesar and Cleopatra*] Hearken to me, Caesar. It may be ignoble; but I also mean to live as long as I can.

CAESAR. Well, my friend, you are likely to outlive Caesar. Is it any magic of mine, think you, that has kept your army and this whole city at bay for so long? Yesterday, what quarrel had they with me that they should risk their lives against me? But today we have flung them down their hero, murdered; and now every man of them is set upon clearing out this nest of assassins—for such we are and no more. Take courage then; and sharpen your sword. Pompey's head has fallen; and Caesar's head is ripe.

APOLLODORUS. Does Caesar despair?

CAESAR [*with infinite pride*] He who has never hoped can never despair. Caesar, in good or bad fortune, looks his fate in the face.

LUCIUS. Look it in the face, then; and it will smile as it always has on Caesar.

CAESAR [*with involuntary haughtiness*] Do you presume to encourage me?

LUCIUS. I offer you my services. I will change sides if you will have me.

CAESAR [*suddenly coming down to earth again, and looking sharply at him, divining that there is something behind the offer*] What! At this point?

LUCIUS [*firmly*] At this point.

RUFIO. Do you suppose Caesar is mad, to trust you?

LUCIUS. I do not ask him to trust me until he is victorious. I ask for my life, and for a command in Caesar's army. And since Caesar is a fair dealer, I will pay in advance.

CAESAR. Pay! How?

LUCIUS. With a piece of good news for you.
Caesar divines the news in a flash.
RUFIO. What news?

CAESAR [*with an elate and buoyant energy which makes Cleo-patra sit up and stare*] What news! What news, did you say, my son Rufio? The relief has arrived: what other news remains for us? Is it not so, Lucius Septimius? Mithridates of Pergamos is on the march.

LUCIUS. He has taken Pelusium.

CAESAR [*delighted*] Lucius Septimius: you are henceforth my officer. Rufio: the Egyptians must have sent every soldier from the city to prevent Mithridates crossing the Nile. There is nothing in the streets now but mob—mob!

LUCIUS. It is so. Mithridates is marching by the great road to Memphis to cross above the Delta. Achillas will fight him there.

CAESAR [*all audacity*] Achillas shall fight Caesar there. See, Rufio. [*He runs to the table; snatches a napkin; and draws a plan on it with his finger dipped in wine, whilst Rufio and Lucius Septimius crowd about him to watch, all looking closely, for the light is now almost gone*]. Here is the palace [*pointing to his plan*]: here is the theatre. You [*to Rufio*] take twenty men and pretend to go by that street [*pointing it out*]; and whilst they are stoning you, out go the cohorts by this and this. My streets are right, are they, Lucius?

LUCIUS. Ay, that is the fig market—

CAESAR [*too much excited to listen to him*] I saw them the day we arrived. Good! [*He throws the napkin on the table, and comes down again into the colonnade*]. Away, Britannus: tell Petronius that within an hour half our forces must take ship for the western lake. See to my horse and armor. [*Britannus runs out*]. With the rest, *I* shall march round the lake and up the Nile to meet Mithridates. Away, Lucius; and give the word. [*Lucius hurries out after Britannus*]. Apollodorus: lend me your sword and your right arm for this campaign.

APOLLODORUS. Ay, and my heart and life to boot.

CAESAR [*grasping his hand*] I accept both. [*Mighty handshake*]. Are you ready for work?

APOLLODORUS. Ready for Art—the Art of War [*he rushes out after Lucius, totally forgetting Cleopatra*].

RUFIO. Come! this is something like business.

CAESAR [*buoyantly*] Is it not, my only son? [*He claps his hands. The slaves hurry in to the table*]. No more of this mawkish revelling: away with all this stuff: shut it out of my sight and be off with you. [*The slaves begin to remove the table; and the curtains are drawn, shutting in the colonnade*]. You understand about the streets, Rufio?

RUFIO. Ay, I think I do. I will get through them, at all events.
The bucina sounds busily in the courtyard beneath.

CAESAR. Come, then: we must talk to the troops and hearten them. You down to the beach: I to the courtyard. [*He makes for the staircase*].

CLEOPATRA [*rising from her seat, where she has been quite neglected all this time, and stretching out her hands timidly to him*] Caesar.

CAESAR [*turning*] Eh?

CLEOPATRA. Have you forgotten me?

CAESAR [*indulgently*] I am busy now, my child, busy. When I return your affairs shall be settled. Farewell; and be good and patient.

He goes, preoccupied and quite indifferent. She stands with clenched fists, in speechless rage and humiliation.

RUFIO. That game is played and lost, Cleopatra. The woman always gets the worst of it.

CLEOPATRA [*haughtily*] Go. Follow your master.

RUFIO [*in her ear, with rough familiarity*] A word first. Tell your executioner that if Pothinus had been properly killed—in the throat—he would not have called out. Your man bungled his work.

CLEOPATRA [*enigmatically*] How do you know it was a man?

RUFIO [*startled, and puzzled*] It was not you: you were with us when it happened. [*She turns her back scornfully on him. He shakes his head, and draws the curtains to go out. It is now a magnificent moonlit night. The table has been removed. Ftatateeta is seen in the light of the moon and stars, again in prayer before the white altarstone of Ra. Rufio starts; closes the curtains again softly; and says in a low voice to Cleopatra]* Was it she? with her own hand?

CLEOPATRA [*threateningly*] Whoever it was, let my enemies beware of her. Look to it, Rufio, you who dare make the Queen of Egypt a fool before Caesar.

RUFIO [*looking grimly at her*] I will look to it, Cleopatra. [*He nods in confirmation of the promise, and slips out through the curtains, loosening his sword in its sheath as he goes*].

ROMAN SOLDIERS [*in the courtyard below*] Hail, Caesar! Hail, hail!

Cleopatra listens. The bucina sounds again, followed by several trumpets.

CLEOPATRA [*wringing her hands and calling*] Ftatateeta. Ftatateeta. It is dark; and I am alone. Come to me. [*Silence*] Ftatateeta. [*Louder*] Ftatateeta. [*Silence. In a panic she snatches the cord and pulls the curtains apart*].

Ftatateeta is lying dead on the altar of Ra, with her throat cut. Her blood deluges the white stone.

ACT V

High noon. Festival and military pageant on the esplanade be-
fore the palace. In the east harbor Caesar's galley, so gorgeously
decorated that it seems to be rigged with flowers, is alongside the
quay, close to the steps Apollodorus descended when he embarked
with the carpet. A Roman guard is posted there in charge of a
gangway, whence a red floorcloth is laid down the middle of the
esplanade, turning off to the north opposite the central gate in the
palace front, which shuts in the esplanade on the south side. The
broad steps of the gate, crowded with Cleopatra's ladies, all in
their gayest attire, are like a flower garden. The façade is lined
by her guard, officered by the same gallants to whom Bel Affris
announced the coming of Caesar six months before in the old
palace on the Syrian border. The north side is lined by Roman
soldiers, with the townsfolk on tiptoe behind them, peering over
their heads at the cleared esplanade, in which the officers stroll
about, chatting. Among these are Belzanor and the Persian; also
the centurion, vinewood cudgel in hand, battle worn, thick-booted,
and much outshone, both socially and decoratively, by the Egyp-
tian officers.

Apollodorus makes his way through the townsfolk and calls to
the officers from behind the Roman line.

APOLLODORUS. Hullo! May I pass?

CENTURION. Pass Apollodorus the Sicilian there! [*The soldiers*
let him through].

BELZANOR. Is Caesar at hand?

APOLLODORUS. Not yet. He is still in the market place. I could
not stand any more of the roaring of the soldiers! After half an
hour of the enthusiasm of an army, one feels the need of a little
sea air.

PERSIAN. Tell us the news. Hath he slain the priests?

APOLLODORUS. Not he. They met him in the market place with ashes on their heads and their gods in their hands. They placed the gods at his feet. The only one that was worth looking at was Apis: a miracle of gold and ivory work. By my advice he offered the chief priest two talents for it.

BELZANOR [appalled] Apis the all-knowing for two talents! What said the chief Priest?

APOLLODORUS. He invoked the mercy of Apis, and asked for five.

BELZANOR. There will be famine and tempest in the land for this.

PERSIAN. Pooh! Why did not Apis cause Caesar to be vanquished by Achillas? Any fresh news from the war, Apollodorus?

APOLLODORUS. The little King Ptolemy was drowned.

BELZANOR. Drowned! How?

APOLLODORUS. With the rest of them. Caesar attacked them from three sides at once and swept them into the Nile. Ptolemy's barge sank.

BELZANOR. A marvellous man, this Caesar! Will he come soon, think you?

APOLLODORUS. He was settling the Jewish question[48] when I left.

A flourish of trumpets from the north, and commotion among the townsfolk, announces the approach of Caesar.

PERSIAN. He has made short work of them. Here he comes. [*He hurries to his post in front of the Egyptian lines*].

BELZANOR [*following him*] Ho there! Caesar comes.

The soldiers stand at attention, and dress their lines. Apollodorus goes to the Egyptian line.

CENTURION [*hurrying to the gangway guard*] Attention there! Caesar comes.

Caesar arrives in state with Rufio: Britannus following. The soldiers receive him with enthusiastic shouting.

---

[48] Mommsen refers to Caesar's role in redressing the grievances of the Jews of Alexandria. Many of them had joined forces with Mithridates of Pergamos, the illegitimate son of Mithridates Eupator, King of Pontus, and thus aided Caesar in his defeat of the Egyptians at the Battle of the Nile.

CAESAR. I see my ship awaits me. The hour of Caesar's farewell to Egypt has arrived. And now, Rufio, what remains to be done before I go?

RUFIO [at his left hand] You have not yet appointed a Roman governor for this province.

CAESAR [looking whimsically at him, but speaking with perfect gravity] What say you to Mithridates of Pergamos, my reliever and rescuer, the great son of Eupator?[49]

RUFIO. Why, that you will want him elsewhere. Do you forget that you have some three or four armies to conquer on your way home?[50]

CAESAR. Indeed! Well, what say you to yourself?

RUFIO [incredulously] I! I a governor! What are you dreaming of? Do you not know that I am only the son of a freedman?

CAESAR [affectionately] Has not Caesar called you his son? [Calling to the whole assembly] Peace awhile there; and hear me.

THE ROMAN SOLDIERS. Hear Caesar.

CAESAR. Hear the service, quality, rank and name of the Roman governor. By service, Caesar's shield; by quality, Caesar's friend; by rank, a Roman soldier. [The Roman soldiers give a triumphant shout]. By name, Rufio. [They shout again].

RUFIO [kissing Caesar's hand] Ay: I am Caesar's shield; but of what use shall I be when I am no longer on Caesar's arm? Well, no matter—[He becomes husky, and turns away to recover himself].

CAESAR. Where is that British Islander of mine?

---

[49] Mithridates VI, or Mithridates Eupator (c. 131–63 B.C.), waged war against the Romans in Asia Minor. He was defeated by Pompey, but rather than face captivity, he had himself stabbed by a slave.

[50] History records only one major battle waged by Caesar before returning to Rome. Caesar defeated Pharnaces, another son of Mithridates Eupator, at Zela, where he later described the action in the words, "Veni, Vidi, Vici." Caesar was in Rome only shortly before he departed for Africa, where he defeated Cato and Juba of Numidia at the Battle of Thapsus. Afterwards he returned to Rome to be hailed conqueror of Gaul, Egypt, Pontus, and Numidia.

BRITANNUS [*coming forward on Caesar's right hand*] Here, Caesar.

CAESAR. Who bade you, pray, thrust yourself into the battle of the Delta, uttering the barbarous cries of your native land, and affirming yourself a match for any four of the Egyptians, to whom you applied unseemly epithets?

BRITANNUS. Caesar: I ask you to excuse the language that escaped me in the heat of the moment.

CAESAR. And how did you, who cannot swim, cross the canal with us when we stormed the camp?

BRITANNUS. Caesar: I clung to the tail of your horse.

CAESAR. These are not the deeds of a slave, Britannicus, but of a free man.

BRITANNUS. Caesar: I was born free.

CAESAR. But they call you Caesar's slave.

BRITANNUS. Only as Caesar's slave have I found real freedom.

CAESAR [*moved*] Well said. Ungrateful that I am, I was about to set you free; but now I will not part from you for a million talents. [*He claps him friendly on the shoulder. Britannus, gratified, but a trifle shamefaced, takes his hand and kisses it sheepishly*].

BELZANOR [*to the Persian*] This Roman knows how to make men serve him.

PERSIAN. Ay: men too humble to become dangerous rivals to him.

BELZANOR. O subtle one! O cynic!

CAESAR [*seeing Apollodorus in the Egyptian corner, and calling to him*] Apollodorus: I leave the art of Egypt in your charge. Remember: Rome loves art and will encourage it ungrudgingly.

APOLLODORUS. I understand, Caesar. Rome will produce no art itself; but it will buy up and take away whatever the other nations produce.

CAESAR. What! Rome produce no art! Is peace not an art? is war not an art? is government not an art? is civilization not an art? All these we give you in exchange for a few ornaments. You will have the best of the bargain. [*Turning to Rufio*] And now, what else have I to do before I embark? [*Trying to recollect*] There is something I cannot remember: what can it be? Well, well: it must remain undone: we must not waste this favorable wind. Farewell, Rufio.

RUFIO. Caesar: I am loth to let you go to Rome without your shield. There are too many daggers there.

CAESAR. It matters not: I shall finish my life's work on my way back; and then I shall have lived long enough. Besides: I have always disliked the idea of dying: I had rather be killed. Farewell.

RUFIO [*with a sigh, raising his hands and giving Caesar up as incorrigible*] Farewell. [*They shake hands*].

CAESAR [*waving his hand to Apollodorus*] Farewell, Apollodorus, and my friends, all of you. Aboard!

The gangway is run out from the quay to the ship. As Caesar moves towards it, Cleopatra, cold and tragic, cunningly dressed in black, without ornaments or decoration of any kind, and thus making a striking figure among the brilliantly dressed bevy of ladies as she passes through it, comes from the palace and stands on the steps. Caesar does not see her until she speaks.

CLEOPATRA. Has Cleopatra no part in this leavetaking?

CAESAR [*enlightened*] Ah, I knew there was something. [*To Rufio*] How could you let me forget her, Rufio? [*Hastening to her*] Had I gone without seeing you, I should never have forgiven myself. [*He takes her hands, and brings her into the middle of the esplanade. She submits stonily*]. Is this mourning for me?

CLEOPATRA. No.

CAESAR [*remorsefully*] Ah, that was thoughtless of me! It is for your brother.

CLEOPATRA. No.

CAESAR. For whom, then?

CLEOPATRA. Ask the Roman governor whom you have left us.

CAESAR. Rufio?

CLEOPATRA. Yes: Rufio. [*She points at him with deadly scorn*]. He who is to rule here in Caesar's name, in Caesar's way, according to Caesar's boasted laws of life.

CAESAR [*dubiously*] He is to rule as he can, Cleopatra. He has taken the work upon him, and will do it in his own way.

CLEOPATRA. Not in your way, then?

CAESAR [*puzzled*] What do you mean by my way?

CLEOPATRA. Without punishment. Without revenge. Without judgment.

CAESAR [*approvingly*] Ay: that is the right way, the great way, the only possible way in the end. [*To Rufio*] Believe it, Rufio, if you can.

RUFIO. Why, I believe it, Caesar. You have convinced me of it long ago. But look you. You are sailing for Numidia today. Now tell me: if you meet a hungry lion there, you will not punish it for wanting to eat you?

CAESAR [*wondering what he is driving at*] No.

RUFIO. Nor revenge upon it the blood of those it has already eaten.

CAESAR. No.

RUFIO. Nor judge it for its guiltiness.

CAESAR. No.

RUFIO. What, then, will you do to save your life from it?

CAESAR [*promptly*] Kill it, man, without malice, just as it would kill me. What does this parable of the lion mean?

RUFIO. Why, Cleopatra had a tigress that killed men at her bidding. I thought she might bid it kill you some day. Well, had I not been Caesar's pupil, what pious things might I not have done to that tigress! I might have punished it. I might have revenged Pothinus on it.

CAESAR [*interjects*] Pothinus!

RUFIO [*continuing*] I might have judged it. But I put all these follies behind me; and, without malice, only cut its throat. And that is why Cleopatra comes to you in mourning.

CLEOPATRA [*vehemently*] He has shed the blood of my servant Ftatateeta. On your head be it as upon his, Caesar, if you hold him free of it.

CAESAR [*energetically*] On my head be it, then; for it was well done. Rufio: had you set yourself in the seat of the judge, and with hateful ceremonies and appeals to the gods handed that woman over to some hired executioner to be slain before the people in the name of justice, never again would I have touched your hand without a shudder. But this was natural slaying: I feel no horror at it.

Rufio, satisfied, nods at Cleopatra, mutely inviting her to mark that.

CLEOPATRA [*pettish and childish in her impotence*] No: not when a Roman slays an Egyptian. All the world will now see how unjust and corrupt Caesar is.

CAESAR [*taking her hands coaxingly*] Come: do not be angry with me. I am sorry for that poor Totateeta. [*She laughs in spite of herself*]. Aha! you are laughing. Does that mean reconciliation?

CLEOPATRA [*angry with herself for laughing*] No, no, NO!! But it is so ridiculous to hear you call her Totateeta.

CAESAR. What! As much a child as ever, Cleopatra! Have I not made a woman of you after all?

CLEOPATRA. Oh, it is you who are a great baby: you make me seem silly because you will not behave seriously. But you have treated me badly; and I do not forgive you.

CAESAR. Bid me farewell.

CLEOPATRA. I will not.

CAESAR [*coaxing*] I will send you a beautiful present from Rome.

CLEOPATRA [*proudly*] Beauty from Rome to Egypt indeed! What can Rome give me that Egypt cannot give me?

APOLLODORUS. That is true, Caesar. If the present is to be really beautiful, I shall have to buy it for you in Alexandria.

CAESAR. You are forgetting the treasures for which Rome is most famous, my friend. You cannot buy them in Alexandria.

APOLLODORUS. What are they, Caesar?

CAESAR. Her sons. Come, Cleopatra: forgive me and bid me farewell; and I will send you a man, Roman from head to heel and Roman of the noblest; not old and ripe for the knife; not lean in the arms and cold in the heart; not hiding a bald head under his conqueror's laurels; not stooped with the weight of the world on his shoulders; but brisk and fresh, strong and young, hoping in the morning, fighting in the day, and revelling in the evening. Will you take such an one in exchange for Caesar?

CLEOPATRA [*palpitating*] His name, his name?

CAESAR. Shall it be Mark Antony? [*She throws herself into his arms*].

RUFIO. You are a bad hand at a bargain, mistress, if you will swop Caesar for Antony.

CAESAR. So now you are satisfied.

CLEOPATRA. You will not forget.

CAESAR. I will not forget. Farewell: I do not think we shall meet again. Farewell. [*He kisses her on the forehead. She is much affected and begins to sniff. He embarks*].

THE ROMAN SOLDIERS [*as he sets his foot on the gangway*] Hail, Caesar; and farewell!

He reaches the ship and returns Rufio's wave of the hand.

APOLLODORUS [*to Cleopatra*] No tears, dearest Queen: they stab your servant to the heart. He will return some day.

CLEOPATRA. I hope not. But I cant help crying, all the same. [*She waves her handkerchief to Caesar; and the ship begins to move*].

THE ROMAN SOLDIERS [*drawing their swords and raising them in the air*] Hail, Caesar!

Notes to Caesar and Cleopatra[51]

CLEOPATRA'S CURE FOR BALDNESS

For the sake of conciseness in a hurried situation I have made Cleopatra recommend rum. This, I am afraid, is an anachronism: the only real one in the play. To balance it, I give a couple of the remedies she actually believed in. They are quoted by Galen[52] from Cleopatra's books on Cosmetic.

"For bald patches, powder red sulphuret of arsenic and take it up with oak gum, as much as it will bear. Put on a rag and apply, having soaped the place well first. I have mixed the above with a foam of nitre, and it worked well."

Several other receipts follow, ending with: "The following is the best of all, acting for fallen hairs, when applied with oil or pomatum; acts for falling off of eyelashes or for people getting bald all over. It is wonderful. Of domestic mice burnt, one part; of vine rag burnt, one part; of horse's teeth burnt, one part; of bear's grease one; of deer's marrow one; of reed bark one. To be pounded when dry, and mixed with plenty of honey til it gets the consistency of honey; then the bear's grease and marrow to be mixed (when melted), the medicine to be put in a brass flask, and the bald part rubbed til it sprouts."

Concerning these ingredients, my fellow-dramatist Gilbert Murray, who, as a Professor of Greek, has applied to classical antiquity the methods of high scholarship (my own method is pure divination), writes to me as follows: "Some of this I dont under-

---

[51] Shaw in a letter to Siegfried Trebitsch, dated September 18, 1903, tells his German translator to "translate the notes. They are of enormous importance: the one on Caesar's character has in it the foundations of a whole philosophy."

[52] Galen (c. 130–c. 200) studied medicine in Greece, Asia Minor, and in Alexandria.

stand, and possibly Galen did not, as he quotes your heroine's own language. Foam of nitre is, I think, something like soapsuds. Reed bark is an odd expression. It might mean the outside membrane of a reed: I do not know what it ought to be called. In the burnt mice receipt I take it that you first mixed the solid powders with honey, and then added the grease. I expect Cleopatra preferred it because in most of the others you have to lacerate the skin, prick it, or rub it til it bleeds. I do not know what vine rag is. I translate literally."

APPARENT ANACHRONISMS

The only way to write a play which shall convey to the general public an impression of antiquity is to make the characters speak blank verse and abstain from reference to steam, telegraphy, or any of the material conditions of their existence. The more ignorant men are, the more convinced are they that their little parish and their little chapel is an apex to which civilization and philosophy has painfully struggled up the pyramid of time from a desert of savagery. Savagery, they think, became barbarism; barbarism became ancient civilization; ancient civilization became Pauline Christianity; Pauline Christianity became Roman Catholicism; Roman Catholicism became the Dark Ages; and the Dark Ages were finally enlightened by the Protestant instincts of the English race. The whole process is summed up as Progress with a capital P. And any elderly gentleman of Progressive temperament will testify that the improvement since he was a boy is enormous.

Now if we count the generations of Progressive elderly gentlemen since, say, Plato, and add together the successive enormous improvements to which each of them has testified, it will strike us at once as an unaccountable fact that the world, instead of having been improved in 67 generations out of all recognition, presents, on the whole, a rather less dignified appearance in Ibsen's Enemy of the People than in Plato's Republic. And in truth, the period of time covered by history is far too short to allow of any perceptible progress in the popular sense of Evolution of the Human Species. The notion that there has been any such Progress since Caesar's time (less than 20 centuries) is too absurd for discussion. All the savagery, barbarism, dark ages and the rest of it of which we have any record as existing in the past, exists at the present moment. A British carpenter or stone-mason may point out that he gets twice as much money for his labor as his father did in the same trade, and that his suburban house, with its bath, its cottage piano, its drawing room suite, and its album of photographs, would have shamed the plainness of his grandmother's. But the descendants of feudal barons, living in squalid lodgings on a salary of fifteen shillings a week instead of in castles on princely revenues, do not congratulate the world on the change. Such changes, in fact, are not to the point. It has been known, as far back as our records go, that man running wild in the woods is different from man kennelled in a city slum; that a dog seems to understand a shepherd better than a hewer of wood and drawer of water can understand an astronomer; and that breeding, gentle nurture, and luxurious food and shelter will produce a kind of man with whom the common laborer is socially incompatible. The same thing is true of horses and dogs. Now there is clearly room for great changes in the world by increasing the percentage of individuals who are carefully bred and gently nurtured, even to finally making the most of every man and woman born. But that possibility existed in the days of the Hittites[53] as much as it does today. It does not give the slightest real support to the common assumption that the civilized contemporaries of the Hittites were unlike their civilized descendants today.

This would appear the tritest commonplace if it were not that the ordinary citizen's ignorance of the past combines with his idealization of the present to mislead and flatter him. Our latest book on the new railway across Asia describes the dulness of the

[53] Hittites were an ancient people of Asia Minor and Syria who flourished from 1600 to 1200 B.C. The artistic work of the Hittites shows a high state of culture.

Siberian farmer and the vulgar pursepride of the Siberian man of business without the least consciousness that the string of contemptuous instances given might have been saved by writing simply "Farmers and provincial plutocrats in Siberia are exactly what they are in England." The latest professor descanting on the civilization of the Western Empire in the fifth century feels bound to assume, in the teeth of his own researches, that the Christian was one sort of animal and the Pagan another. It might as well be assumed as indeed it generally is assumed by implication, that a murder committed with a poisoned arrow is different from a murder committed with a Mauser rifle. All such notions are illusions. Go back to the first syllable of recorded time, and there you will find your Christian and your Pagan, your yokel and your poet, helot and hero, Don Quixote and Sancho, Tamino and Papageno,[54] Newton and bushman unable to count eleven, all alive and contemporaneous, and all convinced that they are the heirs of all the ages and the privileged recipients of THE truth (all others damnable heresies), just as you have them today, flourishing in countries each of which is the bravest and best that ever sprang at Heaven's command from out the azure main.

Again, there is the illusion of "increased command over Nature," meaning that cotton is cheap and that ten miles of country road on a bicycle have replaced four on foot. But even if man's increased command over Nature included any increased command over himself (the only sort of command relevant to his evolution into a higher being), the fact remains that it is only by running away from the increased command over Nature to country places where Nature is still in primitive command over Man that he can recover from the effects of the smoke, the stench, the foul air, the overcrowding, the racket, the ugliness, the dirt which the cheap cotton costs us. If manufacturing activity means Progress, the town must be more advanced than the country; and the field laborers and village artisans of today must be much less changed

---

[54] Tamino and Papageno are a prince and a clown in Mozart's opera, *The Magic Flute.*

from the servants of Job than the proletariat of modern London from the proletariat of Caesar's Rome. Yet the cockney proletarian is so inferior to the village laborer that it is only by steady recruiting from the country that London is kept alive. This does not seem as if the change since Job's time were Progress in the popular sense: quite the reverse. The common stock of discoveries in physics has accumulated a little: that is all.

One more illustration. Is the Englishman prepared to admit that the American is his superior as a human being? I ask this question because the scarcity of labor in America relatively to the demand for it has led to a development of machinery there, and a consequent "increase of command over Nature" which makes many of our English methods appear almost medieval to the up-to-date Chicagoan. This means that the American has an advantage over the Englishman of exactly the same nature that the Englishman has over the contemporaries of Cicero. Is the Englishman prepared to draw the same conclusion in both cases? I think not. The American, of course, will draw it cheerfully; but I must then ask him whether, since a modern negro has a greater "command over Nature" than Washington had, we are also to accept the conclusion, involved in his former one, that humanity has progressed from Washington to the *fin de siècle*[55] negro.

Finally, I would point out that if life is crowned by its success and devotion in industrial organization and ingenuity, we had better worship the ant and the bee (as moralists urge us to do in our childhood), and humble ourselves before the arrogance of the birds of Aristophanes.[56]

My reason then for ignoring the popular conception of Progress in Caesar and Cleopatra is that there is no reason to suppose that any Progress has taken place since their time. But even if I shared the popular delusion, I do not see that I could have made any essential difference in the play. I can only imitate humanity as

[55] "End of the [nineteenth] century."
[56] In *The Birds*, a comedy by Aristophanes, Pisthetaerus talks the birds into building a wall between heaven and earth so that gods and men alike would have to recognize the birds' supremacy.

I know it. Nobody knows whether Shakespear thought that ancient Athenian joiners, weavers, or bellows menders were any different from Elizabethan ones;[57] but it is quite certain that he could not have made them so, unless, indeed, he had played the literary man and made Quince say, not "Is all our company here?" but "Bottom: was not that Socrates that passed us at the Piraeus with Glaucon and Polemarchus on his way to the house of Kephalus?" And so on.

CLEOPATRA

Cleopatra was only sixteen when Caesar went to Egypt; but in Egypt sixteen is a riper age than it is in England. The childishness I have ascribed to her, as far as it is childishness of character and not lack of experience, is not a matter of years. It may be observed in our own climate at the present day in many women of fifty. It is a mistake to suppose that the difference between wisdom and folly has anything to do with the difference between physical age and physical youth. Some women are younger at seventy than most women at seventeen.

It must be borne in mind, too, that Cleopatra was a queen, and was therefore not the typical Greek-cultured, educated Egyptian lady of her time. To represent her by any such type would be as absurd as to represent George IV[58] by a type founded on the attainments of Sir Isaac Newton. It is true that an ordinarily well educated Alexandrian girl of her time would no more have believed bogey stories about the Romans than the daughter of a modern Oxford professor would believe them about the Germans (though, by the way, it is possible to talk great nonsense at Oxford about foreigners when we are at war with them). But I do

---

[57] Shakespeare's *A Midsummer Night's Dream* is set in ancient Athens, but the commoners are generalized Elizabethan types.

[58] George IV (1762–1830) was notorious for his profligacy and extravagance; his cleverness and gracious manners, however, gained him the title "first gentleman in Europe."

not feel bound to believe that Cleopatra was well educated. Her
father, the illustrious Flute Blower, was not at all a parent of the
Oxford professor type. And Cleopatra was a chip of the old block.

BRITANNUS

I find among those who have read this play in manuscript a
strong conviction that an ancient Briton could not possibly have
been like a modern one. I see no reason to adopt this curious
view. It is true that the Roman and Norman conquests must have
for a time disturbed the normal British type produced by the
climate. But Britannus, born before these events, represents the
unadulterated Briton who fought Caesar and impressed Roman
observers much as we should expect the ancestors of Mr. Podsnap[59] to impress the cultivated Italians of their time.

I am told that it is not scientific to treat national character as
a product of climate. This only shews the wide difference between
common knowledge and the intellectual game called science. We
have men of exactly the same stock, and speaking the same language, growing in Great Britain, in Ireland, and in America. The
result is three of the most distinctly marked nationalities under
the sun. Racial characteristics are quite another matter. The difference between a Jew and a Gentile has nothing to do with the
difference between an Englishman and a German. The characteristics of Britannus are local characteristics, not race characteristics.
In an ancient Briton they would, I take it, be exaggerated, since
modern Britain, disforested, drained, urbanified and consequently
cosmopolized, is presumably less characteristically British than
Caesar's Britain.

And again I ask does anyone who, in the light of a competent
knowledge of his own age, has studied history from contemporary
documents, believe that 67 generations of promiscuous marriage

[59] Mr. Podsnap, a character in Dickens' novel *Our Mutual Friend*, is a
wealthy, narrow-minded businessman whose conservative morality and nationalistic attitudes anticipate Shaw's characterization of Britannus.

have made any appreciable difference in the human fauna of these isles? Certainly I do not.

JULIUS CAESAR

As to Caesar himself, I have purposely avoided the usual anachronism of going to Caesar's books, and concluding that the style is the man. That is only true of authors who have the specific literary genius, and have practised long enough to attain complete self-expression in letters. It is not true even on these conditions in an age when literature is conceived as a game of style, and not as a vehicle of self-expression by the author. Now Caesar was an amateur stylist writing books of travel and campaign histories in a style so impersonal that the authenticity of the later volumes is disputed. They reveal some of his qualities just as the Voyage of a Naturalist Round the World reveals some of Darwin's, without expressing his private personality. An Englishman reading them would say that Caesar was a man of great common sense and good taste, meaning thereby a man without originality or moral courage.

In exhibiting Caesar as a much more various person than the historian of the Gallic wars, I hope I have not been too much imposed on by the dramatic illusion to which all great men owe part of their reputation and some the whole of it. I admit that reputations gained in war are specially questionable. Able civilians taking up the profession of arms, like Caesar and Cromwell, in middle age, have snatched all its laurels from opponent commanders bred to it, apparently because capable persons engaged in military pursuits are so scarce that the existence of two of them at the same time in the same hemisphere is extremely rare. The capacity of any conqueror is therefore more likely than not to be an illusion produced by the incapacity of his adversary. At all events, Caesar might have won his battles without being wiser than Charles XII[60] or Nelson or Joan of Arc, who were, like most

[60] Charles XII was King of Sweden from 1697 to 1718. During the Northern War he conducted one of the most brilliant campaigns in history.

modern "self-made" millionaires, half-witted geniuses, enjoying the worship accorded by all races to certain forms of insanity. But Caesar's victories were only advertisements for an eminence that would never have become popular without them. Caesar is greater off the battle field than on it. Nelson off his quarterdeck was so quaintly out of the question that when his head was injured at the battle of the Nile, and his conduct became for some years openly scandalous, the difference was not important enough to be noticed. It may, however, be said that peace hath her illusory reputations no less than war. And it is certainly true that in civil life mere capacity for work—the power of killing a dozen secretaries under you, so to speak, as a life-or-death courier kills horses —enables men with common ideas and superstitions to distance all competitors in the strife of political ambition. It was this power of work that astonished Cicero as the most prodigious of Caesar's gifts, as it astonished later observers in Napoleon before it wore him out. How if Caesar were nothing but a Nelson and a Gladstone combined! a prodigy of vitality without any special quality of mind! nay, with ideas that were worn out before he was born, as Nelson's and Gladstone's were! I have considered that possibility too, and rejected it. I cannot cite all the stories about Caesar which seem to me to shew that he was genuinely original; but let me at least point out that I have been careful to attribute nothing but originality to him. Originality gives a man an air of frankness, generosity, and magnanimity by enabling him to estimate the value of truth, money, or success in any particular instance quite independently of convention and moral generalization. He therefore will not, in the ordinary Treasury bench fashion, tell a lie which everybody knows to be a lie (and consequently expects him as a matter of good taste to tell). His lies are not found out: they pass for candors. He understands the paradox of money, and gives it away when he can get most for it: in other words, when its value is least, which is just when a common man tries hardest to get it. He knows that the real moment of success is not the moment apparent to the crowd. Hence, in order to produce an impression of complete disinterestedness and magnanimity, he has only to act with entire selfishness; and this is perhaps the only sense in which a man can be said to be *naturally* great. It is in this sense that I have represented Caesar as great. Having virtue, he has no need of goodness. He is neither forgiving, frank, nor generous, because a man who is too great to resent has nothing to forgive; a man who says things that other people are afraid to say need be no more frank than Bismarck was; and there is no generosity in giving things you do not want to people of whom you intend to make use. This distinction between virtue and goodness is not understood in England: hence the poverty of our drama in heroes. Our stage attempts at them are mere goody-goodies. Goodness, in its popular British sense of self-denial, implies that man is vicious by nature, and that supreme goodness is supreme martyrdom. Not sharing that pious opinion, I have not given countenance to it in any of my plays. In this I follow the precedent of the ancient myths, which represent the hero as vanquishing his enemies, not in fair fight, but with enchanted sword, superequine horse and magical invulnerability, the possession of which, from the vulgar moralistic point of view, robs his exploits of any merit whatever.

As to Caesar's sense of humor, there is no more reason to assume that he lacked it than to assume that he was deaf or blind. It is said that on the occasion of his assassination by a conspiracy of moralists (it is always your moralist who makes assassination a duty, on the scaffold or off it), he defended himself until the good Brutus struck him, when he exclaimed "What! you too, Brutus!" and disdained further fight. If this be true, he must have been an incorrigible comedian. But even if we waive this story, or accept the traditional sentimental interpretation of it, there is still abundant evidence of his lightheartedness and adventurousness. Indeed it is clear from his whole history that what has been called his ambition was an instinct for exploration. He had much more of Columbus and Franklin[61] in him than of Henry V.

[61] Sir John Franklin (1786–1847) was a noted Arctic explorer who wrote *Narrative of a Journey to the Shores of the Polar Sea* (1823).

However, nobody need deny Caesar a share, at least, of the qualities I have attributed to him. All men, much more Julius Caesars, possess all qualities in some degree. The really interesting question is whether I am right in assuming that the way to produce an impression of greatness is by exhibiting a man, not as mortifying his nature by doing his duty, in the manner which our system of putting little men into great positions (not having enough great men in our influential families to go round) forces us to inculcate, but as simply doing what he naturally wants to do. For this raises the question whether our world has not been wrong in its moral theory for the last 2,500 years or so. It must be a constant puzzle to many of us that the Christian era, so excellent in its intentions, should have been practically such a very discreditable episode in the history of the race. I doubt if this is altogether due to the vulgar and sanguinary sensationalism of our religious legends, with their substitution of gross physical torments and public executions for the passion of humanity. Islam, substituting voluptuousness for torment (a merely superficial difference, it is true) has done no better. It may have been the failure of Christianity to emancipate itself from expiatory theories of moral responsibility, guilt, innocence, reward, punishment, and the rest of it, that baffled its intention of changing the world. But these are bound up in all philosophies of creation as opposed to cosmism. They may therefore be regarded as the price we pay for popular religion.

TWO SHAVIAN REVIEWS

Review of *Antony and Cleopatra*

Shaw was drama critic for the Saturday Review *from 1895 to 1898. His reviews of Shakespeare's* Antony and Cleopatra *and* Julius Caesar *are included here to show the exceptions he took to Shakespeare's characterization of Caesar and Cleopatra, exceptions that presage his own view of these historical figures.*

SHAKESPEAR IN MANCHESTER

ANTONY AND CLEOPATRA. Shakespearean revival by Mr Louis Calvert[1] at the Queen's Theatre, Manchester.

[20 *March* 1897]

Shakespear is so much the word-musician that mere practical intelligence, no matter how well prompted by dramatic instinct, cannot enable anybody to understand his works or arrive at a right execution of them without the guidance of a fine ear. At the great emotional climaxes we find passages which are Rossinian[2] in their reliance on symmetry of melody and impressiveness of march to redeem poverty of meaning. In fact, we have got so far beyond Shakespear as a man of ideas that there is by this time hardly a famous passage in his works that is considered fine on any other ground than that it sounds beautifully, and awakens in us the emotion that originally expressed itself by its beauty. Strip it of that beauty of sound by prosaic paraphrase, and you have nothing left but a platitude that even an American professor of

---

[1] Louis Calvert (1859–1923), a noted Shakespearean and Shavian actor at the turn of the century, was a leading member of the company at the Court Theatre during the Vedrenne-Barker management, playing Broadbent in *John Bull's Other Island* and Undershaft in *Major Barbara*.

[2] Gioacchino Rossini (1792–1868) was an Italian operatic composer whose music was acclaimed for its stirring melody, brilliant effects, and vivacity; Shaw thought the music empty and mechanical.

145

ethics would blush to offer to his disciples. Wreck that beauty by a harsh, jarring utterance, and you will make your audience wince as if you were singing Mozart out of tune. Ignore it by "avoiding sing-song"—that is, ingeniously breaking the verse up so as to make it sound like prose, as the professional elocutionist prides himself on doing—and you are landed in a stilted, monstrous jargon that has not even the prosaic merit of being intelligible. Let me give one example: Cleopatra's outburst at the death of Antony:

> Oh withered is the garland of the war,
> The soldier's pole is fallen: young boys and girls
> Are level now with men: the odds is gone,
> And there is nothing left remarkable
> Beneath the visiting moon.

This is not good sense—not even good grammar. If you ask what does it all mean, the reply must be that it means just what its utterer feels. The chaos of its thought is a reflection of her mind, in which one can vaguely discern a wild illusion that all human distinction perishes with the gigantic distinction between Antony and the rest of the world. Now it is only in music, verbal or other, that the feeling which plunges thought into confusion can be artistically expressed. Any attempt to deliver such music prosaically would be as absurd as an attempt to speak an oratorio of Handel's, repetitions and all. The right way to declaim Shakespear is the sing-song way. Mere metric accuracy is nothing. There must be beauty of tone, expressive inflection, and infinite variety of *nuance* to sustain the fascination of the infinite monotony of the chanting.

Miss Janet Achurch,[3] now playing Cleopatra in Manchester, has a magnificent voice, and is as full of ideas as to vocal effects as

---

[3] Janet Achurch (1864–1916) is best remembered as the first English actress to play Ibsen, creating the role of Nora in *A Doll's House* in 1889. She played in Shaw's *Candida* and *Captain Brassbound's Conversion* at the Strand during the 1900 season. Shaw once referred to her as "the only tragic actress of genius we now possess."

to everything else on the stage. The march of the verse and the strenuousness of the rhetoric stimulate her great artistic susceptibility powerfully: she is determined that Cleopatra shall have rings on her fingers and bells on her toes, and that she shall have music wherever she goes. Of the hardihood of ear with which she carries out her original and often audacious conceptions of Shakespearean music I am too utterly unnerved to give any adequate description. The lacerating discord of her wailings is in my tormented ears as I write, reconciling me to the grave. It is as if she had been excited by the Hallelujah Chorus to dance on the keyboard of a great organ with all the stops pulled out. I cannot—dare not—dwell on it. I admit that when she is using the rich middle of her voice in a quite normal and unstudied way, intent only on the feeling of the passage, the effect leaves nothing to be desired; but the moment she raises the pitch to carry out some deeply planned vocal masterstroke, or is driven by Shakespear himself to attempt a purely musical execution of a passage for which no other sort of execution is possible, then—well then, hold on tightly to the elbows of your stall, and bear it like a man. And when the feat is accompanied, as it sometimes is, by bold experiments in facial expression which all the passions of Cleopatra, complicated by seventy-times-sevenfold demoniacal possession, could but faintly account for, the eye has to share the anguish of the ear instead of consoling it with Miss Achurch's beauty. I have only seen the performance once; and I would not unsee it again if I could; but none the less I am a broken man after it. I may retain always an impression that I have actually looked on Cleopatra enthroned dead in her regal robes, with her hand on Antony's, and her awful eyes inhibiting the victorious Caesar. I grant that this "resolution" of the discord is grand and memorable; but oh! how infernal the discord was whilst it was still unresolved! That is the word that sums up the objection to Miss Achurch's Cleopatra in point of sound: it is discordant.

I need not say that at some striking points Miss Achurch's performance shews the same exceptional inventiveness and judgment in acting as her Ibsen achievements did, and that her energy is quite on the grand scale of the play. But even if we waive the whole musical question—and that means waiving the better half of Shakespear—she would still not be Cleopatra. Cleopatra says that the man who has seen her "hath seen some majesty, and should know." One conceives her as a trained professional queen, able to put on at will the deliberate artificial dignity which belongs to the technique of court life. She may keep it for state occasions, like the unaffected Catherine of Russia, or always retain it, like Louis XIV, in whom affectation was nature; but that she should have no command of it—that she should rely in modern republican fashion on her personal force, with a frank contempt for ceremony and artificiality, as Miss Achurch does, is to spurn her own part. And then, her beauty is not the beauty of Cleopatra. I do not mean merely that she is not "with Phoebus' amorous pinches black," or brown, bean-eyed, and pickaxe-faced. She is not even the English (or Anglo-Jewish) Cleopatra, the serpent of old Thames. She is of the broad-browed, column-necked, Germanic type—the Wagner heroine type—which in England, where it must be considered as the true racial heroic type, has given us two of our most remarkable histrionic geniuses in Miss Achurch herself and our dramatic singer, Miss Marie Brema,[4] both distinguished by great voices, busy brains, commanding physical energy, and untameable impetuosity and originality. Now this type has its limitations, one of them being that it has not the genius of worthlessness, and so cannot present it on the stage otherwise than as comic depravity or masterful wickedness. Adversity makes it superhuman, not subhuman, as it makes Cleopatra. When Miss Achurch comes on one of the weak, treacherous, affected streaks in Cleopatra, she suddenly drops from an Egyptian warrior queen into a naughty English petite bourgeoise, who carries off a little greediness and a little voluptuousness by a very unheroic sort of prettiness. That is, she treats it as a stroke of comedy; and as she is not a comedian, the stroke of comedy becomes in her hands a

---

[4] Marie Brema (d. 1925) was the first English opera singer invited by Wagner to sing at the Bayreuth Festival.

bit of fun. When the bourgeoise turns into a wild cat, and literally
snarls and growls menacingly at the bearer of the news of Antony's marriage with Octavia, she is at least more Cleopatra; but
when she masters herself, as Miss Achurch does, not in gipsy
fashion, but by a heroic-grandiose act of self-mastery, quite foreign to the nature of the "triple turned wanton" (as Mr Calvert
bowdlerizes it) of Shakespear,[5] she is presently perplexed by fresh
strokes of comedy—

> He's very knowing.
> I do perceive 't: there's nothing in her yet:
> The fellow has good judgment.

At which what can she do but relapse farcically into the bourgeoise again, since it is not on the heroic side of her to feel ele-
gantly self-satisfied whilst she is saying mean and silly things, as
the true Cleopatra does? Miss Achurch's finest feat in this scene
was the terrible look she gave the messenger when he said, in dis-
praise of Octavia, "And I do think she's thirty"—Cleopatra being
of course much more. Only, as Miss Achurch had taken good care
not to look more, the point was a little lost on Manchester. Later
on she is again quite in her heroic element (and out of Cleopatra's) in making Antony fight by sea. Her "I have sixty sails,
Caesar none better," and her overbearing of the counsels of
Enobarbus and Canidius to fight by land are effective, but
effective in the way of a Boadicea,[6] worth ten guzzling Antonys.
There is no suggestion of the petulant folly of the spoiled beauty
who has not imagination enough to know that she will be frightened when the fighting begins. Consequently when the audience,
already puzzled as to how to take Cleopatra, learns that she has
run away from the battle and afterwards that she has sold Antony
to Caesar, it does not know what to think. The fact is, Miss
Achurch steals Antony's thunder and Shakespear's thunder and

---

[5] Shakespeare wrote "triple turned whore" (IV, xii, 13).

[6] Boadicea, a warrior queen of ancient Britain, led a revolt against the
Romans. She was defeated and took poison in 62 A.D.

Ibsen's thunder and her own thunder so that she may ride the
whirlwind for the evening; and though this *Walkürenritt*[7] is intense and imposing, in spite of the discords, the lapses into farce,
and the failure in comedy and characterization—though once or
twice a really memorable effect is reached—yet there is not a
stroke of Cleopatra in it; and I submit that to bring an ardent
Shakespearean like myself all the way to Manchester to see Antony and Cleopatra with Cleopatra left out, even with Brynhild-
cum-Nora Helmer[8] substituted, is very different from bringing
down soft-hearted persons like Mr Clement Scott[9] and Mr William
Archer,[10] who have allowed Miss Achurch to make Ibsen-and-
Wagner pie of our poor Bard's historical masterpiece without a
word of protest.

And yet all that I have said about Miss Achurch's Cleopatra
cannot convey half the truth to those who have not seen Mr Louis
Calvert's Antony. It is on record that Antony's cooks put a fresh
boar on the spit every hour, so that he should never have to
wait long for his dinner. Mr Calvert looks as if he not only had
the boars put on the spit, but ate them. He is inexcusably fat:
Mr Bourchier[11] is a sylph by comparison. You will conclude, perhaps, that his fulness of habit makes him ridiculous as a lover.
But not at all. It is only your rhetorical tragedian whose effective-
ness depends on the oblatitude of his waistcoat. Mr Calvert is a
comedian—brimming over with genuine humane comedy. His
one really fine tragic effect is the burst of laughter at the irony
of fate with which, as he lies dying, he learns that the news of
Cleopatra's death, on the receipt of which he mortally wounded

---

[7] The *Walkürenritt* (or "Ride of the Valkyries") is an intensely dramatic
piece of descriptive music in Wagner's opera *The Valkyrie*, named after the
warrior maidens of German myth.

[8] Brynhild (Shaw's spelling) is the heroine of *The Valkyrie*.

[9] Clement Scott (1841–1904) was the conservative drama critic for the
Daily Telegraph.

[10] William Archer (1856–1924) was a distinguished drama critic who
translated Ibsen. See editor's Introduction, pp. ix–x.

[11] Arthur Bourchier (1863–1927) was an actor-manager known for his
Shakespearean roles, especially Falstaff.

himself, is only one of her theatrical, sympathy-catching lies. As a lover, he leaves his Cleopatra far behind. His features are so pleasant, his manner so easy, his humor so genial and tolerant, and his portliness so frank and unashamed, that no good-natured woman could resist him; and so the topsiturvitude of the performance culminates in the plainest evidence that Antony is the seducer of Cleopatra instead of Cleopatra of Antony. Only at one moment was Antony's girth awkward. When Eros, who was a slim and rather bony young man, fell on his sword, the audience applauded sympathetically. But when Antony in turn set about the Happy Despatch, the consequences suggested to the imagination were so awful that shrieks of horror arose in the pit; and it was a relief when Antony was borne off by four stalwart soldiers, whose sinews cracked audibly as they heaved him up from the floor.

Here, then, we have Cleopatra tragic in her comedy, and Antony comedic in his tragedy. We have Cleopatra heroically incapable of flattery or flirtation, and Antony with a wealth of blarney in every twinkle of his eye and every fold of his chin. We have, to boot, certain irrelevant but striking projections of Miss Achurch's genius, and a couple of very remarkable stage pictures invented by the late Charles Calvert.[12] But in so far as we have Antony and Cleopatra, we have it partly through the genius of the author, who imposes his conception on us through the dialogue in spite of everything that can be done to contradict him, and partly through the efforts of the secondary performers.

Of these Mr George F. Black, who plays Octavius Caesar, speaks blank verse rightly, if a little roughly, and can find his way to the feeling of the line by its cadence. Mr Mollison—who played Henry IV here to Mr Tree's[13] Falstaff—is Enobarbus, and spouts the description of the barge with all the honors. The minor parts are handled with the spirit and intelligence that can always be

[12] Charles Calvert (1828–1879), stage manager and principal actor at the Theatre Royal, Manchester, later manager of the Prince's Theatre, where he began a series of Shakespearean "revivals," was famous for his elaborate attention to accuracy and costuming.

[13] Beerbohm Tree (1853–1917), actor-manager, is perhaps best known for his Shakespearean festivals repeated annually at Her Majesty's Theatre.

had by a manager who really wants them. A few of the actors are
certainly very bad; but they suffer rather from an insane excess
of inspiration than from apathy. Charmian and Iras (Miss Ada
Mellon and Miss Maria Fauvet) produce an effect out of all
proportion to their scanty lines by the conviction and loyalty with
which they support Miss Achurch; and I do not see why Cleopatra
should ungratefully take Iras's miraculous death as a matter of
course by omitting the lines beginning "Have I the aspic in my
lips," nor why Charmian should be robbed of her fine reply to the
Roman's "Charmian, is this well done?" "It is well done, and
fitted for a princess descended of so many royal kings." No doubt
the Cleopatras of the palmy days objected to anyone but themselves dying effectively, and so such cuts became customary; but
the objection does not apply to the scene as arranged in Manchester. Modern managers should never forget that if they take care
of the minor actors the leading ones will take care of themselves.

May I venture to suggest to Dr Henry Watson that his incidental music, otherwise irreproachable, is in a few places much
too heavily scored to be effectively spoken through? Even in the
entr' actes the brass might be spared in view of the brevity of the
intervals and the almost continuous strain for three hours on the
ears of the audience. If the music be revived later as a concert
suite, the wind can easily be restored.

Considering that the performance requires an efficient orchestra
and chorus, plenty of supernumeraries, ten or eleven distinct
scenes, and a cast of twenty-four persons, including two leading
parts of the first magnitude; that the highest price charged for
admission is three shillings; and that the run is limited to eight
weeks, the production must be counted a triumph of management.
There is not the slightest reason to suppose that any London manager could have made a revival of Antony and Cleopatra more
interesting. Certainly none of them would have planned that un-
forgettable statue death for Cleopatra, for which, I suppose, all
Miss Achurch's sins against Shakespear will be forgiven her. I begin to have hopes of a great metropolitan vogue for that lady
now, since she has at last done something that is thoroughly
wrong from beginning to end.

Review of *Julius Caesar*

TAPPERTIT ON CAESAR

JULIUS CAESAR. Her Majesty's Theatre, 22 January 1898.

[29 *January* 1898]

The truce with Shakespear is over. It was only possible whilst Hamlet was on the stage. Hamlet is the tragedy of private life— nay, of individual bachelor-poet life. It belongs to a detached residence, a select library, an exclusive circle, to no occupation, to fathomless boredom, to impenitent mugwumpism, to the illusion that the futility of these things is the futility of existence, and its contemplation philosophy: in short, to the dream-fed gentleman- ism of the age which Shakespear inaugurated in English litera- ture: the age, that is, of the rising middle class bringing into power the ideas taught it by its servants in the kitchen, and its fathers in the shop—ideas now happily passing away as the on- slaught of modern democracy offers to the kitchen-taught and home-bred the alternative of achieving a real superiority or going ignominiously under in the class conflict.

It is when we turn to Julius Caesar, the most splendidly written political melodrama we possess, that we realize the apparently im- mortal author of Hamlet as a man, not for all time, but for an age only, and that, too, in all solidly wise and heroic aspects, the most despicable of all the ages in our history. It is impossible for even the most judicially minded critic to look without a revulsion of indignant contempt at this travestying of a great man as a silly braggart, whilst the pitiful gang of mischief-makers who destroyed him are lauded as statesmen and patriots. There is not a single sentence uttered by Shakespear's Julius Caesar that is, I will not say worthy of him, but even worthy of an average Tammany boss.[14] Brutus is nothing but a familiar type of English suburban

---

[14] The Tammany Society, founded originally in New York City in 1789 as a national patriotic and charitable society, was well known for its cor- rupt influence on local politics.

preacher: politically he would hardly impress the Thames Conservancy Board. Cassius is a vehemently assertive nonentity. It is only when we come to Antony, unctuous voluptuary and self-seeking sentimental demagogue, that we find Shakespear in his depth; and in his depth, of course, he is superlative. Regarded as a crafty stage job, the play is a triumph: rhetoric, claptrap, effective gushes of emotion, all the devices of the popular playwright, are employed with a profusion of power that almost breaks their backs. No doubt there are slips and slovenliness of the kind that careful revisers eliminate; but they count for so little in the mass of accomplishment that it is safe to say that the dramatist's art can be carried no further on that plane. If Goethe, who understood Caesar and the significance of his death—"the most senseless of deeds" he called it—had treated the subject, his conception of it would have been as superior to Shakespear's as St John's Gospel is to the Police News; but his treatment could not have been more magnificently successful. As far as sonority, imagery, wit, humor, energy of imagination, power over language, and a whimsically keen eye for idiosyncrasies can make a dramatist, Shakespear was the king of dramatists. Unfortunately, a man may have them all, and yet conceive high affairs of state exactly as Simon Tappertit[15] did. In one of the scenes in Julius Caesar a conceited poet bursts into the tent of Brutus and Cassius, and exhorts them not to quarrel with one another. If Shakespear had been able to present his play to the ghost of the great Julius, he would probably have had much the same reception. He certainly would have deserved it.

When it was announced that Mr Tree had resolved to give special prominence to the character of Caesar in his acting version, the critics winked, and concluded simply that the actor-manager was going to play Antony and not Brutus. Therefore I had better say that Mr Tree must stand acquitted of any belittlement of the parts which compete so strongly with his own. Before going to Her Majesty's I was curious enough to block out for myself a di-

15 Simon Tappertit is an apprentice in Dickens' *Barnaby Rudge*.

vision of the play into three acts; and I found that Mr Tree's division corresponded exactly with mine. Mr Waller's opportunities as Brutus, and Mr McLeay's as Cassius, are limited only by their own ability to take advantage of them; and Mr Louis Calvert figures as boldly in the public eye as he did in his own production of Antony and Cleopatra last year at Manchester. Indeed, Mr Calvert is the only member of the company who achieves an unequivocal success. The preference expressed in the play by Caesar for fat men may, perhaps, excuse Mr Calvert for having again permitted himself to expand after his triumphant reduction of his girth for his last appearance in London. However, he acted none the worse: in fact, nobody else acted so skilfully or originally. The others, more heavily burdened, did their best, quite in the spirit of the man who had never played the fiddle, but had no doubt he could if he tried. Without oratory, without style, without specialized vocal training, without any practice worth mentioning, they assaulted the play with cheerful self-sufficiency, and gained great glory by the extent to which, as a masterpiece of the playwright's trade, it played itself. Some small successes were not lacking. Caesar's nose was good: Calpurnia's bust was worthy of her: in such parts Garrick and Siddons[16] could have achieved no more. Miss Evelyn Millard's Roman matron in the style of Richardson— Cato's daughter as Clarissa—was an unlooked-for novelty; but it cost a good deal of valuable time to get in the eighteenth century between the lines of the first B.C. By operatic convention—the least appropriate of all conventions—the boy Lucius was played by Mrs Tree, who sang Sullivan's ultra-nineteenth-century Orpheus with his Lute, modulations and all, to a pizzicato accompaniment supposed to be played on a lyre with eight open and unstoppable strings, a feat complexly and absurdly impossible. Mr Waller, as Brutus, failed in the first half of the play. His intention clearly was to represent Brutus as a man superior to fate and

---

[16] Sarah Siddons (1755–1831), an English actress who acquired a great reputation as a tragic actress, was greatly acclaimed in the role of Lady Macbeth.

circumstance; but the effect he produced was one of insensibility. Nothing could have been more unfortunate; for it is through the sensibility of Brutus that the audience have to learn what they cannot learn from the phlegmatic pluck of Casca or the narrow vindictiveness of Cassius: that is, the terrible momentousness, the harrowing anxiety and dread, of the impending catastrophe. Mr Waller left that function to the thunderstorm. From the death of Caesar onward he was better; and his appearance throughout was effective; but at best his sketch was a water-color one. Mr Franklyn McLeay carried off the honors of the evening by his deliberate staginess and imposing assumptiveness: that is, by as much of the grand style as our playgoers now understand; but in the last act he was monotonously violent, and died the death of an incorrigible poseur, not of a noble Roman. Mr Tree's memory failed him as usual; and a good deal of the technical part of his work was botched and haphazard, like all Shakespearean work nowadays; nevertheless, like Mr Calvert, he made the audience believe in the reality of the character before them. But it is impossible to praise his performance in detail. I cannot recall any single passage in the scene after the murder that was well done: in fact, he only secured an effective curtain by bringing Calpurnia on the stage to attitudinize over Caesar's body. To say that the demagogic oration in the Forum produced its effect is nothing; for its effect is inevitable, and Mr Tree neither made the most of it nor handled it with any pretence of mastery or certainty. But he was not stupid, nor inane, nor Bard-of-Avon ridden; and he contrived to interest the audience in Antony instead of trading on their ready-made interest in Mr Beerbohm Tree. And for that many sins may be forgiven him nowadays, when the playgoer, on first nights at all events, goes to see the cast rather than the play.

What is missing in the performance, for want of the specific Shakespearean skill, is the Shakespearean music. When we come to those unrivalled grandiose passages in which Shakespear turns on the full organ, we want to hear the sixteen-foot pipes booming, or, failing them (as we often must, since so few actors are naturally equipped with them), the ennobled tone, and the tempo suddenly steadied with the majesty of deeper purpose. You have, too, those moments when the verse, instead of opening up the depths of sound, rises to its most brilliant clangor, and the lines ring like a thousand trumpets. If we cannot have these effects, or if we can only have genteel drawing room arrangements of them, we cannot have Shakespear; and that is what is mainly the matter at Her Majesty's: there are neither trumpets nor pedal pipes there. The conversation is metrical and emphatic in an elocutionary sort of way; but it makes no distinction between the arid prairies of blank verse which remind one of Henry VI at its crudest, and the places where the morass suddenly piles itself into a mighty mountain. Cassius in the first act has a twaddling forty-line speech, base in its matter and mean in its measure, followed immediately by the magnificent torrent of rhetoric, the first burst of true Shakespearean music in the play, beginning—

> Why, man, he doth bestride the narrow world
> Like a Collosus, and we petty men
> Walk under his huge legs and peep about
> To find ourselves dishonorable graves.

I failed to catch the slightest change of elevation or reinforcement of feeling when Mr McLeay passed from one to the other. His tone throughout was dry; and it never varied. By dint of energetic, incisive articulation, he drove his utterances harder home than the others; but the best lines seemed to him no more than the worst: there were no heights and depths, no contrast of black thunder-cloud and flaming lightning flash, no stirs and surprises. Yet he was not inferior in oratory to the rest. Mr Waller certainly cannot be reproached with dryness of tone; and his delivery of the speech in the Forum was perhaps the best piece of formal elocution we got; but he also kept at much the same level throughout, and did not at any moment attain to anything that could be called grandeur. Mr Tree, except for a conscientiously desperate effort to cry havoc and let slip the dogs of war in the robustious manner, with no better result than to all but extinguish his voice, very sensibly left oratory out of the question, and tried conversational sincerity, which answered so well that his delivery of "This was the noblest Roman of them all" came off excellently.

The real hero of the revival is Mr Alma Tadema.[17] The scenery and stage coloring deserve everything that has been said of them. But the illusion is wasted by want of discipline and want of thought behind the scenes. Every carpenter seems to make it a point of honor to set the cloths swinging in a way that makes Rome reel and the audience positively seasick. In Brutus's house the door is on the spectators' left: the knocks on it come from the right. The Roman soldiers take the field, each man with his two javelins neatly packed up like a fishing-rod. After a battle, in which they are supposed to have made the famous Roman charge, hurling these javelins in and following them up sword in hand, they come back carrying the javelins still undisturbed in their rug-straps, in perfect trim for a walk-out with the nursery-maids of Philippi.

The same want of vigilance appears in the acting version. For example, though the tribunes Flavius and Marullus are replaced by two of the senators, the lines referring to them by name are not altered. But the oddest oversight is the retention in the tent scene of the obvious confusion of the original version of the play, in which the death of Portia was announced to Brutus by Messala, with the second version, into which the quarrel scene was written to strengthen the fourth act. In this version Brutus, already in possession of the news, reveals it to Cassius. The play has come down to us with the two alternative scenes strung together: so that Brutus's reception of Messala's news, following his own revelation of it to Cassius, is turned into a satire on Roman fortitude, the suggestion being that the secret of the calm with which a noble Roman received the most terrible tidings in public was that it had been carefully imparted to him in private beforehand. Mr Tree has not noticed this; and the two scenes are gravely played one after the other at Her Majesty's. This does not matter much to our

---

[17] Sir Lawrence Alma Tadema (1836–1912) was famous for his paintings of classical subjects.

playgoers, who never venture to use their common sense when Shakespear is in question; but it wastes time. Mr Tree may without hesitation cut out Pindarus and Messala, and go straight on from the bowl of wine to Brutus's question about Philippi.

The music, composed for the occasion by Mr Raymond Roze, made me glad that I had already taken care to acknowledge the value of Mr Roze's services to Mr Tree; for this time he has missed the Roman vein rather badly. To be a Frenchman was once no disqualification for the antique, because French musicians used to be brought up on Gluck as English ones were brought up on Handel. But Mr Roze composes as if Gluck had been supplanted wholly in his curriculum by Gounod and Bizet. If that prelude to the third act were an attempt to emulate the overtures to Alceste or Iphigenia[18] I could have forgiven it. But to give us the soldiers' chorus from Faust, crotchet for crotchet and triplet for triplet, with nothing changed but the notes, was really too bad.

---

[18] *Alcestis* (1767) and *Iphigenia in Aulis* (1774) were operas on Greek classical themes by Gluck. Shaw admired Gluck's nobly severe style above the sensuous romanticism of Bizet's *Carmen* and Gounod's *Faust* (1859), which were, and remain, much more popular works.

SHAW'S COMMENTS
ON HIS PLAY

Interview in *The Academy*

The following interview, not hitherto reprinted, was published in The Academy *on April 30, 1898, under the title, "Mr. Shaw's Future: A Conversation." The interview contains Shaw's first public statement of resignation as drama critic from the* Saturday Review *and the announcement of his work on a new play,* Caesar and Cleopatra. *The interview was written up by Charles Rook.*

"We are anxious about your future," I remarked to Mr. Bernard Shaw.

"There is really no news about my future," said Mr. Shaw, "except that I am going to throw up dramatic criticism."[1]

"Good gracious! Why?" I asked.

Mr. Shaw, who does not even sit in a chair as other men sit, twisted himself rapidly round a strained foot—the result of over-much cycling.

"Well, I've been writing dramatic criticism in the *Saturday Review* for nearly four years, and really I've said all I've got to say about actors and acting. If I went on I should only repeat myself; I've begun to do that already. After all, when you have written two or three articles about Beerbohm Tree you have said all there is to say about Beerbohm Tree. It doesn't take very long to say all you think of Irving.

"I shall lose my pulpit," continued Mr. Shaw, "and that is a pity. But I fancy the world is rather tired of being preached at. Besides, I suspect it is beginning to find me out. For years I was supposed to be brilliant and sparkling and audacious. That was quite a mistake. I am really slow, industrious, painstaking, timid. Only I have continually been forced into positions that I am

---

[1] Shaw wrote his "Valedictory" to the *Saturday Review* on May 21, 1898.

bound to accept and go through with. I am not clever at all."

Mr. Shaw sat upright and looked at me with complete candour in his eyes, as I made a gesture of polite dissent.

"I am a genius," pronounced Mr. Shaw, sitting upon his shoulder-blades.

"After all," proceeded Mr. Shaw, "I have accomplished something. I have made Shakespeare popular by knocking him off his pedestal and kicking him round the place and making people realise that he's not a demi-god, but a dramatist."

"Then do you think of going in for Parliament?"

Mr. Shaw writhed round his disabled foot.

"I haven't much voice," he said; "but I daresay I might get a place in the chorus at the opera. And I should be doing quite as much good there, and have a deal more fun, than in the chorus at Westminster. Think of the incredible waste of time! And you must remember that for the last ten years I—I and a few of my associates—have practically directed public policy. There's no reason at all for my going into Parliament. But the Vestry—now there is some sense in a Vestry. It does something. Really, my dear fellow [Mr. Shaw nursed his foot in his lap], you ought to be on a Vestry.[2] If you take it humorously, you can laugh at the amazing difficulties it finds in doing the simplest things. If you take it seriously, you learn how things ultimately get done. When you come to think of the muddle-headed way in which affairs are managed, you wonder that the world goes on at all, instead of smashing up in confusion. It does go on, but the waste of life is awful. We worry through—just like the Northern armies in the American Civil War—by sheer force of numbers. If we could ensure that no more people should be born for twenty years, we should very soon find out a way of economising our forces. I have always made it a rule, you know, to be mixed up with practical life; that is where I score and the purely literary man fails. The people who write Adelphi melodramas know life—of a kind. They

[2] Shaw became a member of the Vestry of St. Pancras, a local governing body in London, in 1897 and remained in public service six years.

know the bar-loafing blackguard, and the sort of thing he likes. I know life—the life of action—affairs. The literary man can't write a play, because he knows nothing at all of life. The literary man ought to serve on a Vestry. For my own part I have found my experience of affairs invaluable in the writing of plays."

"Then are we to regard you in the future as a dramatist?"

"I am just in the middle of the first act of a new play."

"What is it about?"

"Well, this time I am going to give Shakespeare a lead. Cleopatra is the heroine, but Caesar, and not Antony, is the hero. And I want to see Forbes Robertson and Mrs. Patrick Campbell in it."

"Then I suppose you have been reading up Mommsen—and people like that?"

"Not a bit of it. History is only a dramatisation of events. And if I start telling lies about Caesar, it's a hundred to one that they will be just the same lies that other people have told about him. I never worry myself about historical details until the play is done; human nature is very much the same always and everywhere. And when I go over my play to put the details right I find there is surprisingly little to alter. 'Arms and the Man,' for example, was finished before I had decided where to set the scene, and then it only wanted a word here and there to put matters straight. You see, I know human nature. Given Caesar, and a certain set of circumstances, I know what would happen, and when I have finished the play you will find I have written history."

Mr. Shaw dug both his hands deep into his pockets, and turned on to one side.

"Criticism is a poor thing to spend your life over," he said. "Four years over the painters of London, four years over the musicians, and four years over the actors—that is quite long enough to express any views you may have. It's an awful labour done as I do it. And you can't make money at that sort of work. Now, you wouldn't think that 'Arms and the Man' was a great success. I don't suppose anyone made much out of it, as things go. But from first to last it has brought me £800. And that was when my percentage of profits was low. The 'Devil's Disciple,' which has been running in America, has drawn £25,000; and on that I get 10 per cent. I should have to write my heart out for six years in the *Saturday* to make as much. It was quite easy to write, too. A young woman I know wanted to make a portrait of me, sitting on the corner of a table, which is a favourite attitude of mine. So I wrote the play in a note-book to fill up the time. I write all my plays on scraps of paper at odd times—on omnibuses and places like that."

"Then," I said gravely, "you are going in frankly for money-making."

Mr. Shaw shifted to his other side and twined one leg round an adjacent chair.

"It is quite time," he said, "that I gave younger journalists a chance."

"It is inexpressibly painful to me," I said, "to find that you, of all men, have succumbed to the temptations of riches."

Mr. Shaw curled himself up until his face and his slippers were within an inch of meeting, and laughed.

"I will not stay to see you swallow yourself," I said.

Two Letters to Golding Bright

Golding Bright, English critic and literary agent, was, according to St. John Ervine, the solitary hisser at the first performance of Arms and the Man *(April 21, 1894). That hiss initiated the famous Shavian retort, "I quite agree with you, sir, but what can we do against so many?" These letters, dated December 15, 1898, and May 2, 1900, are reproduced from* Advice to a Young Critic and Other Letters, *edited by E. J. West, and published by Crown Publishers, Inc., New York, 1955.*

December 15, 1898

. . . In my Caesar & Cleopatra, when it is published, you will find apparently outrageous gags[3] in the aspect of allusions to the foreign politics of the Beaconsfield-Salisbury period, which are nevertheless as "historical" as anything in Addison's "Cato."

I have no information to give you beyond this: that the play and The Perfect Wagnerite have been produced under great difficulties owing to my illness & my chapter of accidents.[4] However, the play is now finished, except for the final revision and the arrangement of the stage business, at which I am at work now at the cost of a serious loss of ground in my recovery. It is in five

---

[3] That is, the anachronistic slogans, "Peace with honor" and "Egypt for the Egyptians." The Marquis of Salisbury was Foreign Secretary in the ministry of Benjamin Disraeli in 1878–80. He later served three terms as Prime Minister.

[4] In April of 1898 a tightly-laced shoe produced an abscess on Shaw's instep that developed into necrosis of the bone. In June he fell down the stairs and broke his left arm. In September he celebrated his improvement in health by riding a bicycle with one foot; he fell and sprained his ankle. Twice more he sprained that ankle and underwent two operations on his foot.

acts, containing eight scenes, & involving considerable variety and splendor of mounting. It begins with the arrival of Caesar in Egypt in pursuit of Pompey after the battle of Pharsalia, & ends with his departure after six months stay in Alexandria with Cleopatra. The whole episode was rejected by Froude as a mere romance; but Mommsen describes it in considerable detail. The famous episode of the carpet in which Appolodorus (sic) the Sicilian conveyed Cleopatra into Caesar's presence is introduced; but in a way which would considerably astonish the French painters who are so fond of the subject.[5]

Nothing whatever has been settled as to the performance of the play. Of course Caesar & Cleopatra suggests Forbes Robertson & Mrs Patrick Campbell; but they are not responsible for this, nor am I. I have read the first act alone to some friends in private, but to no one else. All announcements as to the destination of the play are premature: Nothing has been proposed, nothing is pending. I shall take no trouble to get the play performed, as I shall be busy enough with its successor, which, with "The Devil's Disciple" and C. & C., will form my next volume of plays & will certainly be published without any delay on the chance of production.

May 2, 1900

The Three Plays for Puritans will be published next autumn. There will be quite a collection of prefaces, chief among them a tremendous sermon entitled "Why for Puritans?" In it I give, with exceeding frankness, an account of the London Theatres as I found them during my critical campaign in the Saturday Review from 1895 to 1898, when I collapsed and nearly died of pure inanity and emptiness administered by the managers in large weekly doses. I appeal, of course, to the Puritans to come to the rescue of the stage; and to shew that this is no mere personal eccentricity of mine—no hackneyed Shawism—I find, whilst my preface is still in MS, William Archer in the Morning Leader, cry-

[5] See note 35, p. 79.

ing out for a new Collier[6] to write a new treatise on "the profaneness & immorality etc.," & Massingham[7] immediately afterwards hotly defending George Moore[8] against Walkley[9] from the Puritan point of view.

In a second preface I attack the current critical chatter about the so-called originality of my plays, shewing that the peculiar Diabolonian creed of the Devil's Disciple is as old as William Blake, and had been freshly affirmed by Robert Buchanan[10] in a poem published before the D's D was written; that the contrast between mere knighthood and military capacity which is the theme of Arms & The Man was elaborated years ago in Mommsen's History of Rome, one of the best known books in Europe; that Buchanan was quite right in pointing out that my stage tricks are as old as Charles Mathews[11] in Cool as a Cucumber, & probably centuries older; and that, in short, it is only the criticism that reads nothing, remembers nothing, and knows nothing, that is astonished and bewildered by my sallies.

A third preface deals with Shakespear, and with epoch making authors and artists in general, explaining my view that Shakespear's epoch is over.

I have not yet written any more prefaces; so it only remains to

[6] Jeremy Collier (1650–1726) is chiefly remembered for his Short View of the Immorality and Profaneness of the English Stage, in which he specifically attacked the Restoration dramas of Congreve and Vanbrugh.

[7] H. W. Massingham (1860–1924), journalist and editor of The Star, The Daily Chronicle and The Nation, was a discerning critic of literature and drama. He reviewed many of Shaw's earlier plays.

[8] George Moore (1852–1933), British novelist, poet, dramatist, and critic, was one of the first champions of the naturalistic school in literature.

[9] A. B. Walkley, a formalist critic associated with the London Times from 1900 to 1926, disliked the drama of ideas and insisted that Shaw's comedies were not plays. The preface to Man and Superman is dedicated to Walkley, who is also the original of Trotter in Fanny's First Play.

[10] Robert Buchanan (1841–1901) was a critic and minor poet. The poem referred to here is "The Devil's Case."

[11] Charles Mathews was a comedian during the 1860s and 1870s who was particularly well known for his portrayal of Plumper in Blanchard Jerrold's farce Cool as a Cucumber.

say that the book will conclude with an appendix consisting of the three plays—The Devil's Disciple, Caesar & Cleopatra, and Captain Brassbound's Conversion. Publishers: Grant Richards and H. S. Stone & Co. of Chicago.

Letter to Gilbert Murray

*Shaw had consulted the renowned classicist, Gilbert Murray, on
numerous occasions about his play. Later, Shaw based his characterization of Adolphus Cusins, his professor of Greek in* Major
Barbara, *on Murray. This letter, dated July 28, 1900, was originally published in the Autumn issue of* Drama *(1956).*

Where are you at present? I shall soon submit to you a few
notes which I propose to append to *Caesar and Cleopatra.*

My vestry is in recess; and I shall have a clean run down here
for a few weeks now, though I have to go up for a Housing Conference on Monday and Tuesday.

I have carefully considered your comments on my history, and
have modified accordingly. I am not quite convinced that I have
overdone Cleopatra's ferocity. If she had been an educated lady
of the time I should have made her quite respectable and civilised; but what I was able to gather about her father, the convivial
Flute Blower, and other members of the household, joined with
considerations of the petulance of royalty, led me to draw her as
I did. I submit to you that if a dramatist, 2000 years hence, were
to portray George IV as an ideal First Gentleman of Europe, with
all the culture of his age upon him, he would miss his mark very
considerably.

I also demur to your dictum that we have enough information
about the ancient Britons to shew that they were not like Britannicus. In every line that I have come across concerning them I
see Mr. Podsnap. Surely, if they are like Britannicus now, after
such romantic adulterations as the Roman and Norman invasions
and conquests, how much more like him must they have been then,
when they were the pure products of the climate? I am quite serious.

Further, I suggest that in the Gallic Wars the style is not the man—at least, not the whole man. As a writer, Caesar was an amateur, and could not have achieved complete self expression in letters even if he had lived now, when literature is no longer the game of style it was to Cicero's pals. If the dramatic stories about him are true, such as the burning of the letters after the final defeat of Cato, and the encounter with the mutinous legion—"Comrades: what do you want?" "Our discharge." "*Citizens:* you have it. Sorry you will not be able to share my triumph, etc." and so on, not to mention his personal address in getting round people of all sorts and sizes, he *must* have been an adroit comedian. Now the style-man of the Gallic Wars is not a comedian; but neither is he a dandy; and Caesar *was* a dandy. And I cannot conceive a great man as a grave man: to lack humor is to lack the universal solvent. If my Caesar *can* be guyed, he is a failure. But I believe him to be authentic to the last comma.

Three Letters to Siegfried Trebitsch

Siegfried Trebitsch was Shaw's German translator. He served as Shaw's liaison in the Berlin production of Caesar *and* Cleopatra. *The letters to Trebitsch are from the Henry W. and Albert A. Berg Collection, New York Public Library.*

August 16, 1903

Your letter arrived yesterday—Saturday evening—too late to post the IV and V acts to you. Today is Sunday; and in Scotland nothing can be done on Sunday except go to church. So I cannot post this and register it until tomorrow. Perhaps you will get it on Wednesday.

As to Fischer, there is only one thing I really care about; and that is the time limit of the agreement. It must be limited either to a definite number of copies or to a term of years. The royalty is a very good one—the same as I get in England; but the main thing is that if Fischer turns out badly, if he does not advertize and push the book properly, if he takes to drink, or goes mad, or files a petition in bankruptcy, we must not be tied helplessly to him for ever and ever. I have just paid £60 to secure the American copyright of my new book by printing it in America at my own cost sooner than let the Macmillan Company have it without a time limit.

By the way, if Cotta reproaches you for giving this book to Fischer,[12] you may tell him that I was so dissatisfied with the half-profits agreement that I would not hear of any further dealings with him.

---

[12] Fischer and Cotta were German publishers. Fischer published the *Dramatische Werke von Bernard Shaw*, Berlin, 1911 and 1919; Cotta published *Drei Dramen: Candida, Teufelskerl* [*The Devil's Disciple*], *Helden* [*Arms and the Man*], Stuttgart, 1903.

And now as to C & C. The corrections are very important, because the production in Berlin, whether successful or not—but especially if successful—will not crush Kellner:[13] it will, on the contrary, give him a much better chance than he had before of taking your scalp. His article in the Wiener Tagblatt did not matter outside Vienna: and even in Vienna it was possible to counter it by the Zeit articles, my own,[14] Bahr's[15] etc. But a Berlin production at the Neues Theater will create a demand for magazine articles on me, just as the production of Cyrano here created a demand for magazine articles on Rostand in England and America. Kellner, who lives, I suppose, by his pen, is pretty sure to seize the opportunity to earn the price of a magazine article. And if Kellner sets the fashion of saying that there are blunders in the translation, all the others will follow suit; for 99 out of a 100 of them cannot read English; but all of them will have to pretend that they speak and read it like natives. The bigger the success the more articles there will be. Therefore now is the time to give no chance to the enemy. This is why I have brought down a huge Muret-Sanders dictionary here and spent a month revising a translation in a language that I have never learnt. In future I will make the translation and you shall revise it. The dialogue seems to me to be just as good as the original and sometimes better; but still there are lots of mistakes. Mistakes dont matter: they can always be corrected, and they dont kill a play even if they are left uncorrected; but they are just what Kellner wants for a slashing review. For instance, he could write ten pages about Rufio swearing by Zeus instead of by Jove; and as to the centurion's cudgel being changed into the Dionysiac Thyrsusstab, you would never hear the end of it. You race recklessly through

---

[13] Leon Kellner (1859–1928) was an Austrian literary critic.

[14] Shaw's self-jesting article in *Die Zeit* was *Vornehmlich über mich selbst* ("Mainly about Myself"), which greatly amused the Viennese public.

[15] Herman Bahr (1863–1934), Austrian critic, author, and dramatist, edited the weekly paper *Die Zeit* from 1892 to 1897. The reference is to Bahr's critique of Shaw and his works, which acquainted the German-speaking public with Shaw's dramatic artistry. Bahr produced *Candida* at the Deutsche Volkstheater.

these things, which dont interest you. You care for nothing but the drama. That is just as it should be, as the drama is the main thing. But you give yourself away to the people who are interested in Roman history, Roman politics and Roman institutions. And indeed you ought to be interested in them. A true dramatist should be interested in everything. Kellner would write ten pages of the most erudite Roman history to shew that only the most unge-bildeter Uebersetzer[16] could possibly make Lucius Septimius call the Okkupationsarmée "rebels," or indeed mention such a delicate subject as rebellion to Caesar at all. So be very careful to set all these little things right. I should not have sweated over them all these days if I were not convinced that they would get you into trouble.

Barbarous as my drawings of the scenery are, a great deal de-pends on them. Even an ordinary modern play like Es Lebe das Leben, with drawing-room scenes throughout, depends a good deal on the author writing his dialogue with a clear plan of stage ac-tion in his head; but in a play like Caesar it is absolutely neces-sary: the staging is just as much a part of the play as the dia-logue. It will not do to let a scenepainter and a sculptor loose on the play without a specification on the conditions with which their scenery must comply. Will you therefore tell the Neues man-ager that we will supply sketches. I will not inflict my own draughtsmanship on him; but I will engage a capable artist here to make presentable pictures.

Now as to all this obsolete power and pigtail—Scene VIII—Die Vorige[17] etc.! There is no point in the Schlachtenlenker[18] or in the Drei Dramen at which these silly interpolations are positively in-sufferable; but in the 4th act of C & C there are two places at least

---

[16] "Uneducated translator."

[17] Shaw advised Trebitsch to omit many of the stage directions common in German plays, for example, dividing acts into scenes: Scene VIII—Die Vorige, meaning "The same people on the stage as before." Shaw felt that such interpolations were obsolete and pedantic, and, in particular, an out-rage in Act IV of *Caesar and Cleopatra* where the entrances and exits of characters are quite frequent.

[18] *Schlachtenlenker* is Trebitsch's translation of Shaw's *Man of Destiny*.

in which they are simply an outrage. Believe me, nobody will miss them. If their disappearance would incommode anybody I should not be so cocksure about omitting them; but I am so certain that they will die unlamented and even unnoticed that if I were you I should not even mention the matter in a preface. I only suggested that, in order to break the innovation to you as gently as possible. When you meet a foolish superstition, dont stop to remonstrate or argue or apologize: walk straight through it as if it didnt exist. As the American poetess (Charlotte Stetson)[19] says in her poem "The Prejudice"—

> "I simply walked straight through it
> As if it werent there."

and that is what we must do with this nonsensical pedantry. If anybody points out that we have effected an audacious reform, so much the better for us; but I am afraid the blow will be so completely in the water—in the sense that there will be no resistance to it—that we shall have to do without that useful advertisement.

As to waiting for a success, do you realize that if Caesar fails we shall never have another chance? You must never wait for anything. We must plank everything on this production. We must do everything on the assumption that it is going to be a triumph, and that its failure will be the end of all things. As to thinking twice as to such a trumpery affair as this "Die Vorige etc." business, that would be absurd. Of course the play may fail. Very likely it will; for as you, being an Austrian, very well know, the Germans are as stupid as any people under the sun, and are not a bit likely to treat me better than they treated Wagner—except that they adore foreigners and despise themselves. But what then? We shall simply begin again, and treat the next production in the same way, as if it, too, were the crisis of our destiny. That is the way things are done in this world. Meanwhile be as peculiar

---

[19] Charlotte Stetson Gilman (1860–1935), social reformer, lecturer, and writer, joined the Fabian Socialists and was a spokesman for women. Besides her small volume of poems, *In This Our World* (1893), she is best known for *Women and Economics* (1898).

and as affected and as conceited and as bizarre as you possibly can about the trifles whose importance exists only in the imaginations of the journalists and flaneurs. Reserve your seriousness for the real things of which they know nothing. If the play fails, I hope they will say that my plays are only good to read; for then the public will buy them from Fischer.

I do not object to the cast being published. You will find it in Mrs Warren. But there must not be an idiotic list of nameless characters, ending with "soldiers, citizens, boatsmen, performing dogs etc. etc. etc."

If Hauptamme wont do, let Ftata call herself Kronamme or Koniglichamme or Reichs Amme or something pretentious and prahlerisch.[20]

Now as to Pilum. Mommsen's "Wurfspiess" is vieux jeu: it dates from 1876, when Bismarck and the Germans affected an extravagant Nationalism and called the telephone the Fernsprecher.[21] Nowadays Nationalism has expanded into Imperialism; and ancient Rome is fashionable. The Kaiser will see himself as Caesar; and when Britannus says "Only as Caesar's slave have I found true freedom" he will give an enthusiastic Hoch and decorate you with the Iron Cross. I have carefully considered all this before recommending you to call the Pilum by its Roman name; and I am still of that opinion—more than ever, in fact.

If Bahr disagrees with me on this or any other point, it shews that he needs a holiday. The work of the season has been too much for him.

Yes Du der Du is all right: I became resigned to it after the 6th or 7th time. . . .

[20] Shaw had called Ftatateeta "Chief nurse" (Hauptamme), but is here suggesting other translations: Kronamme, "Crown's nurse"; Koniglichamme, "Royal nurse"; Reichs Amme, "Kingdom's nurse." Prahlerisch means "ostentatious."

[21] Wurfspiess means "javelin" and vieux jeu means "old hat." Shaw's reference to the German translation of Pilum and telephone as nationalistic in origin is based upon the use of German root words for those words other than the original Latin and Greek roots. Fernsprecher is literally "far-speaker"; Wurfspiess is "throw-spear."

I forgot to say that you have not translated the notes to C & C. This is a fearful insult to me. I cherish those notes beyond all the rest of the play. You must translate them.

April 13, 1906

. . . I am sorry Caesar was not more successful in Berlin. It would have been better to omit the third act: the play is too long. Was the Caesar able to rise to the grander moments of the part in Act IV & in the scene with Septimius in Act II? What I dread is that they played it as a comedy all through—five acts of Bluntschli[22] in a bald pate instead of Caesar.

Why on earth does he not induce the Kaiser to pay a visit? Wilhelm would see himself as Caesar, & perhaps write an additional act or play the part himself some night.

May 7, 1906

. . . The secret of Caesar's failure is out at last; and never again shall Reinhardt have a play of mine to ruin. Barker has seen it and told me all about it.

They have cut out the first scene of the 4th act!!! Of course that meant utter failure. It is in that scene that the change in Cleopatra's character is shewn, and the audience prepared for the altered atmosphere and deeper seriousness of the later scene. To omit it is such a hopeless artistic stupidity that the man who would do it would do anything. I will not trust him with the Superman or with anything else after that. Write to him and tell him so. If you dont, I will write myself, not to him, but to the Berlin papers.

He has also cut out the burning of the library, which must make the end of the second act unintelligible. In short, he has done

---

[22] Bluntschli is the practical and sanguine Swiss soldier in *Arms and the Man*.

everything that a thoroughfaced blockhead could do to achieve a failure; and he has achieved it accordingly. If he has advanced any money on the Superman, send it back to him at once; and tell him that I protest against any further performance of Caesar with his abominable mutilation. I told him what to do— to omit the third act. He was too clever to do that; so he spoiled the 2nd, 3rd, 4th acts instead, and wrecked the play. May his soul perish for it.

It is always a mistake to trust to these people to alter a play. They see the effects, but they dont see the preparation of the effects—the gradual leading of the audience up to them. They cut the preparation out, and then are surprised because the effects miss fire. . . .

P.S. Barker says that the Roman army consisted of about half as many men as the crew of Captain Brassbound's ship at the little Court theatre. But that I could forgive. It is the cutting of the 4th act that rouses me to an implacably vindictive fury. My play has been deliberately murdered.

"The Heroic Actors"

Shaw wrote this article as a letter addressed to B. W. Findon, the editor of Play Pictorial, *for its October 1907 issue, which has been reprinted in Mander and Mitcheson's* The Theatrical Companion to Shaw *(New York, 1955).*

Caesar and Cleopatra is an attempt of mine to pay an instalment of the debt that all dramatists owe to the art of heroic acting. Since Shakespeare paid up so handsomely on this score, the British drama has been falling into heavier and heavier arrears. The heroic actor is forced into every-day drama because we cannot spend our whole playgoing lives at *Hamlet* or *Macbeth*; *Virginius, Ingomar* and the *Gamester* are outmoded; and *Richelieu*[23] does not carry a heroic actor very far in the twenty years of eminence which follow his long apprenticeship. Besides, our conception of heroism has changed of late years. The stage hero of the palmy days is a pricked bubble. The gentlemanly hero, of whom Tennyson's King Arthur was the type, suddenly found himself out, as Torvald Helmer in Ibsen's *Doll's House*, and died of the shock. It is no use going on with heroes who are no longer really heroic to us. Besides, we want credible heroes. The old demand for the incredible, the impossible, the superhuman, which was supplied by bombast, inflation and the piling of crimes on catastrophes and factitious rapture on artificial agonies, has fallen off; and the demand now is for heroes in whom we can recognise our own humanity, and who, instead of walking, talking, eating, drinking, sleeping, making love and fighting single combats in a monoto-

---

[23] *Virginius, or The Liberation of Rome* (1820) by James Sheridan Knowles, *Ingomar, the Barbarian* (1851) by Maria Anne Lovell, *The Gamester* (1753) by Edward Moore, and, *Richelieu* (1839) by Edward Bulwer-Lytton, are all plays that have virtuoso roles for the heroic actor.

nous ecstasy of continuous heroism, are heroic in the true human fashion: that is, touching the summits only at rare moments, and finding the proper level of all occasions, condescending with humor and good sense to the prosaic ones, as well as rising to the noble ones, instead of ridiculously persisting in rising to them all on the principle that a hero must always soar, in season and out of season.

I wrote *Caesar and Cleopatra* for Forbes Robertson, because he is the classic actor of our day, and had a right to require such a service from me. He stands completely aloof in simplicity, dignity, grace and musical speech from the world of the motor car and the Carlton Hotel, which so many of the others, clever and interesting as they are, very evidently prefer, or at least think they ought to pretend to prefer, to the Olympian region where the classic actor is at home. Forbes Robertson is the only actor I know who can find out the feeling of a speech from its cadence. His art meets the dramatist's art directly, picking it up for completion and expression without explanations or imitations, even when he follows up the feat by turning to ask what the prosaic meaning of the sentence is, only to find the author as much in doubt as himself on that point. Without him *Caesar and Cleopatra* would not have been written; for no man writes a play without any reference to the possibility of a performance: you may scorn the limitations of the theatre as much as you please; but for all that you do not write parts for six-legged actors or two-headed heroines, though there is great scope for drama in such conceptions.

That Forbes Robertson's Caesar should be famous in America before it has been seen here is a fact which speaks for itself on the subject of theatrical enterprise in London. However, we may be thankful that it has escaped the long-run system, by which it would have been run to death at the first production, and Forbes Robertson run to death's door with it. It will be played at the Savoy for four weeks only this year; but I hope we shall see it every year, as we should see all Forbes Robertson's heroic parts, for the rest of his professional life.

The American notices of the play showed, in spite of all my

warnings to the critics, a widespread and dense ignorance of the nature of great men in general and the career of Julius Caesar in particular. Just as all the military realism and elaborately accurate Balkan local colour of *Arms and The Man* was received in 1894 with incredulous ridicule as mere opera bouffe; so everything in *Caesar and Cleopatra*, which is simply dramatised Mommsen or transcribed Plutarch, has been pooh-poohed as fantastic modern stuff of my own, whilst the few modern topical allusions I have indulged in, including the quotation from Beaconsfield on Cyprus,[24] have passed unchallenged as grave Roman history. As to Caesar, even Shakespeare's Caesar, who is nothing but the conventional tyrant of the Elizabethan stage adapted to Plutarch's Roundhead[25] account of him, would be too modern, too realistic, for some of the New York papers. The fact that Caesar was a real flesh and blood man, and not a statue with a phonograph in its mouth repeating "I came: I saw: I conquered" and "Et tu, Brute" appears to strike the American journalists as a whimsical paradox. Caesar was a very modern man indeed: first a young man about town dressed in the height of fashion; then a demagogue like Wilkes or Bradlaugh,[26] with mobs in his pay; then at forty discovering that handling a provincial army was child's play to a man accustomed to manipulate Roman mobs; then conqueror and explorer; then by force of circumstance and gameness for any destiny, political adventurer gambling with Pompey for the empire of the civilised world and winning; finally dead and turned

[24] See note 26, p. 53.

[25] "Roundhead" was a derisive name for the supporters of Parliament during the English civil war. The name, which originated about 1641, referred to the short haircuts worn by the Puritans in contrast to the fashionable wigs worn by the Cavaliers, who supported King Charles I.

[26] Wilkes and Bradlaugh were both liberal members of the British Parliament who were more popular with their electorate than with their fellow parliamentarians. Middlesex elected Wilkes at least three times before the House of Commons finally seated him in 1774. Bradlaugh, an atheist and free thinker, objected to taking an oath when first elected in 1880; he was thus excluded at least four times before he was allowed to take his seat in 1886.

to clay, assassinated by the Nonconformist Conscience.[27] The reason Shakespeare belittled him, and that no later English dramatist touched this greatest of all protagonists until I saw my chance and took it, was simply that Shakespeare's sympathies were with Plutarch and the Nonconformist Conscience, which he personified as Brutus. From the date of Shakespeare's play onward England believed in Brutus with growing hope and earnestness, until the assassination in the Capitol was repeated in Whitehall,[28] and Brutus got his chance from Cromwell, who found him hopelessly incapable, and ruled in Caesar's fashion until he died, when the nation sent for Charles II, because it was determined to have anybody rather than Brutus. Yet as late as Macaulay and John Morley you find Brutus still the hero and Caesar still the doubtful character. It was Ibsen who killed him at last with the self-same steel that slew the Tennysonian King Arthur.[29] That left the dramatic field free at last for Caesar and Forbes Robertson.

I am sorry we shall have to omit the third act for want of time;[30] but it is perhaps just as well; for when it was played in Berlin in defiance of my instructions, it proved so entertaining that the audience got positively drunk with it and could hardly

[27] By the term "Nonconformist Conscience" Shaw is suggesting that Brutus's stoic morality was as misguided in its application to politics as was that of the Nonconformists or Puritans of the English Free Churches in their day.

[28] Charles I was beheaded in Whitehall in 1649 by the Puritans.

[29] Shaw is here using "Brutus" to symbolize conventional middle-class morality as a force in British reform movements. He sees it as controlling the Puritan Parliament that Cromwell abolished, and in the political writings of Victorian Liberal Party historians like Thomas Macaulay (1800–1859) and John Morley (1838–1923). In Tennyson's *Idylls of the King,* the hero, King Arthur, adopts an air of moral superiority toward his "erring" wife, which, for Shaw, reflected Victorian prejudices. In Ibsen's *A Doll's House,* Shaw thought that the moral posturing of the husband (Helmer) was finally shown up as hollow and self-serving.

[30] Shaw is speaking here of the Forbes-Robertson production of the play at the Grand Theatre, Leeds, on September 16, 1907. It was the first production of the play in England and ran for three performances.

settle down to graver business of the fourth act after it. Some day it may be played as an alternative ending to the play, or before the dinner interval at a complete performance on Bayreuth lines;[31] but for the present it must lie on the shelf as decidedly too much of a good thing.

[31] In 1876 a Festival Hall for the performances of Wagner's operas was opened in Bayreuth, Bavaria. Performances began in the late afternoon with a long break for dinner. Shaw was himself a frequent summer visitor.

Shaw's *New Statesman* Defense

Shaw wrote this defense of his play for the May 3, 1913, issue of the New Statesman *after having experienced much dissatisfaction with the critical responses given the play. He was particularly directing his remarks to the criticisms of A. B. Walkley of the* Times *and Desmond MacCarthy, who wrote a rejoinder to this article in the May 10, 1913, issue of the* New Statesman.

I do not think the critics have criticised *Caesar and Cleopatra* worth a cent. I could have done it better myself. They discuss the invention of a story which is not invented, or at least was not invented by me; and they are still busy with the question of whether I can write plays and whether Mr. Forbes Robertson can act, and, generally, how soon Queen Anne's death may be expected. Why did Nature curse me with this fatal gift of driving critics out of their senses? It is enough to drive me out of mine to see clever men mumbling over controversies that are as dead as The Music of the Future of the last "passing craze" but six (it would be Ibsen or thereabouts). I can stand the young bloods who declare, with a flattering air of paradox, that I am a dotard, or that pitiable thing The Old Pioneer; but these middle-aged and elderly contemporaries of mine, who, after twenty years of my plays, still cannot settle down to me and recognise that I am as inevitable as Shakespear and much more to their own taste, positively annoy me, which I am sure is the last thing in the world they intend.

The technically interesting part of *Caesar and Cleopatra* is that it is "a history": the old term for a chronicle play. It is a long time—some centuries, in fact—since anyone but Masefield[32] and

---

[32] John Masefield's *Pompey the Great* was first produced by the London Stage Society in 1910.

Laurence Housman[33] (censored for it) has put a chronicle on the
stage as Shakespear put the chronicles of Holinshed and Plutarch.
We have had Virginius, and Richelieu, and Louis XI,[34] and
Charles V[35] figuring in invented dramatic incidents; and the plays
in which these occur have been called historical. But the real
thing, the play in which the playwright simply takes what the
chronicler brings him and puts it on the stage just as it is said to
have happened—which is just what I have done in *Caesar and
Cleopatra* and what Masefield has done in *Pompey*—is a revival
curious enough to interest as such a critic with any feeling for
his profession. How far is it possible to interest playgoers in
chronicle pure and simple? Take this old rigmarole about Caesar
going to Egypt in pursuit of Pompey; finding Pompey dead and
trying to collect the old debt due by the not highly respected Mon-
arch Auletes (who, like Frederick the Great, played the flute):
taking the side of Cleopatra in her quarrel with her little brother
Ptolemy for the throne of Egypt solely because she attracted him
personally; nearly getting killed in an insurrection provoked by
the murder of the eunuch Pothinus; getting rescued in the nick
of time by Mithridates of Pergamos; and going off on his travels
and campaigns again! All this is not drama: it is mere anecdote.
Indeed, it is so scatterbrained, insignificant, and, consequently,
undramatic, that some authorities contend that it never happened at all, and that Caesar's expedition to Alexandria after
Pharsalia is a fable.

My friend Walkley, whose ignorance of history is a disgrace to
the *Times* and joy to its readers, has all along insisted that *Caesar
and Cleopatra* is comic opera invented by myself. To him, Caesar
asking for barley water instead of hock or claret is farce pushed

[33] Laurence Housman (1865–1959) has been called "England's most censored playwright." Thirty-two of his plays in all were censored because they
represented either Biblical personages or living members of the royal family.
His most successful history play, *Victoria Regina*, was yet to be written.

[34] *Louis XI* by Casimir Delavigne was adapted for the British stage by
Dion Boucicault in 1855.

[35] Charles V, or Don Carlos, appears in Victor Hugo's *Hernani* (1830).

to the limit. Other critics think that Caesar might have drunk barley water because they never drink it themselves, but are sure that he never ate oysters. Others are shocked by what they take to be the puerile invention of Caesar wearing the large wreath to conceal his baldness. They say "What a cynic you are" not knowing, poor dears, that the story is as hackneyed as that of King Alfred and the cakes. Others complain that the plot is ill constructed, rambling, inconclusive, and so forth, as if I had made Roman history. As far as I can recall,[36] only two critics, Mr. Massingham and Mr. Desmond MacCarthy, knew that what they were looking at was a chapter of Mommsen and a page of Plutarch furnished with scenery and dialogue, and that a boy brought to see the play could pass an examination next day on the Alexandrian expedition without losing a mark.

But both Mr. Massingham and Mr. MacCarthy express one feeling in common with the ignoramuses. This feeling is that the Caesar shewn at Drury Lane by Mr. Forbes Robertson and myself is not the Caesar who was so like Mahomet in his susceptibility to sexual attraction that his soldiers sang ribald songs about his baldness, and his enemies in the Senate accused him of being every woman's husband and something worse to boot. Mr. MacCarthy, too, objects that my Caesar is too squeamish about killing people, and says "if Mr. Shaw had lifted from Plutarch that speech of Caesar's to Metellus, who tried to prevent him from appropriating the treasury of Saturn: 'Thwart me, young man, and I shall kill you.'" Now, as it happens I *have* lifted that speech from Plutarch. In the play, Caesar, in the Alexandrian treasury, is asked by Pothinus where his right is. He replies: "In Rufio's scabbard," which is a fair paraphrase of his remark to Metellus. To confess the truth, if there is a point in the play on which I pride myself more than another, it is the way in which I have shewn how this readiness to kill tigers, and blackguards, and obstructive idealogues (Napoleon's word) is part of the same character that

---

[36] Shaw's memory failed him, for the most ardent defender of Shaw's play as history was Arthur A. Bauman, whose defense, "Mr. Shaw Run to Waste," appeared in the November 30, 1907, issue of the *Saturday Review*.

abhors waste and murder, and is, in the most accurate sense of the word, a kind character. Caesar throughout expresses the greatest horror of judicial academic murder and cruelty, whether committed by himself on Vercingetorix and the Gauls or imagined by him as what Rufio might have done to the savage Egyptian nurse whose throat he has cut as he would that of a mad dog. A murder of a higher man by a lower one, as Pompey by Septimius, or a treacherous and spiteful murder like that of Pothinus, revolts him; but his readiness to remove human obstacles by the sword if they will not step out of the way of the Gods is not a contradiction of this side of his character, but a part of it. I protest I have done this bit of my job extremely well; and I call on Mr. MacCarthy to prostrate himself and admire the genius of the dramatist he has rashly disparaged.

As to my alleged failure to present the erotic Caesar, that is a matter almost too delicate for discussion. But it seems to me that the very first consideration that must occur to any English expert in this connection is that Caesar was not Antony. Yet it is precisely because Caesar in my play is not Antony that I am told he is not Caesar. Mr. MacCarthy says that Caesar stayed too long in Alexandria for Cleopatra's sake. But the fact remains that Caesar did not think it too long, and that, as the upshot proved, he was right. Antony let Cleopatra disgrace and ruin him: when he left her he came back to her like the needle to the magnet. She influenced Caesar's affairs so little that few people know that he ever met her; and when he left her she had to go after him to Rome to get hold of him again. Antony was Cleopatra's slave: Julius was "every woman's husband." I have no doubt he stayed in Alexandria just as long as he dared; but he went in the nick of time at last; and he would never have seen Cleopatra again if she had left it to him.

The truth, if you insist on my blurting it out, is that theatrical critics are a much misunderstood class. Their profession obliges them to pose as experts in gallantry, as veritable Ovids and Don Juans who know all about love and consider the world well lost for it. But they never write a line about it that does not betray a lamblike innocence. If they met Mahomet or Caesar in the flesh they would put him down as a cold ascetic. They often express that view of me; and I am very like Caesar except for an unfortunate personal timidity and a certain want of readiness as to the right thing to do or say at a moment's notice. And Mr. Forbes Robertson is more like Caesar than Caesar was like himself. Whether the strength and continence that enable a man to be dignified and decent before the world are rooted in impotence is a question I cannot here discreetly discuss, so many eminent persons now alive being both dignified and decent. I trust that "whatever records leap to light, we never shall be shamed;[37] so let us hope that our executors will burn our private correspondence.

---

[37] The quotation is from Tennyson's "Ode on the Death of the Duke of Wellington."

Letter to Hesketh Pearson

Shaw's letter of 1918 to Pearson first appeared in the latter's G.B.S.: A Full-Length Portrait (*Harper & Row*) *in 1942. The book was republished with thirteen additional chapters as* George Bernard Shaw: His Life and Personality *in 1951 after Shaw's death.*

Why did it need a colossal war to make people read my books? The whole army seems to do nothing else, except when it lays down the book to fire a perfunctory shot at Jerry or to write me a letter asking me what I meant by it. . . .

I wrote *Caesar and Cleopatra* for Forbes Robertson and Mrs Patrick Campbell when they were playing together. But it was not played by him until they had gone their several professional ways; and Cleopatra was "created" by Gertrude Elliott, who had already played in *The Devil's Disciple* with Robertson, and is now Lady Forbes Robertson. It is what Shakespeare called a history: that is, a chronicle play; and I took the chronicle without alteration from Mommsen. I read a lot of other stuff, from Plutarch, who hated Caesar, to Warde-Fowler; but I found that Mommsen had conceived Caesar as I wished to present him, and that he told the story of the visit to Egypt like a man who believed in it, which many historians dont. I stuck as closely to him as Shakespeare did to Plutarch or Holinshed. I infer from Goethe's saying that the assassination of Caesar was the worst crime in history, that he also saw Caesar in the Mommsen-Shaw light. Although I was forty-four or thereabouts when I wrote the play, I now think I was a trifle too young for the job; but it was not bad for a juvenile effort.

It may interest you, now that you are enduring the discomforts and terrors of active service, to know that when I wrote Caesar I was stumbling about on crutches with a necrosed bone in my

foot that everybody believed would turn cancerous and finish me.
It had been brought on by an accident occurring at the moment
when I was plunging into one of those breakdowns in middle-life
which killed Schiller and very nearly killed Goethe, and which
have led to the saying that every busy man should go to bed for
a year when he is forty. In trying to come downstairs on crutches
before I was used to them I shot myself into empty space and fell
right down through the house on to the flags, complicating the
useless foot with a broken arm. It was in this condition that I
wrote *Caesar and Cleopatra;* but I cannot see any mark of it on
the play. I remember lying on the top of a cliff in the Isle of
Wight with my crutches in the grass beside me, and writing the
lines:

> The white upon the blue above
> Is purple on the green below

as a simple memorandum of what I saw as I looked from the cliff.
The Sphinx scene was suggested by a French picture of the Flight
into Egypt.[38] I never can remember the painter's name; but the
engraving, which I saw in a shop window when I was a boy, of
the Virgin and child asleep in the lap of a colossal Sphinx staring
over a desert, so intensely still that the smoke of Joseph's fire
close by went straight up like a stick, remained in the rummage
basket of my memory for thirty years before I took it out and
exploited it on the stage.

[38] Martin Meisel identifies the painting as "Repos en Égypte" by Luc
Olivier Merson. A sketch of that painting appeared in *Scribner's Monthly*
for December 1880, under the title "The Flight into Egypt." See *The Shaw
Review,* VII (May 1964), 62–63.

Letter to the Editor of the *Times*

Shaw's letter to the Times *appeared in the Monday, December 31, 1945, issue. The letter was undoubtedly prompted by remarks made about the Gabriel Pascal motion picture production of the play, which had its premiere showing on December 13, 1945, at the Odeon Theatre, London.*

My play was written primarily for the sake of its subject. Shakespeare had created a Cleopatra so consummate that the part reduced the best actresses to absurdity.[39] But he made a mess of Caesar under the influence of Plutarch, and made Brutus his hero. Goethe corrected this by declaring that the assassination of Caesar was the greatest crime in history, but did not write a play about him. The field was open for a play about him the hero, but not for the mature Cleopatra. She was available only as a child.

It happened just then that we had a classical actor of the first rank working with an actress of extraordinary witchery: Forbes Robertson and Mrs. Patrick Campbell. It was the moment for my play! and I seized it accordingly. But it was not yet the moment for me as a classic author. Mrs. Campbell made fun of the play and lost an opportunity.

Meanwhile the success of my play *The Devil's Disciple* in New York had confirmed Richard Mansfield's position as the leading actor in America; and his claim as such to Caesar was clear. But neither his physique nor his very peculiar idiosyncrasy was suited to the part. He cried off; and a postcard from me inscribed "Farewell, Pompey" ended our relation professionally, though not personally.

A playwright has to consider the talent at his disposal as well as the other limitations of the stage. He does not write a part for an Indian god with seven or eight arms and legs, however interesting it might be dramatically. Without Forbes Robertson at hand I might not have written C & C just then: that is all. It was a misfit for Mansfield.

[39] See Shaw's review of *Antony and Cleopatra*, pp. 145–152.